THE WAR IN SOUTH AFRICA

THE ADVANCE TO PRETORIA AFTER
PAARDEBERG, THE UPPER TUGELA
CAMPAIGN, Etc.

VOLUME 2

THE WAR IN SOUTH AFRICA

THE ADVANCE TO PRETORIA AFTER PAARDEBERG, THE UPPER TUGELA CAMPAIGN, Etc.

PREPARED IN THE HISTORICAL SECTION OF THE GREAT GENERAL STAFF, BERLIN.

AUTHORISED TRANSLATION BY
COLONEL HUBERT DU CANE, R.A., M.V.O.,
MILITARY ATTACHÉ AT SOFIA.

WITH MAPS AND ILLUSTRATIONS.

The Naval & Military Press Ltd

Published by

The Naval & Military Press Ltd
Unit 5 Riverside, Brambleside
Bellbrook Industrial Estate
Uckfield, East Sussex
TN22 1QQ England

Tel: +44 (0)1825 749494

www.naval-military-press.com
www.nmarchive.com

Cover image: Military Attachés To The Boer War.

When the Boer War broke out in October 1899 the Foreign Office granted permission for one officer from each 'friendly power' to act as an observer in South Africa. Together with their grooms and servants the attachés were later awarded the Queen's South Africa Medal.

In reprinting in facsimile from the original, any imperfections are inevitably reproduced and the quality may fall short of modern type and cartographic standards.

CONTENTS.

I.

THE OCCUPATION OF BLOEMFONTEIN.

Chapter	Page
I. After Cronje's Surrender	3
II. Action at Poplar Grove on March 7th, 1900	9
III. Comments on Poplar Grove	18
IV. Action at Driefontein on March 10th, 1900	23
V. Occupation of Bloemfontein	39
VI. Comments on Driefontein and the Advance on Bloemfontein	46

APPENDICES.

No. I. Losses of the Sixth Division at Driefontein on March 10th, 1900	54
No. II. Casualties in the 6th and 9th Divisions, from February 12th to March 13th, 1900	55

II.

EVENTS IN NATAL AFTER THE BATTLE OF COLENSO UP TO THE RELIEF OF LADYSMITH.

PART I.—THE SECOND ATTEMPT AT THE RELIEF ON THE UPPER TUGELA.

Chapter	Page
I. The Situation after the Battle of Colenso	59
II. British Preparations for the Second Attempt at Relief	67
III. The Passage of the Tugela	87
IV. The Fight at Thaba Myama. Events from 20th to 22nd January	113
V. The Battle of Spion Kop and the Retirement of the Natal Army across the Tugela	132

CONTENTS.

PART II.—THE THIRD ATTEMPT AT RELIEF (VAALKRANZ).

CHAPTER	PAGE
VI. THE THIRD ATTEMPT	186

PART III.—THE FINAL ATTEMPT AT THE RELIEF EAST AND NORTH OF COLENSO.

VII. THE ENGAGEMENTS SOUTH OF THE TUGELA	221
VIII. THE FIGHTING ON THE NORTH OF THE TUGELA	246

III.
SURVEY OF THE EVENTS DURING THE SUMMER OF 1900.

PART I.—THE OPERATIONS IN THE SOUTH-EAST OF THE FREE STATE.

IX. PREPARING FOR FURTHER ADVANCE	290

PART II.—THE MARCH ON PRETORIA.

X. THE ADVANCE OF LORD ROBERTS AND SIR R. BULLER	296

PART III.—THE OPERATIONS NORTH-WEST AND SOUTH-WEST OF PRETORIA.

XI. DE WET'S MOVEMENTS	308

PART IV.—EVENTS IN THE EASTERN TRANSVAAL. THE MARCH TO KOOMATI POORT.

XII. SIR R. BULLER'S OPERATIONS	314

IV.
TACTICAL RETROSPECT OF THE COURSE OF THE SOUTH AFRICAN WAR.

XIII. TACTICAL RETROSPECT	324

APPENDICES.

No. I. ORDER OF BATTLE OF THE NATAL ARMY DURING THE FIGHTING ON THE UPPER TUGELA	346
No. II. ORDER OF BATTLE OF THE NATAL ARMY AT THE BEGINNING OF THE LAST ATTEMPT TO RELIEVE LADYSMITH	350
INDEX	357

LIST OF MAPS.

1. GENERAL MAP OF THE OPERATIONS TO NOVEMBER, 1900 . . . . *to face p.* 1
2. POSITIONS IN NATAL, JANUARY, 1900 . . ,, 8
3. BATTLE OF POPLAR GROVE, 7TH MARCH, 1900 . ,, 16
4. BATTLE OF DRIEFONTEIN, 10TH MARCH, 1900 . ,, 38
5. FIGHT AT THABA MYAMA, 20TH JANUARY, 1900 . ,, 130
6. BATTLE OF SPION KOP, 24TH JANUARY, 1900 . ,, 180
7. ACTIONS AT VAALKRANZ, 5TH—7TH FEBRUARY, 1900 . . . . ,, 220
8. THE FIGHTING AT MONTE CHRISTO ON THE 18TH, AND AT WYNNE'S HILL ON THE 22ND FEBRUARY, 1900 . . . . . . ,, 256
9. FIGHT NORTH OF COLENSO ON THE 27TH FEBRUARY, 1900 . . . . . . ,, 322

LIST OF ILLUSTRATIONS.

VIEW OF SPION KOP FROM THE SOUTH . . *to face p.* 132
THE SUMMIT OF SPION KOP . . . . ,, 140
A BRITISH COLUMN CROSSING THE TUGELA . . ,, 180
VAALKRANZ . . . . ,, 198
HART'S HILL . . . . ,, 265
PIETER'S HILL FROM THE SOUTH-WEST . . ,, 278

ERRATA.

Page 183. To read—* " Not quite accurate. Thorneycroft's decisive consultation with Crofton and Coke took place before 9.30 p.m."

,, 219. Last para., line 4, to read—" The loss in killed, wounded, and missing,* . ."

,, 230. Last para., line 2—" Lower Tugela" to read "Little Tugela."

,, 233. Last para., line 1—" 15th" to read " 13th."

,, 311. Last para., line 2—" Schœmann's" to read "Schoemann's."

,, 325. First para., line 14—"they also often caused it" to read "it was often forced."

THE OCCUPATION OF BLOEMFONTEIN.

CHAPTER I.

After Cronje's Surrender.

By order of the Commander-in-Chief the British troops were, on February 28th, 1900, granted a day of complete rest in the positions which they were then occupying, but a new camp was pitched some distance up stream on March 1st. The fourteenth brigade and the artillery of the seventh division were moved to a spot about one mile and a-quarter to the east of their former position and quite close to the river on its south bank; the ninth division was immediately opposite on the north bank, while the sixth division was near Osfontein Farm, where the Headquarter Staff was housed. The mounted infantry was to the east of Kitchener's Kopje, and the cavalry division remained at Koodoesrand Drift. The latter had already commenced to reconnoitre towards Petrusberg on the south and towards Poplar Grove on the east.

Lord Roberts went to Kimberley on March 1st to arrange about the Lines of Communications, and there he met Lord Kitchener, who had arrived from Naauwpoort. It was quite impossible for the former to carry out his original intention of marching immediately on Bloemfontein after Cronje's surrender; the horses were still greatly exhausted, and had not been able to recover from the excessive exertions to which they had been subjected during the preceding fortnight, when they had suffered besides from a want of good and sufficient forage. It was also necessary to take very extensive precautions to ensure the army being punctually and sufficiently supplied between

Kimberley and Bloemfontein, a distance exceeding 90 miles, and without railway communication. The difficulty of forwarding supplies from Kimberley to the army had become extreme owing to the heavy rain which had lasted since February 22nd, and which had utterly spoilt the roads with their clay soil, although under ordinary circumstances these were quite tolerable. At this time rations were required daily for 40,000 men, 12,000 horses, and 10,000 mules in round numbers. The Commander-in-Chief was, therefore, compelled to halt for a week, in spite of the great advantage which this gave to the Boers in concentrating the Commandos approaching from Ladysmith and the Orange River.

On March 6th the fifteenth brigade of the seventh division, which had hitherto remained at Jacobsdal, joined the army, as did also the Brigade of Guards from Klip Drift, and the three batteries of the ninth division. The 65th (Howitzer) and the 82nd Batteries, which had hitherto been attached to the last named, joined the sixth division. Reinforcements had arrived daily for the mounted infantry, and Lord Roberts reorganised it into four brigades.* The combatant strength of the army now amounted to 30,000 men in round numbers with 116 guns.

During this period of quiescence the cavalry division had ascertained that the heights to the west of Poplar Grove were strongly held by the enemy, and Lord Roberts had, therefore, personally reconnoitred the Boer position carefully on March 5th. It extended for more than nine miles, its right flank being on Leeuw Kop, situated to the north of the Modder River, while the left reached as far as a row of hills, called Seven Hills, which fell away towards the south-west. This very extensive position, which ran roughly in a south-westerly direction, was not

---

* Appendix II.

occupied continuously; it was only on the flanks at Leeuw Kop and Seven Hills, and on the commanding Tafelberg, situated somewhere about the centre of the position, that considerable bodies of the enemy were observed; artillery was also seen at these three localities. The British Headquarters estimated that the strength of the Boers exceeded 14,000 men.

The ground in front of the position on the south bank was completely open for a distance of nearly five miles; it afforded a splendid field of fire, and the Boers on the Tafelberg could distinguish the British camps clearly. The ground in front of Leeuw Kop, however, being more rolling, the field of vision was restricted to barely 1,000 yards, and it was very difficult to climb this hill on account of its steep and rocky sides. The Boers had with great trouble brought a 3-inch Krupp gun on to its summit, and Kaffirs had to carry up the ammunition for it. There were entrenchments at the foot of the hill which reached, but not continuously, as far as the river, the defence on the north of which was entrusted to the Bethlehem and Potchefstroom Commandos. The kopjes immediately to the south of the river were held by the Heidelberg and a portion of the Bloemfontein Commandos, while the defence of the Tafelberg, and of the ground between it and these kopjes, was confided to the remainder of the Bloemfontein, and to the Ladybrand and Edenburg Commandos. Gun emplacements had been made for the three guns on the steep and rocky Tafelberg. This hill and the neighbouring kopjes had been well entrenched and prepared for a stubborn defence by infantry. The Philippolis and Ficksburg Commandos, with one Krupp and one Maxim-Nordenfelt gun, formed the left wing to the east and north of the Seven Hills. The Boers were under cover immediately in rear of their positions, the Winburg Commando with two guns being in reserve at a very high kopje, on which there was a signal station, to the south of Poplar Grove Drift.

The Boer position was very strong on the right, and especially in the centre against a frontal attack, but the left wing on the somewhat projecting Seven Hills was quite isolated and this, as it could be easily turned, was the weak point of the whole position. The total Boer force amounted to about 7,000 men.* General Christian de Wet, who had been appointed acting Chief Commandant by President Steyn at the commencement of March, was in command. He had occupied himself energetically with the concentration at Poplar Grove of all the Commandos which were hurrying up from the south and from the east during the lull in the British operations, and he was firmly resolved stoutly to resist, on the heights to the west of the drift, the advance of the English on Bloemfontein.

Lord Roberts assembled all the divisional commanders on March 6th, and communicated to them the result of his reconnaissance and his plans for the morrow.†

"I have," he said, "called you together in order to communicate to you my plans for to-morrow. The enemy is, as you know, holding a strong but somewhat extended position immediately to our front. He intends to oppose our advance on Bloemfontein, and, so far as we can tell, this is apparently the only place between here and Bloemfontein where he could do this with success. It is difficult to ascertain his exact strength, but it can scarcely exceed 14,000 men and about 20 guns. On the other hand we have at our disposal some 30,000 men and 116 guns. I intend to threaten the enemy's line of retreat to Bloem-

---

* Captain Reichmann, the American Military Attaché, who was present with the Boers during the action, reported to his Government that the Boers only had 2,500 men and 7 guns at Poplar Grove, but this is evidently an error. If the strengths of the separate Commandos which were present be added together, then there is still a total of nearly 7,000 men, after deducting 50 to 60 per cent. from their strength at the outbreak of the war.

† These were taken down simultaneously in writing.

fontein with the cavalry division, Alderson's and Ridley's mounted infantry, and seven batteries of horse artillery. In order not to come under the enemy's fire during its advance the cavalry will have to make a circuit of about 17 miles; it will endeavour to gain the Modder River two or two and a-half miles above Poplar Grove Drift, but General French will probably find some favourable opportunities to attack before he reaches the river. Experience has shown that the destruction of their laagers alarms the Boers to an extraordinary degree. Three or four laagers are shown on the plan, of which copies will be issued to officers in command, and it will be worth while to direct the fire of 42 guns against these. The Boers are extremely adroit in preparing cover for themselves, but they cannot conceal their horses, carts, and transport animals, the destruction of which will be all the more serious for them the more their line of retreat on Bloemfontein be threatened. The sixth division, together with its artillery, the howitzer battery, and Martyr's mounted infantry (except the detachment which is to join the seventh division) will advance in the same direction as the cavalry for about six miles; it will then be to the south of Seven Hills, the extreme left flank of the Boers. General Kelly-Kenny will not, I think, have much difficulty in driving the enemy from these hills. The Boers will already have become uneasy on learning that the cavalry is advancing in their rear, and proper use of the mounted infantry, in conjunction with the fire of 24 guns, will still further discourage them. The first position to which the Boers can retire from Seven Hills is the Tafelberg, about five miles distant. The sixth division will follow closely the retreating enemy. During its advance against the Tafelberg it will be supported by the Brigade of Guards, with which are four 4·7-inch naval guns and Le Gallais' mounted infantry. This force will be ready at daybreak at the outposts, about two miles to the east of Osfontein Farm. The Tafelberg is the key of the enemy's position; when once it is in our possession the Boers will retreat towards the river valley, as Cronje also did, and will endeavour to cross the river.

"The seventh division will assemble where the cavalry division is now. Its artillery, Nesbitt's Horse, the New South Wales, and Queensland Mounted Infantry will accompany it. The duty of the seventh division will be to threaten the enemy as much as possible and to distract his attention from the main attack directed against the Tafelberg. If there should be signs that the enemy wishes to retire across the river the seventh division is to move at once in the direction of the drift and cause him as much damage as possible.

"The ninth division will advance with the same object on the north bank of the river. It is to devote special attention to the enemy's right wing, where there was a gun a day or two ago. Three 12-pounder naval guns will be attached to the division, and Lieutenant-Colonel de Lisle with two regiments of mounted infantry will cover its left flank.

"Lieutenant-Colonel Rhodes will see that there is signal communication throughout the day between Headquarters and the infantry divisions. The Headquarter Staff will accompany the Brigade of Guards and will take up its position at the spot where Le Gallais' mounted infantry now is. The Principal Medical Officer will make his arrangements in accordance with these movements of the troops.

"Commanding officers are to arrange that the men take cooked rations with them and that they are, as far as circumstances permit, provided with water.

"All the trains will remain in camp."*

---

* The fifteenth brigade was left as baggage guard.

CHAPTER II.

ACTION AT POPLAR GROVE ON MARCH 7TH, 1900.

In accordance with these instructions the cavalry division moved off from its bivouac at 2 a.m. on March 7th, in line of brigade columns, protection being afforded by one squadron in front and by one on the left flank. It was still dark when, about 5 a.m., the division reached a small pan situated a couple of miles or so to the west of the Seven Hills, and halted there for three-quarters of an hour. When the division resumed its march, and was making a circuit round the hills on their south side about six o'clock, it was fired into by a Boer gun which had come into action on the kopje situated furthest to the south. The common shells did no damage, although they fell in the middle of the mass of horsemen, because, as was often the case, they did not burst;* the division encountered shrapnel fire soon afterwards, but this also had no effect, the penetration of the bullets being so trifling that the men and horses who were struck only received slight contusions. A fresh halt was made towards 7 a.m. behind a sheltering hill in rear of the Seven Hills, and beyond the range of the enemy's fire. According to Lord Roberts' orders the division should have been in rear of the Boers at daybreak. General French, accompanied by his Staff, rode on to a hill situated further to the north in order to reconnoitre the hostile position. Meanwhile, the sixth division was approaching, and it deployed for

---

* An officer who was present at the engagement states that the greater number of the shells did burst—in one case under a horse—but, strange to say, no damage was done.

attack to the south-west of the Seven Hills, and far beyond the range of the Boer fire; the thirteenth brigade was on the right, and the eighteenth brigade on the left, the divisional artillery being in the centre between them. There was nothing to be seen as yet of the enemy. Each brigade of four battalions formed a kind of open double column, the distance between each column and between each battalion varying from 300 yards to a quarter of a mile. Each battalion extended all its eight companies one behind the other in one thin line, with two or three paces interval between each man, while the distance from one company to the next in front of it was 100 or 120 yards. The brigades were thus quite ready for action, on going into which it would only be necessary to increase the intervals between the various units and between the individual men in the firing line. This formation was subsequently adopted frequently in commencing an action, but it did not, it is true, allow of changes of front being carried out.

FORMATION OF A BRIGADE FOR ATTACK.

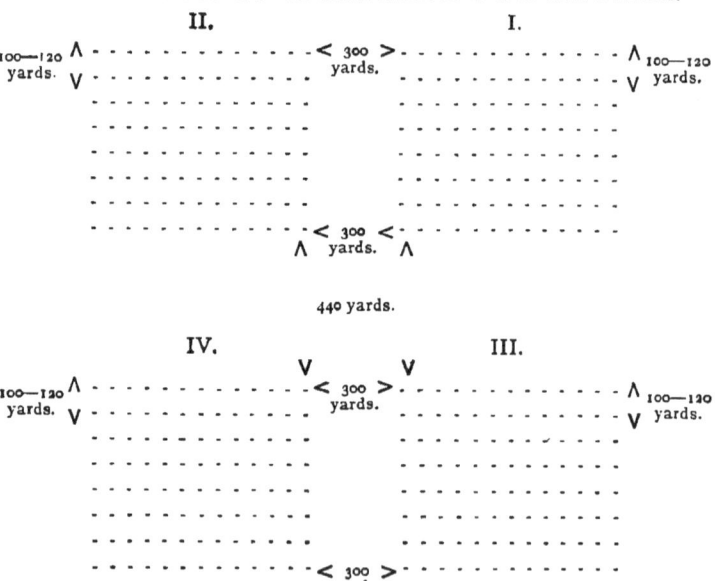

The infantry advanced in this formation "slowly and cautiously," according to Captain Reichmann, the American Military Attaché with the Boers.* After a short time another lengthy halt was made beyond the range of the Boer fire; the desire was to wait until the advance of the cavalry division should have made itself felt, but this body had not yet arrived on the scene.

The artillery of the sixth division had meanwhile come into action two and a-half or three miles to the southwest of the Seven Hills, while the naval guns of the centre column and the artillery of the seventh division had taken up a position about five miles to the west of the Tafelberg. Their fire was quite ineffective owing to the extreme ranges, which, however, appeared to be much less than they really were, on account of the atmosphere which was unusually clear, even for South Africa, on the day in question. The Boers on the Seven Hills very soon discovered the danger which threatened their flank, and did not wait till the turning movement of the British should become effective. They withdrew their advanced left wing, without firing a shot, to the Tafelberg, but evacuated the latter soon afterwards, and commenced their retreat along the Modder River in the direction of Abraham's Kraal. The hour was about 11 a.m. On the south bank the Heidelberg Commando alone stood fast, and it afterwards covered the retreat with several guns. Just as the Boer left wing was commencing its retreat President Krüger arrived from Bloemfontein at Poplar Grove in order to stimulate the Burghers to energetic resistance, but disorganisation had already begun to spread in their ranks. They were terrified all the more by the unexpected loss of their position on the left, for they had expected the British

---

* "Reports on Military Operations," p. 191.

again to make a frontal attack on their strong position. Once the retirement had commenced, the Burghers were no longer to be stopped; each hurried to his cart in order to try and save his property. The President was also obliged to return hurriedly so as to avoid being captured.

Christian de Wet has described very vividly the flight of the Boers:* "When the President had again entered his carriage, I mounted my horse and hastened to the positions. But what bitter fruit I was obliged to gather there from Cronje's surrender! Terror had penetrated into the bones of the Burghers and, although the British had not even approached so near that they could have turned their guns on us with any effect whatever, there was a wild flight from all the positions. Splendid as these were, the Burghers did not make the slightest attempt to hold them. It was a flight such as I had never seen before, and was not to see again in the future. Notwithstanding my efforts, and those of the officers, we were unable to stop a single one of the Burghers who were streaming away behind the guns and their carts. I exhausted myself in my endeavours, and wore out two excellent horses on this day, but all in vain. Fortunately the British followed us very slowly, otherwise they would have captured everything. . . ." When General French observed the retreat of the Boers from his position to the east of the Seven Hills, he at once appreciated the extremely favourable opportunity which presented itself, but one glance at his completely exhausted horses, and the distance of nearly three miles which still separated him from the enemy, made him understand to his sorrow that there was no possibility of profiting by the situation. He was obliged to allow the utterly disorganised Boers to stream past his front, a few

---

* "The struggle between Boer and Briton."

thousand yards away, without being able to reach them with his men.

In spite of their seven days' rest the horses had not yet been able to recover from the great exertions and the scarcity of forage during the preceding weeks, and the results of this now showed themselves. The animals could not charge, for they were already worn out by the night march. Some of Broadwood's horses, indeed, had dropped down dead during the march, a large number lay exhausted on the ground, and it was not even possible to get these in the evening to the bivouac ground on the Modder River. General French resolved to ride straight ahead as soon as the condition of the horses should allow him to do so and, by fighting on foot, to do as much damage as possible to the enemy. Broadwood's horses could not even trot, so that his brigade had to follow at a walk. There ensued only a somewhat ineffective fire action with the Boer rear-guard, which had taken up a position on the heights to the south and south-west of Salderpoort. The cavalry division followed the enemy, who was retiring from position to position, slowly as far as Slagkraal Hill, where it bivouacked in the evening not far from the river. The fatigue of the horses rendered it impossible for the horse artillery to pursue the Boers, although ten horses were hooked in to each gun.

The sixth division had only followed the enemy very slowly across the Seven Hills in the direction of Poplar Grove Drift, and had halted on several occasions for considerable periods. Its artillery took no part whatever in the pursuit of the Boers, but continued to direct a hot fire on the hills at a range of nearly three miles, although the enemy had evacuated the Seven Hills a long time before. A considerable time elapsed before a heliogram from Headquarters could make it comprehend its mistake.

Owing to the loss of time which was thus occasioned, touch was lost with the adversary.

Meanwhile, the ninth division had advanced on the north side of the river, the Highland Brigade on the right moving along the bank in the direction of Leeuw Kop, while the nineteenth brigade on the left advanced towards the Steinberg. When the brigades reached their outpost line they halted to await the advance of the seventh division on the south of the river, for, so the Divisional Commander understood, the Highland Brigade was thus to be supported from the south. On the other hand the seventh division and the Brigade of Guards delayed their advance, waiting for the attack of the sixth division on the enemy's left to become effective. Most valuable time was thus lost by each body remaining inactive and waiting for the other. General Colvile has written as follows on this subject in his book The Work of the Ninth Division: "About five miles to our front a line of Boers stood out darkly against the rising sun, and we saw their horses grazing close to them. 'They will not stand,' I remarked to my aide-de-camp. If I could have acted in accordance with this pure supposition, Poplar Grove would have been the most glorious day for the ninth division; as it was, it was its worst day. It should not, however, be forgotten that the enemy had, hitherto, not only always stood fast, but had done so with the greatest stubbornness; his position was an extremely strong one; he had a special predilection for river banks, and the Highland Brigade had not forgotten in the last seventeen days what the banks of the Modder River had cost it. . . ."

At last the ninth division received a heliographic order about 10 a.m. from Headquarters to advance immediately, so as to cut off, at Poplar Grove Drift, the Boers retreating from the Tafelberg in a north-easterly direction, when crossing the river. It was not until then that this division advanced in the direction which had been ordered. As soon as the Boers observed this, they evacuated their position on Leeuw Kop without waiting to fire; they retreated towards the east, and the naval guns, which had unlimbered quickly on the Cactus Berg, sent some shells after them, but without much effect as the range exceeded 6,500 yards. The Boer gun on Leeuw Kop had to remain there, as it was impossible to get it down the rocky slopes rapidly enough. It opened fire on the two naval guns, and an artillery duel went on for an hour without much result to either side. When the ninth division at last approached the Leeuw Kop, the gun detachment fled hastily, when the gun fell into the hands of the Shropshires. On the arrival of the division at Poplar Grove Drift about 3 p.m. there was nothing more to be seen of the enemy: the mounted infantry attached to the division was unable to pursue the Boers, as it had been charged with the duty of protecting the left flank of the division, and had been skirmishing all day long with small parties of Boers on that side. The ninth division bivouacked soon after 3 p.m. to the north of Poplar Grove Drift. The seventh division and the Guards Brigade, the latter being accompanied by the Headquarter Staff, bivouacked on the south bank near Poplar Grove a couple of hours afterwards; they had not commenced their advance until the sixth division had reported that the enemy had evacuated the Tafelberg. The artillery attached to them had hurried forward so as to fire into the retreating Boers, but this led to no result, and the batteries then joined the sixth division, which was advancing to the south of the Tafelberg. It was after six o'clock in the evening when this division arrived to the south of Poplar Grove, where it bivouacked, its artillery being scarcely able to move at a walk.

On the cavalry division, which was in front, devolved

the duty of providing for the security of the force, but its horses were so exhausted that it was impossible to send even patrols after the enemy. Colonel Gourko, the Russian Military Attaché with the Boers, had remained behind with Lieutenant Thomsen, the Dutch Military Attaché, in order to claim the aid of the British; Colonel Gourko's baggage cart had its axle-tree broken not far from Sandpoort during the retreat. On their way from the scene of this accident to Poplar Grove they did not meet one single British patrol, and suddenly found themselves to their astonishment in the immediate neighbourhood of the Headquarter Camp.

The large quantity of ammunition and other articles which were found by the English in the abandoned positions led to the conclusion that the strong entrenchments had been quitted in great haste. The Boers, who had been nowhere pressed by their adversary, continued their retreat, or rather flight, towards Abraham's Kraal, and it was only there that the leaders succeeded in halting and assembling some individual Commandos. The old and venerable President Krüger, on whose " rugged and heavy features despair seemed on that evil day to be portrayed,"* endeavoured to infuse courage again into the Boers, who were streaming past him in a disorganised mass; he raised his heavy stick threateningly against the fugitives, but could not stop them. At last he gave orders to shoot anyone who should attempt to pursue his flight further, but the leaders of this undisciplined militia had not the heart to do this, and the order, which could alone have brought salvation, was not carried out. Soft words were useless in such circumstances; most of the men declared they had had enough, and wanted to return to their homes. It was only with extreme difficulty that

---

* V. Lossberg: "With Saint Barbara."

de Wet and de la Rey managed to induce a portion of the Commandos to hold out and to occupy the heights of Abraham's Kraal.

The British loss at Poplar Grove amounted to 2 officers and 3 men killed, and 50 men wounded, nearly all of whom belonged to the cavalry division; the English captured no prisoners, and the Boers lost about 50 men killed and wounded.

CHAPTER III.

COMMENTS ON POPLAR GROVE.

The British plan at Poplar Grove had been to turn the enemy, who was entrenched on the heights, in order to force him to evacuate his strong position, and so to pave the way for a second Paardeberg when he should be crossing the Modder River. Lord Roberts himself has said on this subject that the day of Poplar Grove was for him one of sore disillusion, as he had confidently reckoned on cutting off the Boer retreat on Bloemfontein, and on holding the enemy fast at the difficult drifts of the Modder River, and of destroying him there. " In spite, however, of the comparatively long rest which the horses had had since Cronje's surrender, they were in exceedingly wretched condition, besides which, the ground was very heavy in consequence of the rain storms of the preceding days. If the mounted troops had been capable of advancing somewhat more quickly, they would undoubtedly have cut off the enemy's retreat. . . ." The failure of Lord Roberts' plan was due to the unfortunate way in which it was executed. In order that the cavalry division should carry out its task it was indispensable that it should have been ready for action at daybreak in rear of the Boers. Instead of this, however, it did not reach the extreme left of the Boer position, on the heights to the south of the Seven Hills, until after sunrise; being then completely exhausted by the night march, and almost incapacitated for fighting, it was obliged to rest for a considerable time in order to let the horses recover. The Boer line of retreat, therefore, remained quite unmolested during the early hours of the morning. But if the cavalry division had moved off on the evening before, it could by midnight have been to the west of Schuinshoek, even if, in order not to be observed by the enemy, it had made a long circuit southward in the direction of Emmaus. There would thus have been time for the men to get some food, and for the exhausted horses to be rested, fed, and watered, so that the whole could have gone fresh into action. The heights to the south of Poplar Grove Drift ought then to have been occupied before daybreak, and the guns and dismounted cavalrymen would have been ready to receive the Boers.

If the infantry had attacked then, it would have driven the enemy into the fire of the cavalry division; escape would have been impossible, and the adversary would have been obliged to fight just where he stood. But, in order to prevent the Boers as far as possible from evacuating their position prematurely, and in order to make it a certainty that the turning movement of the cavalry should be effective, it would have been necessary for the infantry to hold the Boers fast by means of a resolute attack delivered simultaneously in front and flank. In this way only could success have attended the turning movement. But there was no trace whatever of such an attack; on the contrary the British did nothing but feel their way cautiously and wait. One man was waiting for the other, and with this delay the most precious moments for action slipped by. The defender, who threw up the sponge before a shot had been fired, showed, indeed, no more desire to fight than did the attacker. The attacking infantry, which was so splendid at Paardeberg, was scarcely to be recognised a fortnight later at Poplar Grove. But it is quite wrong to assume that the explanation for this lies in the losses at Paardeberg, on the ground that the burnt child dreads the fire. The moral value of the British infantry at Poplar Grove was the same as at Paardeberg, and the proof of this is the dash with which these same troops attacked the enemy at Driefontein three days later. They demonstrated there that, when they were properly led against the Boers, they understood how to attack.

The action at Poplar Grove, however, shows the fatal endeavour on the part of the British leadership to avoid serious losses under all circumstances. The men had felt only too quickly that the faith of the Commander-in-Chief in their ability was shaken, and that it was no longer believed that a frontal attack against modern firearms could succeed. This was the main reason for the dallying uncertainty displayed by the leaders of all ranks. The strong determination to conquer, cost what it might, regardless of loss, threatened to disappear from among the troops which had hitherto been animated by such a spirit.

The rapid and easy success of Poplar Grove was due essentially to the sudden disorganisation which spread among the Boers with overpowering force, but this piece of good fortune, attained without loss of blood, betrayed the British Commander-in-Chief into the error that he had discovered in these tactics an infallible means of victory. His plans for Poplar Grove were typical of future actions, and consisted solely in threatening the enemy's flanks or rear and thus, while avoiding bloody but crushing blows, compelling him to evacuate his positions; to push him back was sufficient. The occupation of the country and of the towns, not the destruction of the living hostile forces, became the objective of the operations, and manœuvres took the place of battles. Weighty reasons must certainly have decided a general like Lord Roberts to adopt this mode of warfare in such exceptional circumstances; reasons connected with the difficulty of maintaining the army at its proper strength, the peculiarities of the Boers, and the great extent of the theatre of war must have specially influenced him. It is, however, difficult to justify it when viewed from the standpoint of European warfare.

But, as the course of events was to show afterwards, the success which at first attended this method of making war was only apparent and not real. The English did indeed, manage to occupy the enemy's capitals without much trouble, but this in no way broke down the power of resistance of the living Boer forces.

The Boers recovered very soon from their moral collapse at Poplar Grove. The gallant little band of heroes, which, purified and constitutionally invigorated by the exfoliation of the bad and of the campaign-sick, remained in the field under the leadership of men like Louis Botha, Christian de Wet, and de la Rey, made war its profession. In order to break down their strength a long struggle was necessary, during which the issue of the campaign seemed only too often to be in doubt. The long duration of the South African War was due, above all other causes, to the tactics adopted by the British, who wished to gain decisive victories without suffering bloody losses. " To sacrifice ruthlessly, when necessary, the life of the soldier in battle is the great law of war, to which both the soldier and the officer must conform with equal readiness."[*]

The loosely organised and undisciplined Boer Commandos met with the same fate as every other militia army which has to deal with similar serious military complications. Their units, which were devoid of all internal stability, dissolved completely, and a long and severe military apprenticeship, crammed with hard fighting and bitter experiences,

---

[*] Boyen: "Memoirs II."

was needed before the Boers who still remained in the field became real soldiers. It was not until a later stage of the war that the Boer army, purged by previous misfortune, developed really military virtues in the conduct of detachment warfare.

CHAPTER IV.

Action at Driefontein on March 10th, 1900.

The British troops remained at Poplar Grove on March 8th and 9th, but it has not been ascertained whether this fresh halt was rendered necessary by the difficulties of supply or by the exhaustion of the horses. In consequence of repeated intelligence concerning insurrectionary movements in the north-west of Cape Colony, Lord Roberts despatched Lord Kitchener on March 8th to De Aar to provide for the safety of the Lines of Communication. All the troops belonging to the Lines of Communication, which were already at that place and which were reinforced by others from England, were placed under his orders, and Lord Kitchener remained at De Aar until the end of September. That Lord Roberts should have parted with his principal adviser at such a time during the very height of the operations shows what importance he attributed to the state of affairs in rear of the army.

The first cavalry brigade, together with a brigade of mounted infantry, was pushed forward to Waaihoek, on the road to Abraham's Kraal, on the afternoon of the 8th, in order to reconnoitre in front of the army.* The sixth division was also sent to the former place on the following day in support of them. But as an encounter both with the Boers retreating from the north of Cape Colony and those flying from Poplar Grove to Bloemfontein was

---

* *See* Map of the Battle of Driefontein.

reckoned upon during the advance on that capital, the army was to be divided into three columns. The left one under General French received orders to march *viâ* Baberspan and Venter's Vlei on Leeuwberg, which is situated to the east of the railway and to the south of Bloemfontein; the right column, under General Tucker, was to move on Venter's Vlei *viâ* Petrusberg, Driekop, and Panfontein, while the centre column, under the immediate command of Lord Roberts, was to march on Leeuwberg by way of Driefontein, Aasvogel Kop, and Venter's Vlei. The Commander-in-Chief learned, by the evening of the 9th, that the Boers were occupying a strongly entrenched position near Abraham's Kraal, and were apparently resolved to offer renewed resistance to the British advance on Bloemfontein. Lord Roberts thereupon decided, in case the enemy should stand his ground, to turn the Boer position from the south. The left and centre columns, therefore, were to carry out a tolerably hazardous flank march along the front of the Boer position at Abraham's Kraal, but the British Headquarter Staff assumed, apparently, that the enemy, who had shown so little desire to fight at Poplar Grove, would adopt his usual method of a purely passive defence of the summits of the kopjes.

The columns were composed as follows:—

Left Column. General French.	*Centre Column.* Field-Marshal Lord Roberts.	*Right Column.* General Tucker.
Sixth Division. First Cavalry Brigade. Alderson's M.I.	Ninth Division. Guards Brigade. Second Cavalry Brigade. Martyr's and Le Gallais' M.I. 65th Howitzer Battery. Naval guns. 7th Co. R.E. Ammunition Park. Supply Park.	Seventh Division. Third Cavalry Brigade. Ridley's M.I.

The itinerary was as follows:—

Date.	Left Column.	Centre Column.	Right Column.
Mar. 10 ...	Baberspan.	Driefontein.	Petrusberg.
,, 11 ...	Doornboom.	Aasvogel Kop.	Driekop.
,, 12 ...	Venter's Vlei, cavalry to Leeuwberg.	Venter's Vlei, cavalry to Leeuwberg.	Panfontein or Waltevreede.
,, 13 ...	Leeuwberg.	Leeuwberg.	Venter's Vlei.

It was intended to effect a junction of the three columns to the south of Bloemfontein in order, as soon as possible, to acquire assured possession of the railway from East London and Port Elizabeth, so as to provide the army with a fresh channel of supply.

In accordance with the orders the right column reached its destination unopposed on March 10th; the left column, on the other hand, had a serious action near Driefontein. It had moved off from its bivouac at 6 a.m. on the 10th, its cavalry brigade and mounted infantry, which had started at 4.30 a.m. to reconnoitre, being far in advance to the front. The order of march of the sixth division was as follows: The advanced guard was formed by the Welch Regiment, while the main body was composed of the eighteenth brigade, the divisional artillery, and the thirteenth brigade, the transport following immediately in rear of the last named. The road to Baberspan was *via* Abraham's Kraal, and it, generally speaking, followed the course of the Modder River. General Kelly-Kenny, who was riding ahead of his advanced guard, received a report soon after 9 a.m. that the kopjes, which commanded the road to Baberspan, were strongly held by the enemy at and to the south of Abraham's Kraal.

General Christian de Wet had betaken himself to Bloemfontein early on the 8th in order to discuss with Presidents Krüger and Steyn the measures to be adopted for the defence of the capital. Both Presidents insisted on an attempt being made to hold the town, which, for political as well as military reasons, could not be allowed to fall into the hands of the enemy without a struggle. General de Wet resolved, therefore, to venture on this attempt in the favourable position at Abraham's Kraal. During his absence large Boer Commandos, reinforced from Colesberg and Ladysmith, had been again collected between Abraham's Kraal and Driefontein Farm under Piet de Wet, de la Rey, Andries Cronje, Philip Botha, and Fronemann, and they were strongly entrenched on the heights. They were divided into three groups, namely, the main body under de la Rey at Abraham's Kraal, and two weaker forces under Piet de Wet and Philip Botha on Alexandra Berg and the Boschrand Kopjes. Christian de Wet was in chief command on the left wing, and the Pretoria and Johannesburg Police Corps* was with the northern force. The Boers had altogether more than 6,000 men,† with 16 guns, of which four were Maxim-Nordenfelts (Pom-Poms). The old warlike spirit of the Burghers was rekindled. In the short time available they had recovered remarkably quickly from the Poplar Grove panic, and were firmly resolved to offer a stout resistance. General de Wet himself praises in the warmest manner the good spirit which animated the Burghers in the action: "It was scarcely conceivable that they were the same men who had fled so shamefully from Poplar Grove." Captain von Lossberg, a former Prussian officer, who was present during the action on de la Rey's Staff, also wrote as follows: "De la Rey collected the Commandos more or less on the 8th and 9th of March, allotted them their positions on the hills, had gun emplacements made for the artillery, and in 48 hours an entirely new picture presented itself. The impression of a flying

---

* This body had been organised in peace time as a kind of nucleus. It was, with the exception of the artillery, the sole really disciplined military force which the Boers had.

† Christian de Wet gives their strength as 5,000 Burghers, but he has not, apparently, included in this total the Pretoria and Johannesburg Police Corps, of which he makes no mention, so that the number, 6,000, is certainly not too high an estimate.

horde of free-shooters, which had at first existed, had given place to what seemed, even to a military eye, almost a disciplined force."*

The right wing of the main body, which was at Abraham's Kraal, rested on the river; strong entrenchments, facing towards the south-west, had been made on a hill situated between the river and the road to Baberspan; similar works, but facing N.W., had been made on two other hills lying south of the road. All these entrenchments had been most carefully concealed, and were difficult to discover, while the Boer Commandos themselves also lay hidden further to the rear. It was the intention of de la Rey to lay an ambush for the British who were marching on the road to Baberspan, but the watchfulness of the English cavalry, which was reconnoitring carefully, and had kept contact squadrons in touch with the enemy, not only on the 9th, but also during the night of the 9th-10th, prevented this project from being carried out.

General French ordered the first brigade (Porter's) to leave some squadrons and mounted infantry to observe the enemy in front, and to turn off in a southerly direction with the remainder of his troops in order to turn the Boer left wing. But de la Rey, as soon as he perceived the change of direction of the cavalry, abandoned his plan of an ambush and galloped off with his men to Viehkraal Hill to reinforce the centre group. Several Boer guns came into action on the commanding Signal Hill, situated to the north-east of Viehkraal Hill, and fired with good effect at the cavalry. The two horse artillery batteries " T " and " O " took up position on the heights to the west of the Modderpan, and replied to the enemy's guns, but could only with difficulty maintain themselves against the superior artillery fire of the Boers, especially

---

* V. Lossberg: "With Saint Barbara," p. 23.

as they, at a distance of more than three miles, were beyond effective range. The batteries were protected in front and flank by the squadrons of Porter's brigade, which had been left behind, and by the mounted infantry.

General French, who was with the batteries, perceived a number of Boers, on Alexandra Berg; he took them for a rear-guard, and thought the enemy there would not offer any serious resistance. He therefore declined the aid of the cavalry with the centre column, which was offered to him. The remainder of Porter's Brigade, when endeavouring to turn this part of the Boer position from the south by making a circuit *viâ* Driefontein Farm, met the cavalry of the centre column, namely, Broadwood's Brigade and Martyr's Mounted Infantry, to the east of the farm at noon. These troops had been in action since 10 a.m. against the most southerly group of the Boers under de Wet, who were holding the Boschrand kopjes strongly. The two batteries of Broadwood's Brigade were firing from the heights of Driefontein at a Boer gun on the most northerly Boschrand kopje. In attempting to turn the Boer position from the south, the first cavalry brigade now prolonged the second towards the right of the latter. During the course of the afternoon Broadwood succeeded in getting possession of the Boschrand kopjes, while de Wet with his main body retired to Aasvogel Kop, whence he commanded the main road to Bloemfontein, leaving only a weak force opposite the English cavalry. The latter contented itself with the occupation of the Boschrand kopjes, and remained there throughout the whole of the rest of the day.

Meanwhile the sixth division had also come into action. When, about 9 a.m., it had first heard of the occupation of Abraham's Kraal by the Boers, and when still five miles away from it, a long halt was made, during which General Kelly-Kenny rode on ahead in order to reconnoitre. On his way he met an orderly officer from French, who informed him of the change in the enemy's dispositions, and gave him an order to continue his advance, and to hold the Boers fast in front until the cavalry should have succeeded in turning their left from the south. About the same time a heliographic order was received from Lord Roberts to avoid making an attack on the enemy's position at Abraham's Kraal, and to turn off in a south-easterly direction, paying special attention to the safety of the transport.

The sixth division thereupon continued its advance in the direction of Driefontein Farm, leaving behind, however, a strong escort for the transport, consisting of the Oxfordshires, the West Ridings, the 82nd Battery, and Alderson's Mounted Infantry, the whole being under General Knox, who commanded the thirteenth brigade. The Welch regiment formed the advanced guard, and extended four companies in the front line while the remainder followed, likewise extended, one behind the other with a considerable interval between each. The main body of the division also advanced in extended formation, the two remaining battalions of the eighteenth brigade, the Essex and Yorkshires, flanking the Welch to left and right, being in front. The remainder of the divisional artillery, namely, the 76th and 81st Batteries, was in the centre between these two battalions, and the rest of the thirteenth brigade, the Buffs, and Gloucesters, followed in second line under Colonel Hickson.

The two batteries were soon pushed forward to the support of the horse artillery, and, coming into action on an eminence to the south of the latter, they at once directed their fire against the Boer guns on Signal Hill. General Kelly-Kenny had ridden forward in order to discuss the situation with General French, but did not find him, as he had already gone on to the heights to the west of Driefontein Farm. General Kelly-Kenny was, therefore, obliged to make his own plans independently; he saw that the Boers held Alexandra Berg and the hills in front of it in force, while artillery was also observed on Signal Hill and Alexandra Berg. The latter forms a long and high ridge from south to north, and commands the whole of the surrounding country. At its northern extremity there is a row of low hills, which subside gradually into rolling country. Towards the south Alexandra Berg terminates abruptly in a valley, which extends between it and the Boschrand kopjes. In front of the hill were two lower ones, which were afterwards called Viehkraal and Yorkshire Hill respectively. A col, 1,200 yards broad and perfectly level, connects the former with Alexandra Berg.

The main body of the Boers was in position on the slope of Alexandra Berg, where, in spite of the short time available, they had thrown up slight entrenchments facing towards the west and north-west, while smaller bodies had been pushed forward on to Viehkraal and Yorkshire Hills. Nearly all the guns, under the escort of a Commando several hundred strong, were in position on Signal Hill, only a few guns being on Alexandra Berg.*

General Kelly-Kenny became convinced that the enemy would offer a stout resistance, and he decided first to drive him from his advanced position, and then to hold him fast in his main position on Alexandra Berg, until the turning movement of the cavalry from the south should have become effective. He therefore ordered the eighteenth brigade to capture the kopjes in front of Alexandra Berg. The brigade at once extended, at noon, three battalions for the attack on the hills, the Welch Regiment being in the centre and opposite Viehkraal Hill, while the York-

---

* It has not yet been possible to ascertain the exact distribution of the sixteen Boer guns in these two artillery positions.

shires were on its right, and the Essex on its left. All the battalions had great depth of formation, and each company was extended. In no instance was close order maintained when once within the extreme range of the Boer fire. The Yorkshires received special instructions to seize the more southerly hill of the two advanced ones by means of a turning movement. The two battalions of the thirteenth brigade, which were still available, were ordered to follow in reserve in rear of the centre.

When the battalions were crossing the heights to the south of their guns, they were met by an extremely hot infantry and artillery fire. After a brief fire action, and supported by the 81st Battery, which had for a short time diverted its fire from the Boer guns in order to turn it against the enemy in the advanced position, the battalions made a resolute charge and drove the Boers from this position. The eighteenth brigade climbed the two hills in front of the main Boer position about 1 p.m., but had scarcely reached their summits when the main body of the Boers on Alexandra Berg and Signal Hill opened a hot artillery fire on it, the enfilade fire from the latter being especially damaging. In order to divert this artillery fire from the attacking infantry, the 81st Battery quitted its protected situation, whence it had not done much execution, and advanced nearer to the enemy's position. The battery came into action on the slope to the northwest of the Viehkraal Hill where there was no cover at all, and again opened fire against the guns on Signal Hill, which soon afterwards concentrated their fire on the British artillery, and particularly on the advanced 81st Battery. They poured a regular hail of well-aimed shrapnel shells into the last-named, but, although more than thirty shells fell in the middle of the battery, the damage done was very slight, as most of the shells did not burst, so that only two men and two horses were wounded. The

Boers, however, thought that their fire had completely crushed this battery. Captain von Lossberg,[*] who was with them, describes in the following language his impressions concerning the effect produced by the Boer artillery: " Our pom-poms had an enormous effect on the British artillery. Two English batteries were standing without any cover whatever on the long ridge which stretched towards Abraham's Kraal Farm. The pom-poms fired systematically at them, and silenced one gun after the other, knocking them down like nine-pins." Similar illusions concerning the results of an artillery duel are nothing new in military history, and will always recur in the future. Spoilt by the favourable results which are easily obtained on the practice ground, we are, after a long peace, only too much inclined to expect, in every instance, a result from the artillery fight which will be but too seldom attained in battle.

Meanwhile, the eighteenth brigade was in a good position, and was hotly engaged with the Boers on the slope of Alexandra Berg. It had worked its way with difficulty as far as the eastern edge of the ridge, where it halted and awaited the turning movement of the cavalry, but it was three o'clock in the afternoon and the latter had not come into action from the south as arranged. Touch with it had been completely lost, and an Intelligence officer, despatched from the Staff of the sixth division, had not been able to find it. An order from General French had been received about 2 p.m. to the effect that the sixth division was to resume its advance immediately, as the enemy was in full retreat, but French, on the heights of Driefontein, had lain under a complete misapprehension concerning the situation when he sent this order. General Kelly-Kenny felt that, if a decisive result was to be attained

---

" With Saint Barbara," p. 28.

on that day,* there was no more time to be lost, and he resolved, therefore, to capture the Boer position with the sixth division alone without the co-operation of the cavalry.†

He ordered the officer commanding the eighteenth brigade to make a determined attack at once on Alexandra Berg. General Stephenson thereupon directed the Welch Regiment to advance across the col connecting Viehkraal Hill and Alexandra Berg, and to make a frontal attack on the Boers, while the Essex Regiment, covering the left flank of the division towards Signal Hill, was to turn the Boers on Alexandra Berg from the north. The Yorkshires were to advance against the enemy's left flank, and the two battalions in reserve were to follow in rear of the centre.

The divisional artillery was pushed forward to the col between Viehkraal and Yorkshire Hills, and in rear of the Welch Regiment, in order to support the infantry attack; the guns directed their fire partly against the Boer artillery and partly against the enemy on Alexandra Berg; the two horse artillery batteries opened fire on the Boer guns on Signal Hill, but their fire slackened more and more as their ammunition became exhausted.

While the Yorkshires were making a long circuit towards the south in the direction of Driefontein Farm, the Welch Regiment was endeavouring to work its way further to the front by rushes and by crawling. In order to strengthen the firing line all the supports were gradually brought up into it, and, thanks to the effective aid rendered by the 76th and 81st Batteries to the south-east of Viehkraal Hill, the Welch Regiment managed to advance across the perfectly bare ground of the broad col until within about 650 yards of the enemy. Their frontal advance was made easier by the attack of the Essex Regi-

---

* Sunset was about 6 p.m.
† "To force the enemy's line."

ment from the north, which had extended for attack against the Boer right while leaving some companies to the east of Viehkraal Hill to observe Signal Hill. The ground was more rolling on the Boer right, and this assisted the advance of the Essex Regiment considerably, the Boers soon turning a very hot fire on to it, which relieved the pressure on the hard-pushed Welchmen in no small degree. Nevertheless, the latter found it impossible to advance any further, numerous attempts being repulsed with heavy loss. Captain von Lossberg, who watched the fight at Alexandra Berg from his place on Signal Hill, has written with regard to this determined frontal attack of the Welch Regiment:* " Over and over again we saw the well-extended British firing line rise, run forward 40 or 50 yards, dash back 80 yards or more, and again renew the attempt with bull-dog tenacity."

General Stephenson, recognising that only a determined attack by the Essex Regiment could give breathing time to the Welchmen, brought up the companies which had been left behind at Viehkraal Hill to protect the left flank; he considered this step to be all the less hazardous since the two reserve battalions were by this time in rear of that hill. It was, however, 4.30 p.m. before the attacking battalions managed to make any further progress whatever, and a scarcity of ammunition was beginning to make itself felt in the Welch Regiment. The Yorkshire Regiment, which was to operate against the enemy's left flank, and which had been so anxiously awaited, had not arrived, having made much too long a circuit; when it did advance in the direction of the farm to the south of Alexandra Berg it became entangled, at very long range, in a fight with the Boers who were to the east of the Boschrand kopjes. The attack of this battalion was, therefore, very

---

* "With Saint Barbara," p. 29.

much delayed. The superiority of the Boer fire at Alexandra Berg became more and more marked, and it seemed as if the action there would terminate unfavourably for the English.

The situation had become extremely critical, and General Kelly-Kenny, who was on Yorkshire Hill, resolved, therefore, to put his last reserves into the fight, especially as he counted upon the early arrival of the centre column. The Buffs pushed themselves partly into the Welch right, which they also partly prolonged, while the Gloucestershires, still further to the right, advanced against the Boer left wing. The arrival of the Buffs pulled the tired Welch line forward again, and their powerful fire gave renewed strength to the wavering fighting line. The Buffs, and the Welch Regiment, which had been supplied with fresh ammunition by the reinforcements, now poured in an overpowering fire against the front of the enemy's position, while the Essex battalion, by means of its flanking fire from the north, weakened the Boer fire in the front, and continually diverted thence fresh numbers of the enemy. The artillery likewise, the range being only 1,650 yards, concentrated the whole strength of its extremely effective shrapnel fire against the Boer riflemen on the slope.

On both sides the firing grew more and more intense; there was one last struggle for victory. The Boers threw their last reserve, which consisted of a few hundred men, who had been, hitherto, kept back on Signal Hill, into the wavering fight on the slope of Alexandra Berg. Several of their guns were also hurried from the former to the latter.

The strong and united fire of the British from front and flank gradually gained the mastery; the Buffs and the Welch managed to work their way to within 400 or 500 yards of the enemy, while the left wing of the Essex, whose advance had also been very much favoured by the ground, had approached to within about 350 yards of the Boers. From the English firing line it was already possible to observe the effect of the superiority of its fire, for the Boers were seen to be hastening, at first singly and then in continually increasing numbers, from the fighting line across the ridge to their horses. Many of these fugitives paid the penalty of their behaviour with their lives. The Yorkshire Regiment then appeared on the left flank of the enemy not far from the farm, and its volleys, which commenced at long range, appeared to crush finally the enemy's power of resistance.

As the Gloucestershires, who, by making a circuit to the right, had advanced against the Boer left, were approaching the firing line, the following order resounded on the right wing of the Welch Regiment: "The enemy is retiring—the whole to advance!" This ran like wildfire through the British ranks; bayonets were fixed, the whole line rose as one man, and charged madly with loud cheering. The enemy did not face this united and powerful assault; not waiting for the bayonet attack they evacuated their entrenchments in all haste, and hurried to their horses. When the British infantry reached the summit of Alexandra Hill the Boers were seen to be galloping off in a north-easterly direction. A hot fire was sent after them, but the rapidly flying enemy soon disappeared behind the kopjes south of Signal Hill.

"The English fought with the greatest bravery," says Captain von Lossberg; "but their frontal attacks had to be repeated five or six times, in spite of their strong firing lines, which were being continually reinforced, before late in the afternoon the assault on the stoutly defended kopjes was successful."

The defeated enemy was not pursued, as the cavalry, although at hand, was not in the right place. Long after the Boers had disappeared from view, the 10th

Hussars and 12th Lancers attempted to pursue towards the north, but they soon desisted as darkness came on.

General Broadwood with the first and second brigades had remained inactive during the whole of the afternoon at the Boschrand kopjes opposite some weak Boer forces; he had omitted altogether to get into touch with the sixth division, and was, consequently, ignorant of the state of the severe action which was proceeding some thousands of yards to the north of him. When he had learned in the morning that the Boers were occupying the Boschrand kopjes and Alexandra Berg, he sent to ask General French about 9.30 a.m. whether he was to operate in conjunction with him. General French, however, having erroneously supposed that the Boers would not offer any serious resistance to the British advance, had replied: "No support necessary," and as he, at Driefontein Farm, sent Broadwood no further orders, the latter thought he had fulfilled his duty by capturing the Boschrand kopjes, which rendered it possible for the centre column to complete its march to Driefontein without interruption.

The British lost 17 officers and 404 men,* of whom 6 officers and 52 men were killed; the Boers lost about 300 men, of whom at least 102 men were killed.† The Boers on Alexandra Berg had at least 2,000 men in action, while the combatant strength of the four English battalions

---

* Appendix I.

† In the deserted hostile position alone the British found 102 Boers, whom they buried on the following morning. A farmer in the neighbourhood, who visited the battlefield soon after the departure of the British, also discovered quite a number of unburied Boers, so that, if the statement of this man be correct, the Boers may have had 150 dead. The number of their wounded can only be estimated, because the Boers on this, as on other occasions, carried them off. In comparison with the number of dead the number of wounded may be taken as being from 350 to 400. In their official report on the action the Boers gave the number of killed and wounded as 7 and 18 respectively. This is another proof that the reports which they circulated, and which were, as a rule, accepted absolutely unreservedly by the European Press, should be received with caution.

which actually took part in the fight amounted to scarcely 3,000 troops.

The sixth division bivouacked near the scene of action, the Essex and Yorkshire battalions finding the outposts. The Boers continued their retreat during the night *viâ* Baberspan and Bainsley on Bloemfontein, where they arrived about noon on the following day. A Council of War was held there in the evening, when it was decided to make one last effort before the gates of Bloemfontein to defend the capital. The arrangements for this were entrusted to General de Wet. He caused a line of strong entrenchments to be made at a distance of five or six miles from the town on its western and southern sides; he also endeavoured, by every possible means, to raise the drooping courage of the Burghers and to strengthen their desire to hold Bloemfontein at all costs.

CHAPTER V.

OCCUPATION OF BLOEMFONTEIN.

The British columns reached their destinations unmolested on March 11th and March 12th. The cavalry division concentrated again on the 12th at Venter's Vlei, and moved on that day to Ferreira Siding on the railway from Springfontein to Bloemfontein; the railway and the telegraph line had been destroyed in several places in order to cut off communication between the Boers who were still in the north of Cape Colony and Bloemfontein. A few horsemen and a small mounted detachment of engineers likewise destroyed the railway some miles to the north of Bloemfontein during the night of March 12th-13th for a similar reason. The result of this was not only to cut off communication between that capital and Pretoria, but at the same time to prevent the Boers in Bloemfontein from removing thence the railway material, supplies, and military stores towards the north. Consequently the British, when they occupied Bloemfontein, captured there no less than eleven locomotives, and twenty passenger carriages and goods wagons, a most valuable booty.

When the English cavalry was approaching the town, there began again to spread among the Boers, who were to hold the entrenchments in front of the capital, a feeling of despondency, and during the night of March 12th-13th a panic-stricken flight occurred, similar to that at Poplar Grove a few days previously. The Boers fled from their positions, at first singly and secretly, but afterwards in large bodies, so that in the early morning of the 13th only a few of them remained in the entrenchments. These men also quitted the field-works in all haste, and without offering any resistance, as soon as some horse artillery batteries belonging to the cavalry division came into action in the positions on the Boer right wing, which had been already evacuated. Bloemfontein was to be taken by the British without a shot being fired.

The British Headquarter Staff arrived at Ferreira siding at 9.40 a.m., where it was met by representatives of the capital who had hastened thither to negotiate about the surrender. Both the Presidents, Krüger and Steyn, had already quitted the town, and had gone to Kronstadt, to which place the seat of government was now removed. The result of the negotiations was the unconditional surrender of the town with a guarantee of protection for the personal property of the inhabitants. Lord Roberts made his solemn entry into Bloemfontein at the head of the third cavalry brigade.

The Brigade of Guards was the first to arrive there late in the evening after a forced march, having covered the last 42 miles in 26¾ hours. The sixth division reached Brand Kop on the same day, the seventh, Panfontein, and the ninth, Ferreira Siding. The sixth division marched into Bloemfontein on March 14th, but the seventh and ninth divisions remained where they were. The cavalry division, which was charged with the duty of securing the safety of the British, pitched a camp from two to two and a-half miles from the town, with one brigade to the north, west, and east of it respectively.

The Boer Commandos still in the field in this part of the theatre of war began to disperse. Their leaders, Christian de Wet and de la Rey, perceived that it was no longer possible to carry on a campaign with such demoralised men, and they resolved, therefore, to send all the Commandos home on furlough for three weeks. " I saw," writes de Wet,* "that the Boer, who had already been away from his wife and child for six months, must be granted an opportunity of recuperating." When Commandant General P. Joubert reproached him bitterly some days later for this somewhat unusual step during the middle of a campaign, he replied: "Do you not know the Afrikander? It is neither your fault nor mine that our discipline is in such a sad state; the burghers *must* now go home, and those who return will then fight with renewed courage. I would sooner have ten men who fight cheerfully than a hundred who do so with reluctance." This reply represents better than anything else the ropes of sand which bind an undisciplined militia army.

The Boer Commandos on the Orange River were ordered to withdraw in a northerly direction, but their line of retreat was already threatened from that quarter. Two days after the entry into Bloemfontein Lord Roberts had despatched General Pole-Carew with a portion of the Guards Brigade, several guns, and a small body of mounted infantry by train to Springfontein,† in order to effect communication between Generals Gatacre and Clements, and to facilitate their passage across the Orange River. Until these passages should be in the assured possession of the English, it would not be possible to work traffic on the railways from East London and Port Elizabeth, and so to provide the army with a new and important line of communication.

When the Boers on the Orange River heard of the despatch of British forces against their rear they fled in all haste and, after destroying the two railway bridges at Bethulie and Norval's Pont, retreated in a north-easterly direction towards Thabanchu and Ladybrand. So hurriedly

---
* "The Struggle between Boer and Briton."
† Map I.

was this retreat carried out that the Boers omitted to destroy the road bridge at Bethulie. Generals Gatacre and Clements crossed the river without opposition on the same day, the former by means of the uninjured stone bridge at Bethulie, and the latter by means of a pontoon bridge which had been rapidly thrown across at Norval's Pont. They both then advanced on Bloemfontein in order to join Lord Roberts. General Brabant, moving *viâ* Jamestown, had already crossed the river at Aliwal North some days previously with his force of mounted volunteers.

The restoration of the railway bridges which had been destroyed was commenced immediately, and the first through train was able to leave Port Elizabeth on March 27th for Norval's Pont and Bloemfontein. Traffic had, however, already commenced on that line by transhipment at Norval's Pont, as the British had captured a valuable quantity of rolling stock by their timely destruction of the railway to the north and south of Bloemfontein. The importance of this was all the greater as the transport of supplies for the whole army from Kimberley, solely on the country roads, threatened to break down in time.

During the short space of one month the military situation had changed completely in favour of the British. In the western theatre of war Kimberley had been relieved; the main body of the enemy at Magersfontein had been compelled to lay down its arms; the forces which had been assembling for the defence of Bloemfontein had been completely scattered, and that capital had been taken without a blow. In the centre the resistance of the enemy on the Orange River had been broken, the passages across the river opened to the English, and the railway to Bloemfontein was being worked by them. In the eastern theatre of war Ladysmith had been relieved, and the Natal army under Sir Redvers Buller was engaged in a victorious advance.

These great results had certainly been obtained at the cost of heavy sacrifices, which had been rendered unavoidable by the rapid delivery of a deep thrust into the heart of the enemy's country. The readiness for action of the British army had suffered considerably, and it was, therefore, fortunate for the English that the Boers were for the time being incapable of any military enterprise. Even small expeditions directed against the Bloemfontein railway in rear of the English would have caused them the greatest difficulties, in the condition they were in at the moment. An immediate resumption of the operations, and of the advance on Pretoria were not yet to be thought of. The Commander-in-Chief was just then concerned only with assuring the safety of the Lines of Communication, collecting a sufficient quantity of supplies in Bloemfontein* for the further advance, and making good the losses which had been heavy, especially among the horses.† The mounted troops, and particularly the cavalry division, were, for the moment, practically useless.‡ The latter alone had lost, between February 12th and March 13th, more than 2,000

---

* Colonel Richardson, the Director of the Army Service Corps, had managed to purchase supplies for the army for twenty-seven days, a few days after the entry into Bloemfontein, and to collect them there. This was all the more meritorious as the supply of the army at that time was a care which lay heavily on the Headquarter Staff, which did not think the railway could be relied upon before the beginning of April.

† Appendix II. shows the casualties in the sixth and ninth divisions from February 12th to March 13th.

‡ In Lord Roberts' opinion the main cause of the great mortality among the horses was their not having been acclimatised before being put to hard work. Most of the horses had been brought direct from a northern to a southern zone, where the change of coat did not correspond with its accustomed season. From his long experience in India he was satisfied that horses imported from Australia into India broke down if in any way over-exerted before being acclimatised, for which he considered ten or twelve months to be necessary. On board ship horses must be kept short, and they are therefore in bad condition on landing, as a rule, and quite unfitted for hard work. It was a fact that the horses belonging to the great London omnibus companies showed the most endurance. They were in good condition before embarkation, and the three or four weeks' quiet during the voyage gave them a rest, and they became fit for duty much more rapidly than the other horses. As there was an urgent demand for mounted troops,

horses, of which the majority had perished from utter exhaustion. Some squadrons only had from 20 to 30 horses left, and even these were mostly overworked and unfit for duty. The difficulties in the way of replacing them were all the greater, because the distance from Cape Town to Bloemfontein exceeded 750 miles, while the only available railway was fully occupied, for the time being, in bringing up the supplies, clothing, and equipment which were quite indispensable, especially as winter was approaching.*

All these difficulties compelled the British army to halt for more than six weeks at Bloemfontein, in spite of the fact that the military situation demanded a rapid advance on Pretoria, mainly so as to leave the Boers no time to recover from their shattered condition, and to assemble again. If it had been possible to continue the operations at once, the Boer

---

especially at the beginning of the war, it was impossible to give the horses time to rest after landing. Want of good food was another cause of the great loss of horseflesh, for there was no other forage in South Africa except grass of the worst quality. This was all the more serious as the war commenced during the hot season, when the grass on the veldt was frequently withered, and the supply of water was also extremely limited. An ample and regular supply of oats would have compensated to some extent for the bad grass; but it was at first impossible, and afterwards very difficult, to assure sufficient transport so that each horse with the army might have a full ration of oats daily, especially if we remember that transport which would carry supplies for 12,000 men could only carry forage for 1,000 horses. This was the main reason why the supply of oats was often inadequate. The horses were, besides, in the opinion of most of the British cavalry leaders, always too heavily laden; and Lord Roberts attempted to improve matters by means of various army orders. In these he issued strict instructions, among other points, that horses on the march should be led occasionally, but, as a rule, not much attention was paid to them. The mounted troops disliked marching on foot. All experts, however, are unanimous that the chief cause of the great loss of horses was due to the fact that neither officers nor men were properly acquainted with the management of horses, and that they did not take that care of them which was necessary, if, in spite of the extreme demands which the campaign was making on their strength, they were to retain their efficiency. Up to April, 1900, 49,641 horses were sent to South Africa, viz., 27,600 from England and 22,041 from North and South America and Russia.

* By direction of the Commander-in-Chief the tents were brought up in the first trains which arrived from Cape Colony. Since leaving Modder River Camp the troops had been obliged to do without them, and had suffered greatly from the sharp change of temperature from broiling hot days to cold nights, as well as from the subsequent rain, which lasted for days together.

Republics would have been compelled to conclude in the summer of 1900 the peace which they were not driven to make, after a severe struggle, until two years later.

The British Commander-in-Chief experienced the truth of the words of Clausewitz: "A pause in military operations is, strictly speaking, contradictory to the nature of the case, because both armies, like two hostile elements, must continue to destroy one another without ceasing; the military operations should, therefore, be continued just as clock-work, which has been wound up, goes until it runs down. Yet, savage as is the nature of war, it is nevertheless chained by human weaknesses."

CHAPTER VI.

COMMENTS ON DRIEFONTEIN AND THE ADVANCE ON BLOEMFONTEIN.

One of the senior British officers has very rightly described the action at Driefontein as the most instructive of the whole campaign. One reason is that, in this instance, the rare case happened that the opposing forces were, as regards numbers and value, approximately equal. The action also shows the mobility of the Boers, as the Commandos entrenched at Abraham's Kraal left their original position, and hurried to Viehkraal Hill, the possession of which the English cavalry threatened to dispute with them. The hasty entrenchments thrown up on this hill were not, therefore, so strong as elsewhere.

The remarkable supineness displayed throughout the whole day by the senior British officer present, General French, who was, as a rule, so enterprising, can only be explained by his complete misconception of the situation. Until late in the afternoon he had clung with curious obstinacy to his preconceived idea, namely, the improbability of the Boers offering serious resistance. At first he attached no importance at all to the action which was developing, and which he took to be a trifling skirmish with a weak rear-guard of the enemy. He reported in this sense to the Commander-in-Chief, who thereupon took no steps whatever towards a timely support of the sixth division, which was hotly engaged. Shortly before 4 p.m.

General Kelly-Kenny received from Lord Roberts, who had hastened on ahead to Driefontein, orders to force his way on, as the Commander-in-Chief believed the enemy in Kelly-Kenny's front to be only "very weak." The centre column, therefore, ate its rations quite undisturbed, and did not arrive at its destination, Driefontein, until about 6 p.m.

The preconceived conclusion, erroneous in itself, to which the British leaders had jumped, was the improbability of encountering any serious resistance; as so easily happens in war they clung to it, and this might have had disastrous results. If the sixth division, whose victory was, up to the last, entirely in doubt, had been beaten, its defeat could not have been repaired owing to the great distance of the centre column from the battle-field.

The false impression formed concerning the enemy can alone explain the action of the British Commander-in-Chief in laying down in detail the marches for four days in advance, without it being possible to effect a timely concentration of the army towards one of its two flanks. These plans had been drawn up beforehand without making sufficient allowance for the unfettered will of the adversary, and they increased immensely General Kelly-Kenny's difficulties in conducting the action.

It also looks as if the use of "local rank" rendered unity of command more difficult: Kelly-Kenny and French are close personal friends, but, by an order of March 8th, the latter was appointed to the command of the left column instead of General Kelly-Kenny, who was the senior general officer present with the army. This may perhaps explain why French kept himself so much in the background, and also the want of co-operation between the two commanders during the fight.

The action of General Kelly-Kenny, when French remained passive, in cheerfully undertaking the responsibility of conducting the action in accordance with his better knowledge of the situation, due to careful personal reconnaissance, was especially praiseworthy; by making a resolute frontal attack he was knowingly acting in opposition to the views of the Commander-in-Chief, whose slight faith in the success of such attacks was quite well known to him, and who desired also to evade a decisive action on the day in question. It was the force and the energy of the attack of the sixth division which first made the Boers realise the superiority of the British; it was this victory which first crushed their power of resistance, and which opened the gates of the capital to the English. Without this decisive success, which so disorganised the Boers, the situation of the British would have become very much more difficult after the entry into Bloemfontein than it already was; even a few Commandos, really fit for action, would have sufficed to place the British army in a critical position by operations against its rear.

The dispositions adopted by Kelly-Kenny for the action were thoroughly well adapted to the purpose, except that a baggage escort of excessive strength was detached. But this may have been due to the repeated and urgent reminders of the Commander-in-Chief to make careful arrangements for the safety of the transport. The best way to protect it would have been undoubtedly the simple plan of diverting it at once towards the south, as the veldt was passable everywhere, and by making it march some distance to the right of the main body of the division advancing on Driefontein. The latter would then of itself have ensured the safety of the transport by its own advance. Alderson's Mounted Infantry would have sufficed amply to protect the train towards the north, and it was not necessary to keep nearly one-third of the total combatant strength away from the decisive point where the whole force should have been in hand. The mania of the British leaders for detaching troops for minor undertakings, and thus weakening themselves prior to a crisis, often had disastrous results, and might easily have led to a catastrophe at Driefontein also.

The mode of attack there differed considerably from that adopted at Paardeberg. Whereas at Paardeberg the troops were isolated and scattered, they were, at Driefontein, put into action uniformly and simultaneously against the front and flank of the enemy. In some instances at Paardeberg all the units were extended in the firing line simultaneously, and there was no depth of formation; at Driefontein, on the other hand, the firing line was reinforced gradually, and was at first only strong enough to keep up a powerful fire, while a strong reserve was retained in the hands of the officer in command. Unlike former occasions, when the reserve took no part whatever as a rule in the final result, it was very skilfully employed at Driefontein down to the last man, in order to increase the strength of the fire to the utmost extent, and to acquire superiority in it. The battalions making the frontal attack were supported in the most effective manner by the enfilade fire of the Essex Regiment. The ground favoured the advance of the latter, which made the most skilful use of the cover available, and facilitated considerably the purely frontal attack of the Welch Regiment across the completely bare plain. The superior frontal and enfilade fire of the British, which was marked by unity of command, overcame at last the resistance of the enemy. Except Elandslaagte, Driefontein was, indeed, really the first action of the campaign in which the British, appreciating correctly the importance of fire as the one decisive factor in the modern battle, fought with a definite plan, and with a determination to acquire the superiority in fire.

The artillery likewise intervened in a very effective manner in the infantry fight, and the co-operation of the two arms towards acquiring the mastery in fire was a model of how this should be attained.

The 81st Battery, regardless of its own losses, advanced closer to the enemy's artillery, and came into action on the slope which was absolutely destitute of cover, in order to relieve the hard-pressed infantry from the enfilade fire of the Boer guns on Signal Hill. When the final struggle to obtain the mastery in fire commenced, two batteries accompanied the attacking infantry, and took up a position 1,650 yards from the enemy, in order to concentrate the whole force of their fire at decisive range against the Boer riflemen. They did not cease firing when the infantry attack was approaching nearer and nearer to the hostile position, although, according to an eye-witness, some of their shrapnel shells are said to have burst, at last, close in front of the assaulting infantry. Until the Boers fled from their position, the batteries kept their entrenchments under fire.

When the effect of this violent fire became apparent, and individual Boers began to evacuate the position, the whole of the infantry dashed forward, not in isolated parties, as had been invariably the case previously, but simultaneously as if by word of command. The adversary, who had already been shaken by the British fire, was unable to withstand the crushing weight of this general charge.

It will always be uncommonly difficult, often, indeed, impossible for the troops in action and for the directing head in rear simultaneously to discern the exact moment for the further progress of the attack or for the final charge. The course of several actions has shown that in most cases, especially at the commencement of a war, the attacker had deceived himself as to the effect of his fire, and had advanced prematurely against the hostile position, an error which was generally punished with extremely bloody losses. The rapid and abbreviated course of our manœuvre combats creates only too easily among the troops false views concerning the duration of the modern battle. This is inevitable, but conceals the danger that, in real war, especially in the first battles, there will result illusions as to the effect of the fire, and repulses will follow. Such unavoidable incidents, however, should neither surprise nor disorganise in any way well-trained and well-disciplined troops. The proper course to pursue then will be, without letting go of the enemy, to recommence the fire action with renewed vigour, and to give our own fire fresh strength by bringing up reinforcements. This is what the Welch Regiment did at Driefontein; after its numerous and premature attempts to approach nearer to the Boers had been repulsed with severe loss, it reopened fire, reinforced by the Buffs, from its original position at Viehkraal Hill.

The victory of Driefontein was due chiefly to the correct use made of deep formations, and to the unity of command which characterised the proceedings throughout. This was the only possible way of conducting the long and costly fire action, while continually increasing the strength of the fire, and then hurling the shaken enemy from his position by means of a resolute assault.

In all the principal actions hitherto the British had sought for victory in shock rather than in fire tactics, either, as at first, in more closed formations, or, as at Paardeberg, in long, thin, and widely extended lines. This was the most important cause of their original tactical failures. It was at Driefontein for the first time that the endeavour first to beat down the enemy by the co-operation of infantry and artillery fire and then crush him finally by means of a united charge was displayed.

Although the British had hitherto preferred shock tactics to fire tactics, the importance of the effect of fire was now beginning to make itself gradually felt. Bloody experience had been necessary, however, before they were forced to this significant conclusion after much groping and frequent vacillation.

Driefontein will always remain a glorious day for the Sixth Division and its General. The tactics which he employed there were, however, based substantially on the same principles which the German regulations, evolved from the experiences of the campaign of 1870-1871, have laid down for the attack for a long time past. These regulations embody the conviction that fire is the essence of the modern battle, and their leading principles aim at nothing else than the carrying out, in a well-planned, uniform, and powerful manner, of a long and wasting fire action until the mastery be obtained. The shock of the charge is merely intended to pluck the fruit when ripe for picking.

A thorough study of the successes and failures of the war in South Africa leads us to the significant and confident conclusion that the principles of the German regulations have retained all their worth where modern fire-arms are concerned. Their substance is as valuable now as formerly, even if several external tactical forms be capable of improvement, in consequence of the experience gained during that war, and there is, besides, a certain elasticity inherent in the spirit of our broad-minded German regulations. Among other points it should be especially noted that the limits of distance within which modern battles will be fought are much greater than formerly, and that the possibility of employing closed formations on that part of the field which is exposed to the enemy's fire appears open to question. More consideration must also be paid to the adversary's fire in the formations of the firing lines and in the movements of the latter during the progress of the attack; but the great strength due to combined action, especially where our own fire effect is concerned, must not be lost by troops being scattered.

All this, however, affects in no way the essence of the matter; in the leading principles of our regulations the German army has a possession, the incomparable intrinsic worth of which has been in no degree lessened by the experiences of the South African War, however deserving of attention these may otherwise be. Notwithstanding the effect of small calibre rifles with smokeless powder, success will not be denied in the future to the attack, provided that its standard principles be understood in the proper spirit, and that the innumerably manifold demands of the battle be skilfully met.

APPENDIX I.

LOSSES OF THE SIXTH DIVISION AT DRIEFONTEIN ON MARCH 10TH, 1900.

REGIMENT.	Officers.		N.C.O.'s and Men.			Total.		Percentage.	
	Killed.	Wounded.	Killed.	Wounded.	Missing.	Officers.	N.C.O.'s and Men.	Officers.	N.C.O.'s and Men.
Royal Artillery	1	—	2	5	—	1	7	—	—
The Buffs	1	3	17	79	5	4	101	6	1·3
Yorkshire	—	—	1	27	—	—	28	—	3·4
Essex	2	4	11	79	16	6	106	27	1·2
Welch	2	5	17	109	5	7	131	39	16·3
Gloucestershire	—	1	4	19	—	1	23	4·3	3·3
Total	6	13	52	318	26	19	396	—	—

Total losses 415

APPENDIX II.—CASUALTIES IN THE 6TH AND 9TH DIVISIONS, FROM FEBRUARY 12TH TO MARCH 13TH, 1900.

Brigade.	Regiment, &c.	Strength on Feb. 12th.		Strength on March 13th.		Killed or died of wounds.		Wounded.		Sick.		Missing.		Decrease.		Percentage.	
		Officers.	N.C.O.'s and Men.	Officers.	N.C.O.'s and Men.	Officers.	N.C.O.'s and Men.	Officers.	N.C.O.'s and Men.	Officers.	N.C.O.'s and Men.	Officers.	N.C.O.'s and Men.	Officers.	N.C.O.'s and Men.	Officers.	N.C.O.'s and Men.

SIXTH DIVISION.

13th	2nd East Kent (Buffs)	18	787	10	576	2	25	6	105	—	81	—	—	8	211	44·4	26·9
	2nd Gloucestershire	23	717	19	573	—	12	3	46	1	80	—	6	4	144	17·4	20·1
	1st West Riding	23	790	17	597	1	24	4	124	1	45	—	—	6	193	26	24·4
18th Minus 2nd R. Warwickshire Regt.	1st Oxfordshire Light Infantry	20	596	14	431	3	17	2	74	1	74	—	11	6	165	30	27·7
	1st Yorkshire	21	954	12	724	—	46	7	131	1	42	—	—	9	230	43	24
	1st Essex	23	937	11	758	2	21	5	128	3	8	2	22	12	179	52	19
	1st Welch	23	876	10	661	2	32	10	165	—	5	1	13	13	215	56·5	24·5
	Divisional troops	38	1,008	36	879	—	4	1	17	—	65	1	43	2	129	5·3	12·8
	Total	189	6,665	129	5,199	11	181	38	790	7	400	4	95	60	1,466	31·7	22

NINTH DIVISION.

						Killed and wounded.											
						Officers.	N.C.O.'s and Men.										
3rd Highland Minus 1st Light Infantry.	2nd R. Highlanders (Black Watch)	19	714	13	516	5	93			1	105	—	—	6	198	31·6	28
	2nd Seaforths	20	832	12	562	7	144			1	126	—	—	8	270	40	32·4
	1st Argyll and Sutherland	22	805	12	633	6	100			4	72	—	—	10	172	45·4	21·3
19th	2nd Duke of Cornwall's Lt. Inf.	21	801	16	648	5	73			—	80	—	—	5	153	24	19·1
	2nd King's Shropshire Lt. Inf.	24	889	21	768	3	46			1	75	—	—	3	121	12·5	13·6
	1st Gordon Highlanders	24	839	22	743	1	20			1	76	—	—	2	96	8·3	11·4
	Royal Canadians	40	878	33	706	4	123			3	49	—	—	7	172	17·5	19·6
	Divisional troops	26	743	25	730	—	—			1	13	—	—	1	13	3·8	1·7
	Total	196	6,501	154	5,306	31	599			11	596	—	—	42	1,195	21·4	18·4

EVENTS IN NATAL AFTER THE
BATTLE OF COLENSO UP TO
THE RELIEF OF LADYSMITH.

PART I.

THE SECOND ATTEMPT AT THE RELIEF ON THE UPPER TUGELA.

CHAPTER I.

THE SITUATION AFTER THE BATTLE OF COLENSO.

The first attempt to relieve White's Division shut up in Ladysmith, had failed owing to the reverse at Colenso. The British troops, unmolested by the Boers, had withdrawn to their old encampment between the Tugela and Chieveley Road. The impression of a severe defeat was felt by all. The General Commanding-in-Chief, Sir Redvers Buller, considering a fresh attempt at relieving Ladysmith useless, wished the garrison of that place to do the best it could for itself. In his despondency he telegraphed on the evening of 15th December to the Secretary of State for War in London in the following sense:—" My unfortunate undertaking of to-day raises grave questions. I do not believe that I am strong enough at present to relieve White. Colenso is a fortress which, if it cannot be carried by storm, can, in my opinion, only be taken after a regular siege. There is no water within a mile and a-half of the point of attack, and in this weather that exhausts Infantry. The place is strongly entrenched. I do not believe that during the whole day we have seen one Boer or one gun, although we were under very heavy fire. The Infantry were keen to fight, but completely worn out by the great heat. My opinion is that I must let Ladysmith go and take up a good defensive position in Southern Natal in order to let time come to our assistance. But that is a step about which I must first ask your advice. I reckon that 20,000 men were opposed to me to-day. They had the advantage of me in weapons as well as in position. They admit that they have suffered severely, but my people have not seen a single dead Boer. That discourages them. My losses were not very heavy. I might have made them much heavier by continuing the fight, but that would in no way have altered the result, as my attempt was doomed the moment that I failed to cross the river with my troops. I feel that I cannot say that I am in a position to relieve Ladysmith with the troops now at my disposal, and the best suggestion I can make is that I should take up a defensive position and fight the battle out on ground better suited to our tactics."

It was hardly to be expected that the situation would be viewed more favourably in London than in Natal. The Secretary of State for War was, nevertheless, obliged to look at the political side of the question, though naturally more disinclined than the General in Command to take the responsibility for a step which the latter thought impracticable.

He replied by wire on the 16th:—" The Government would consider it the gravest national misfortune if White's troops were abandoned and were, in consequence, forced to surrender. We must urgently beg of you to prepare another plan for his relief. It is not essential to make a fresh attempt by way of Colenso. You can, if you think well, make use of the reinforcements now on their way."

On receipt of this answer Sir Redvers Buller turned to White, and on the 16th December the following enquiry was addressed to the latter by flash-light:—" My attempt to break through *viâ* Colenso yesterday failed. The enemy is too strong for my troops unless a regular siege is undertaken. A full month would, however, be needed for the preparation for a siege. Can you hold out as long as that? How many days can you hold out? I suggest you should fire away as much ammunition as you can and then capitulate on the most favourable terms possible. I can remain here if you have any other proposal to make, but without support I cannot break through. I find that my infantry cannot fight further than 10 miles from camp, and even then only if water is to be had, and it is scarce. Whatever happens, remember to burn your ciphers and all ciphered messages."

This communication took Sir George White completely by surprise. Could his Chief be really advising him to lay down his arms before every resource had been exhausted? It was more natural that he should assume that the cipher-key had fallen into the hands of the Boers who were trying to mislead him. The reply was, therefore, so drafted that it should, if necessary, make an impression on the Boers.

"Your message of to-day received and understood. My advice is that you should take up the strongest possible position which will enable you to keep touch with the enemy, and to harass him uninterruptedly with artillery and as far as you can in other ways. I can arrange so that my supplies shall last much longer than a month, and I will not think of capitulating before I am forced to. Perhaps you have caused the enemy more severe losses than you think. All our native spies report that your artillery fire made a great impression on him. Were your losses really very severe? If you lose touch with the enemy it will be much easier for him to crush me. This would re-act adversely elsewhere. So long as you are in touch with the enemy and in communication with me he has to reckon with both our forces. Try to get support as quickly as possible, also from India; raise every man in the Colony who is willing to serve and who can ride. The situation may take a more favourable turn. If 12,000 men are lost here it would be a heavy blow for England. We cannot think of such a thing. I am afraid I am not strong enough to fight my way through to you. Enteric is increasing here in an alarming way. In the last month we have had 180 cases. Answer in detail. I am keeping everything secret till I learn your plans."

On the 17th Buller repeated his enquiry, thus:—"I am convinced that I cannot capture Colenso. Nor can I stay here long with any larger force, for there is no water. I shall leave as many troops as possible here to support you; remember that in the present weather my Infantry cannot march more than 10 miles. Can you make any proposal? I believe I can take Colenso in three weeks, but I can never reach Onderbrook."

To the request of his Chief for proposals as to what he should do, the General Officer Commanding the Fourth Division (Sir G. White) replied as follows on the 18th December:—"Your despatch of 17th received and understood. As I do not know the situation outside, nor whether you have made a serious effort to capture Colenso, nor what were your losses, it is difficult for me to make proposals. Your communications at first seemed confident. I had made preparations for action towards Onderbrook, and could still carry them out at any time if you took Colenso. I cannot advise you to leave a small body of troops in advance of your main body. It would probably be cut off and would offer no serious menace to the enemy. You should keep your advanced line in full strength. To abandon this garrison appears to me, on political grounds, to be a very hazardous solution of the difficulties. If Ladysmith should fall the strength of the enemy on the Tugela will be doubled. I can only advise you to get every obtainable reinforcement in troops and guns and as soon as possible to renew the attack with all your force. Meanwhile, I will do everything in my power to carry on an active defence and will, as far as I can, co-operate with you if you resume the offensive. What progress have you made in the Free State? We know nothing. Precise information is requested that we may be able to contradict mischievous rumours."

Buller did not wait for this answer; he had already on the 17th December, under cover of darkness, withdrawn his troops further south from the camps between the Tugela and Chieveley, viz., to Chieveley, the Second Brigade (Hildyard), the Sixth Brigade (Barton), as well as the 13th Hussars, the Mounted Infantry, 3 Field Batteries, and some of the heavy guns; and to Frere, the Fourth Brigade (Lyttelton), the Fifth Brigade (Hart), the Royal Dragoons, and the rest of the heavy guns. Cavalry secured the line Weenen-Springfield. Buller decided to postpone the resumption of operations till January, and on the 18th December informed General White that he would, in about three weeks, be reinforced by the Fifth Division which had already arrived at Capetown, and which had been immediately ordered on to Natal, and that he would then make another attempt to relieve Ladysmith by way of Potgieter's Drift.

As the rainy season would set in from the middle of January and would hinder all movements and make the

Tugela a really serious obstacle, the advantage to be derived from the contemplated increase of force would appear to be small in comparison with the far greater difficulties with which the attack would later have to contend on account of unfavourable conditions of weather. Moreover, the Boers, if they were left quite at their ease on the Tugela, would have a free hand to direct all their strength against Ladysmith. But the great disadvantage lay in the fact that the withdrawal of the troops and the postponement of any further decisive action gave to the failure at Colenso an altogether exaggerated importance.

The feeling of success raised the Boers' self-esteem and confidence in their own strength to a high pitch. They felt themselves able to cope with any British attack. At the same time, however, nobody among them thought of turning the success to advantage or of taking the offensive. Quite contented with what they had done they remained inactive in their position, which extended from Robinson's Farm to Hlangwane. They limited their efforts to occupying Colenso and to strongly entrenching Hlangwane on the south of the Tugela. A bridge was thrown over the Tugela above the Falls to connect Hlangwane with the northern bank.

Beyond taking these measures, as an eyewitness with the Boers reports, they sank into a condition of absolute lethargy. Many burghers asked for and obtained leave to go to their homes, others tried to get off military service on the plea of sickness, "scrimshanking" or shirking began to be the fashion. Even the leaders, and among them the energetic General Louis Botha, took up to fourteen days' leave.

Nothing was done in the way of reconnaissance: although the British were so close, all touch with them was lost. The following observation, under date 20th December in the War Journal, of Major Freiherr von

Reitzenstein, who, as a spectator on the Boer side, was present at all these occurrences:—" General Botha, who is in command at Colenso, has no idea as to where the British are. Not even the slightest reconnaissance is attempted by the Boers; this is a form of activity which is quite foreign to their nature, and which in no way suits their passive temperament. I have frequently begged the General to give me 20 Boers, with knowledge of the country, so as to work a strong patrol round the flanks and in rear of the British, but he will have absolutely nothing to do with such a scheme, and is afraid that we should be rounded up. Neither does one hear or see anything of British patrols." The Boers and the British received most of their information, and that the best, from the Kaffirs, who did very good work as spies.

Another quotation: " Day by day, morning and evening, the British thunder out at us their customary benediction at Matins and Evensong from their heavy long-range naval guns; but they never get near a Boer in these performances. I am firmly convinced that the whole cannonade is nothing more than a ruse, and that the British have withdrawn the whole of their main body. The reconnaissance is pitiable."

As the Boers were in constant expectation of a night attack, they always occupied their position towards evening with the greater part of their force. About 6 a.m. the burghers were dismissed, and during the day-time the positions were only weakly held.

The sanitary conditions obtaining among the Boers left much to be desired; there were many cases of enteric and dysentery. In consequence of the numbers absent on leave, and of the constant endeavours to withdraw from service, their fighting strength was continually changing and cannot be accurately recorded. It was, however, said that at this time some 6,000 or 7,000 were along the

Tugela, while about 9,000 invested Ladysmith. It was not till the beginning of January that the Boers began to display some activity. Patrols were sent towards Weenen and Springfield, and these, scouting round flanks and rear of the British, brought back reports on their situation.

CHAPTER II.

BRITISH PREPARATIONS FOR THE SECOND ATTEMPT AT RELIEF.

Depression of spirits ruled in the British force. Leaders and men had lost confidence in one another. There was a feeling that it was impossible to fight against an enemy who, concealed from view, understood how to make the most of his excellent weapons, and who seemed himself to be quite insensible to the heaviest artillery fire. Officers and men declared that they had not seen a single Boer in action. A British officer describing this "emptiness of the battle-field" as the most uncanny feature in the modern attack, says that one had during an action the paralyzing sensation of advancing to meet an invisible fate against which no weapon could avail; when firing, it was only possible to aim at random in the general direction from which the enemy's bullets appeared to come; his invisibility fostered the suspicion that he was everywhere. The sensation of fighting against an enemy who had all the advantages of the conditions soon produced its impression; every attempt to rise made by those in the attack was immediately met by some shots fired from above; consequently it was not long before any sort of movement—forwards, to a flank or rearwards—just died away.

Such were the first impressions in action. It was necessary to give the troops some rest before leading them forward again against the enemy. The period of the halt was employed in completing the training of the troops, in adapting their methods of fighting to the special characteristics of the enemy and to the peculiar environments of the scene of the fighting.

Great pains were also taken in the development of the arrangements on the Lines of Communication and to the creation of the train of transport needed in the forthcoming operations. The railway running from the Port of Durban through Pietermaritzburg to Frere, formed the Army's chief channel of supply. The working capacity of this single line of railway, however, was small, for on account of steep banks which had to be climbed in the here and there extremely mountainous country, it was impossible to make up trains of more than five or at most six wagons. As, however, the rationed strength of the Natal Army at that time scarcely exceeded 50,000 men, the railway sufficed to bring up the supplies. Three months' supply was stored in Pietermaritzburg, where also a large ammunition depôt and a base hospital were established. Frere was made the provisional rail-head, and at the beginning of the operations was to remain occupied by a fairly strong garrison consisting of $1\frac{1}{2}$ battalions of Infantry and several Guns. Food and fuel for 15 days were stored there, and a permanent field hospital was established there, as well as a remount depôt and a depôt of ordnance stores of all descriptions. The field-bakeries which were constructed there, were able to furnish more than the daily needs in bread.

As has already been mentioned the field transport was based on the regimental system, and by this was effected the transfer of supplies from the field magazines to the troops, while the magazines were kept filled from the stores on the Lines of Communication by means of Brigade,

Division, and Corps Supply-Columns. Owing to the unexpectedly early commencement of operations, it had not been possible to create these Supply-Columns in full strength or to organise them systematically; consequently, beyond the regimental transport which furnished three days' supply, the troops were only in part provided with adequate resources for the transport of subsistence. Hence it resulted that it was impossible to move troops further than a few days' march away from the Lines of Communication on the railway, and, therefore, that all operations were tied to it; effective freedom of movement was out of the question. Should Buller wish to operate for more than a few days clear of the railway, he must either wait for the systematic organisation of the whole of the requisite Supply-Columns, or he must try, as Lord Roberts did later with success, to make more complete use of the transport already available by means of a fresh distribution which should, in the first place, ensure a regular despatch of supplies from the Lines of Communication to the troops, and so free their operations from the incubus of problems as to how they should get their daily subsistence.

Buller meanwhile thought that he must continue to work on the existing foundation of the obsolete system of supply and transport, and as, in his opinion, no duly regulated and reliable adaptation to fresh conditions could be introduced, he determined to have all the supply stores which should be needed for the next phase of the operations, collected and deposited in the intended theatre as a preliminary measure; in this decision he was evidently influenced by his recollection of previous colonial campaigns. Such a measure could not have been thought of for a moment in operations against an enemy possessed of more initiative than were the Boers. If, thanks to the absolute want of any offensive spirit in the enemy, the British troops were able, in spite of the inappropriate application of General Buller's experiences, to feed abundantly and well, the operations, as the course of events proved, fell all the same under the influence of supply-considerations owing to the General's rigid adherence to the customary system of replenishment from the rear which was unsuited to the circumstances. On the other hand, in the western theatre of war, where the talent for organisation of Lord Roberts and Lord Kitchener created, in the middle of operations and in the shortest time, a completely new constitution of the transport, well adapted to altered conditions, all requirements were amply fulfilled in spite of difficulties just as great. There the troops were always well and abundantly rationed, and at the same time the operations were not unnecessarily hampered by considerations for supply.

On account of the difference between the local conditions and those prevailing at home, colonial warfare will always demand from those conducting it a superior standard of adaptability of mind as regards organisation and, above all, the capacity to adopt under strange conditions and, if necessary, even during the operations, fresh arrangements suited to the particular local conditions in place of such as are found impracticable there.

For the projected operations, and as a preliminary to them, 16 days' supplies were to be stored at Springfield. With this in view during the lull in the operations several columns of transport train were improvised out of the already available transport. These were to be loaded up and in 4 days to convey to Springfield all the requirements. In addition to these, 7 road-traction steam-engines with 7 loaded trains were available; these, however, stuck in the mud before they had really quitted the camp. There was a project for laying a light railway from Frere to Springfield before operations should begin, and the material was collected in Frere; but no steps were actually taken later on towards the construction.

Early in January the Fifth Division, under Lieut.-General Sir Charles Warren, reached Durban as reinforcements. It had reached Capetown on the day of Colenso, and 2 Battalions and a Battery were immediately landed.* The disembarkation of the rest of the troops was postponed as soon as the first news of Buller's failure at Colenso came to hand. The following day orders were received that those troops which were still on board should continue the voyage to Durban and should there be disembarked to reinforce the Natal army. On the 7th January the Division, now consisting of only six Battalions, one Squadron and two Field Batteries, was united at Estcourt.

By an order, dated 8th January, an entirely new distribution of the Natal Army was effected by the breaking-up of the existing formations.† The fighting strength was at this date about 27,000 men with 76 guns, of which 14 were heavy Field.

On the 9th January Warren's Division reached Frere Camp. The British troops were now distributed as follows: At Chieveley, Staff of the Second Division (Clery), Second Brigade (Hildyard), and Sixth Brigade (Barton), 13th Hussars, Mounted Infantry and 22 Guns; at Frere, Headquarter Staff, Staff of Fifth Division (Warren), Fourth Brigade (Lyttelton), Fifth Brigade (Hart), Tenth Brigade (Coke), Eleventh Brigade (Woodgate) and 54 guns.

On the 10th January Lord Roberts reached Capetown and took up the Chief Command in South Africa, *vice* Buller.‡ On the 17th December, two days after the Battle of Colenso, the latter had been relieved of the command of the British Forces in South Africa, but retained

---

* These units were employed in the western theatre of war.
† See Appendix I.
‡ *See* p. 125 Waters' Translation "War in South Africa."

the command of the Natal Army; this was arranged on the assumption that all his attention would be needed in this theatre of the war.

With the beginning of the New Year the Boers, too, had begun to rouse themselves from their inactivity. General Joubert, who was in command at the siege of Ladysmith, finally yielding to repeated pressure from Presidents Krüger and Steyn, decided to employ in a vigorous attack on Ladysmith the uninterrupted leisure which the British troops south of the Tugela allowed the Boers to enjoy. This attack, fixed for the 6th January, was to be directed against the south front of the British defences formed by the Tafelberg, Cæsar's Camp and Wagon Hill. Three assaulting columns, each about 1,000 men strong, were formed for the attack, viz., on the right the Krugersdorp and Lydenburg Commandos, in the centre the German Corps and the Utrecht and Vryheid Commandos, on the left the Free Staters, reinforced by the Johannesburg and Pretoria Commandos. Under cover of darkness the columns advanced noiselessly almost up to the British position, and at break of day threw back in hot haste the weak line holding the southern edge of the Tafelberg. But instead of immediately following up the British, so as to reach with them the northern edge of the Tafelberg (whence they would have commanded the town), the Boers halted and occupied the abandoned position on the southern edge, and thence opened and maintained a fire-action against the British, who had halted in a position on the northern edge in which they soon received considerable reinforcements, particularly in artillery. After this and during the whole day there was no energetic resumption of the offensive by the Boers. The projected surprise became an indecisive fire-action which lasted till nightfall when the Boers evacuated their position of their own free will and withdrew behind the line of investment.

This attack cost the Boers 162 killed and wounded, while the British lost 45 officers and 379 men.

From early morning the firing of guns near Ladysmith had been heard in the camps at Chieveley and Frere; movement in the Boer position on the Tugela was also noticed, and single horsemen were seen hurrying away northward in the direction whence the firing was heard.* About 7 a.m. Buller received information from White that the British position had since 3 a.m. been under a heavy but so far unsuccessful assault. The situation demanded a prompt decision on the part of the commander of the Natal Army. Was it not distinctly apparent that an immediate attack ought to be made on the Boers at Colenso, either to chain them down there and so embarrass their attack on Ladysmith, or if their force had been weakened there to profit by the favourable opportunity for crossing the Tugela? The troops in camp, keen for a fight, impatiently awaited orders for action; their Commander, however, could not decide what form, if any, this action should take.

About 9.30 a.m. a second and more urgent message arrived from White: "Attack continues; enemy has received reinforcements from south; whole of my reserve is in action. Consider enemy must have reduced his force in front of you." About 12.45 p.m. this opinion was confirmed in the following heliograph message: "We know for certain that a considerable force of the enemy left Colenso yesterday with the intention of capturing Ladysmith before you could get into action. Have, up to the present, repulsed them, but they surround me more and more; their numbers are increasing, particularly towards the South. I consider a fresh attack very probable."

---

* As a matter of fact, several commandos and guns under Louis Botha had already proceeded to Ladysmith during the night of the 6th January.

Towards noon the noise of the guns echoing down from Ladysmith appeared to increase in intensity; grave alarm was expressed that the assault would overwhelm White. At last, towards 1.30 p.m., came Buller's order that General Clery's troops at Chieveley were to turn out to advance towards Colenso. But according to Buller's own expression this advance was only to have the object of a demonstration. He also said before the Commission of Enquiry, "I sent every available (!) man to produce the impression of an attack on Colenso with the object of holding there as many of the enemy as possible. Their entrenchments were, however, fully manned."

About 2 p.m. 5 Battalions and 3 Batteries advanced from Chieveley Camp. It was not till 4.30 p.m. that these Batteries, posted on Gun Hill, opened fire on Hlangwane and the ground lying between that mountain and Fort Wylie. The Boers remained under cover ready for action, but without making any reply to the fire.

The Battalions deployed under cover of the Artillery fire. Each Battalion was extended in four loose ranks following one another far apart, with intervals of 6 or 7 paces between files; in this formation they all advanced up to within 2,000 yards from the enemy's position and lay down without firing. An hour passed; the battalions turned about and marched back into the camp at Chieveley.*

The British Headquarters remained all day completely in the dark as to the fate of Ladysmith. It was only during the 7th January that messages were received from White to announce the successful warding off of the attack. But they went on: "The troops have been severely handled; a large number of officers are killed,

---

* It is astonishing that this British advance, quite unmistakably a simple demonstrative movement though it was, induced Louis Botha to march back to their position at Colenso his commandos, with which till it took place he had been inactively looking on at the fight round Cæsar's Camp.

wounded, or sick. I would rather not lead the troops out of Ladysmith to co-operate with you. . . . I beg that our casualties may not be published in the local papers lest they should encourage the enemy."

The Boer attack on Ladysmith, coupled with this message from White, betraying as it did a state of great dejection, drew Buller's attention to the urgent necessity of undertaking, without further delay, measures for the early relief of Ladysmith. He therefore decided to abandon his passive and waiting attitude as soon as ever reinforcements should arrive.

He had, even in December, been considering whether any, and if so, what further efforts could be made for the relief of Ladysmith. Lord Roberts, on the 23rd December, while still in London, had thus communicated to him by telegraph his own appreciation of the situation: "Co-operation between you and me after my arrival in South Africa will, in my opinion, be most effective if the original plan of campaign is carried out, and if we advance in force through the Free State. I would like to make this co-operation easier by formulating my views as follows: I gather from the intelligence with which I am provided here that you are only waiting for sufficient reinforcements to turn the enemy's strong position on the Tugela, while you occupy an entrenched camp near Chieveley Road. If you succeed in this the situation changes distinctly in our favour. Subsequently* it would, in my opinion, be desirable to evacuate Ladysmith and to limit yourself to holding the line of the Tugela until the general advance begins. How many troops could you spare if you act in this way? If Methuen succeeds in relieving Kimberley he should come back to me on the line of the Orange River, where I would wait for him, so that all the

---

* *i.e.*, after the Relief of Ladysmith.

forces could be assembled on that line before the commencement of the advance on Bloemfontein. We must always keep before us the importance of assembling in Cape Colony all available troops for the last-named operation."

Buller did not adopt Lord Robert's suggestion to turn the Boers' strong position at Colenso, as he rightly recognised that a simple flank march round the enemy could bring about no decisive success. It seemed to him to be, before all things, requisite that the Boers should be defeated before Ladysmith could be relieved and "that the Boer position must be forced." Moreover, a turning movement on the Tugela, such as Roberts a few weeks later planned for the relief of Kimberley, was not possible. The unbroken chain of heights, which stretched like a belt of forts along the northern bank of the Tugela as far as the Drakensberg, allowed a mobile defence, such as that of the Boers, always to show front against an enemy pushing across the Tugela. Buller had, with clear military insight, recognised all this, but after his failure at Colenso he had felt himself too weak for a fresh frontal attack. However, after the Boers' attack of the 6th January, he determined to attempt once more the relief of Ladysmith, and that without further delay.

As it was known that the Boers had been busily employed during the pause in the operations in further strengthening their entrenched positions near Colenso, a second attempt to cross the Tugela there appeared to hold out but small prospect of success. An advance below Colenso did not appear advisable as it would lead into very bushy country, which Buller at that time thought unfavourable for his operations. The passage of the river above Colenso held out the prospect of bringing on an engagement in a more open country, which would favour the British method of fighting and in which, moreover, the Boers were not so strongly entrenched. Buller, therefore, determined to make a flank march to his left on Springfield and to cross the Tugela at Potgieter's Drift with a view to joining hands with White in the open country south-west of Ladysmith. White was informed of the plan, of which the execution was to be begun on the 9th January, and was, moreover, told that in any fighting which might ensue, his support in the direction of Lancers' Hill would be counted on. All movements of troops were to be carried out by night with a view to effecting the surprise of the Boers and to concealing from them the flank march on Springfield.

Meanwhile the Boers, expecting that the British would cross the river above Colenso, had for some time turned their special attention to this portion of the Tugela; it also appears that they had been warned by Kaffirs of the danger which threatened them there. Early in January several observation posts were established at the drifts on the Tugela in that quarter, and from these reconnaissances were carried out *viâ* Springfield towards Frere and Chieveley Road; the horse-drifts were made impassable with barbed-wire entanglements; two of the British guns captured at Colenso were, moreover, brought into a position commanding Potgieter's Drift, and shelter trenches were constructed on Spion Kop and on the Brakfontein heights for the defence of the passages of the river. In the next few days, as early in fact as 9th January, when the original suspicion had been confirmed by the appearance of numerous British patrols in the neighbourhood of Springfield, several commandos were sent from the Colenso position to the Upper Tugela; of these the Vryheid Commando took up their position on and entrenched Spion Kop, the Free Staters the Brakfontein heights, the Johannesburg Commando Vaalkrantz.

The following orders for the flank march to the left

on Springfield were issued from the British Headquarters to the Troops on the evening of 8th January:—

Frere Camp, 8th January, 1900.

1. A distribution of the Army is published with this Order.*

2. The following movements will be carried out during the night, 9th-10th January, 1900, under the orders of Lieut.-General Sir C. F. Clery:—

Second Division and attached Troops.

(*a*) Major-General Hildyard's Column, viz.:—

400 men of the Mounted Brigade (including a squadron 13th Hussars),
Second Infantry Brigade,
Divisional Troops: a Field Battery,
Corps Troops: two 12-pr. naval guns,

will march from Chieveley, passing south of the Doorn Kop to the camp already selected near Pretorius' Farm.

(*b*) Major-General Hart's Column, viz.:—

400 men of the Mounted Brigade,
Fifth Infantry Brigade,
73rd Field Battery,
17th Field Company Royal Engineers,
Corps Troops: six 12-pr. naval guns,

will march from Frere, along the Frere-Springfield Road to the camp already selected south of Pretorius' Farm.

(*c*) The Divisional Staff and the Divisional Troops of the Second Division:—

Staff, Main Body, Supply Column (from Frere) and Hospital Detachment of the Mounted Brigade,

Divisional Troops: one Field Battery, Ammunition Column, Supply Column (from Frere), Field Hospital (from Frere),

---

* See Appendix I.

Corps Troops: two (?*) squadron 13th Hussars, two guns 66th Field Battery, two 4·7-in. naval guns,

Supply Column (from Frere),

will march from Chieveley (with the exception of those units, etc., for whom a different place of departure is appointed), along the Frere-Springfield Road to the camp selected south of Pretorius' Farm. The squadron 13th Hussars belonging to the Fifth Division and the two guns of the 66th Field Battery remain in Frere.

3. On the evening of the 10th January the following troops, under the command of Lieut.-General Sir C. Warren, will march from Frere to Springfield:—

Fifth Division and attached Troops.

Fifth Division.
Fourth Infantry Brigade.
Eleventh Infantry Brigade.
Divisional Troops.

Corps Troops:
Tenth Infantry Brigade.

Artillery:
61st Field Battery (Howitzer).
78th Field Battery.
Ammunition Column.

Royal Engineers.
Pontoon Train.
Balloon Section.
Field Telegraph Section.
Supply Park.

---

* According to the Distribution of Troops only one Squadron belonged to the Corps troops.

4. Ammunition :—

(a) Ammunition will be taken on the following scale :—

Type of Gun.	Rounds per Gun.		Total.
	With the Battery.	With the Ammunition Column.	
15-pounder Field Gun	150	150	300
5-inch Howitzer	88	130	218
4·7 inch Naval Gun	150	100	250
12-pounder Naval Gun	250	50	300

Rifle and carbine ammunition according to the Equipment Regulations.

(b) There will be held in readiness in a small Ammunition Park in Frere :—

1,260 rounds per 15-pr.,
300 rounds per 5-inch Howitzer, and
125,000 rounds rifle and carbine ammunition.

The personnel of the Ammunition Park (1 Officer, 20 N.C.O.'s and men Royal Artillery) will be furnished from the principal depôt under orders of the Inspector of the Lines of Communication.

5. Medical details :—

(a) The Corps Troops are to obtain surgical assistance from the nearest Divisional Field Hospital.

(b) No. 4 General Hospital will accompany the Army in order to take over wounded and sick from the Field Hospitals under the direction of the Principal Medical Officer of the Army.

(c) The European Volunteer Ambulance Corps is divided into four sections, which are distributed among the Brigade Field Hospitals of the Second and Fifth Divisions. The Commandant of the Corps will accompany the Principal Medical Officer of the Army and receive orders from him.

(*d*) 100 men of the Native Ambulance Corps will accompany No. 4 General Hospital; the remainder will halt, till further orders, in Estcourt.

6. Supply:—

Arrangements for supply are to be in accordance with instructions issued as an appendix herewith to the Commanders of Divisions and of the Corps Troops.

7. Heavy Baggage:—

The following will be carried on the regimental wagons—tents, one blanket for every two men, a waterproof sheet per man, 50 cartridges per rifle, 3 days' rations (only two meat rations), 750 lbs. fuel (3 days' supply), 3 days' rations of corn, officers' baggage, and all stores considered necessary for the troops which can be carried without raising the maximum load above 3,000 lbs.

Orders for Supply.

Supply-Columns and Supply-Parks each carry 4 days' supplies.

A Ration and Forage Depôt is to be established in Springfield as follows:—

First Day—The Supply-Park will proceed to Pretorius' Farm, will there off-load and return to Frere. The troops camping at Pretorius' Farm will draw supplies with their regimental transport wagons, which are to be replenished daily at Frere.

Second Day—All Supply-Columns will proceed to Springfield and will there off-load. The Supply-Park will go to Pretorius' Farm, there off-load and return to Frere.

Third Day—All Supply-Columns will proceed from Springfield to Pretorius' Farm, there load up and march back to Springfield. The Supply-Park will move from Frere to Pretorius' Farm, remain there loaded, and be held in readiness to march again on the following day.

Fourth Day—The Supply-Columns will proceed from Springfield to Pretorius' Farm, there load up and return to Springfield. The Supply-Park will move from Pretorius' Farm to Springfield.

The troops camping at Springfield will draw supplies from the regimental transport wagons which are to be replenished from the magazine there.

The troops at Pretorius' Farm will move to Springfield with loaded transport wagons.

The following supplementary order was published on the 9th:—

Frere Camp, 9th January, 1900.

1. With the object of relieving Ladysmith, the General intends to effect the passage of the Tugela in the neighbourhood of Potgieter's Drift.

2. The units already detailed* remain in Chieveley and Frere to hold these places while the rest of the army operates against the enemy's right flank.

3. Springfield will be taken and occupied. The march of the Army and of the Columns to that place will be covered by a detachment posted at Pretorius' Farm.

4. The principal task of Hildyard's Column (see Army Order of 8th inst., para. 2a) is the protection of the advance of the troops from Frere to Springfield during the establishment of a magazine at Springfield. The movements of this Column must further be so arranged that the enemy may be induced to believe that our intention is to cross the Tugela at Poreit's Drift.

5. The remainder of Lieut.-General Clery's Troops will occupy a camp south of Pretorius' Farm in accordance with paras. 2b and c of the above-quoted order. Major-General Hart, under the instructions of Lieut.-General Clery, is to afford every assistance to the

---

* In the fresh distribution of the Natal Army which was simultaneously published (Appendix I.).

Columns as they pass his camp, and is to hold himself in readiness to support General Hildyard if necessary.

6. In the afternoon of the 10th General Clery will send a sufficiently strong detachment of the Mounted Brigade, with Artillery, to reconnoitre and, if possible, to occupy Springfield.

7. The Troops under General Warren (see Army Order dated 8th inst., para. 3) will reach Springfield on the morning of the 11th and will support the detachment of the Mounted Brigade, referred to in para. 6 above.

8. It is calculated that the magazine, which it is intended to establish in Springfield, will be completed on the 13th instant, and that on that day General Clery's troops should march to Springfield.

9. The Commanding Royal Engineer will establish telegraphic communication between Frere and Springfield, with an intermediate station at General Clery's Camp south of Pretorius' Farm.

10. The General Officer Commanding Tenth Brigade will detail a signalling detachment under the Brigade Signalling Officer for service with Army Headquarters.

11. The General Commanding will move on the 11th instant to Springfield.

The advance was carried out in the following manner:—

On the 9th January the supply wagons started on the march from Frere to Pretorius' Farm. During the night, 9th-10th, the Infantry of Clery's Division followed on, viz., Hildyard's Brigade from Chieveley and Hart's Brigade from Frere; the former was to protect the flank of the transport and of the main Column, while Hart's Brigade acted as rearguard and gave assistance to the column of wagons on its march.

In consequence of heavy rain the roads were so soft, and several small streams which had to be crossed were so swollen, that progress was frequently delayed for several hours at a time. The roads were blocked with foundered wagons abandoned by the Supply-Columns sent ahead, which impeded the march of the Troops following them. In consequence of this it was not till the evening of the 10th, after a march of only 9 or 10 miles, that the Brigades of Clery's Division reached their appointed goal at Pretorius' Farm, and there went into camp in order to protect the passage of the Supply-Columns to Springfield during the two succeeding days.

On the evening of the same day Warren's Division, with the greater part of the Corps Troops, set out on the march to Springfield as ordered; it too was delayed owing to the blockage on the soft and muddy roads caused by the transport wagons; the Infantry and Artillery had to thread their way wearily through the endless columns of wagons halted along the road, and so it was not till late in the afternoon of the 11th that the Troops reached the end of their march.

In accordance with Clery's orders, Dundonald's Mounted Brigade with the 66th Field Battery had been already sent forward on the afternoon of the 10th for "the occupation of Springfield and reconnaissance"; it had crossed the Little Tugela by a bridge which had been left intact, had reached Springfield, and after posting there a small detachment and 2 guns, had continued its march to Spearman's Heights unmolested by the enemy. Only the patrols sent towards the Tugela were fired on, from the opposite bank; these patrols noticed a signalling station on Spion Kop flashing messages to Ladysmith and Colenso.

On the 12th Warren's Division crossed the Little Tugela, and Lyttelton's Brigade was pushed forward to Spearman's Farm as a support to Dundonald's detachment which, from this day onwards, was placed under Warren. The heights near Spearman's Farm and at Zwart Kop were occupied and entrenched. The remainder of the Division halted in camp on the northern bank of the Little Tugela. Sir Redvers Buller moved from Frere to Springfield, where the following Army Order of the day was issued:—

"Springfield, 12th January, 1900.

"The Army is about to advance to the relief of Ladysmith, where our comrades, surrounded by superior forces, have been valiantly defending themselves these last ten weeks. The General in Command knows that every man in the Army is inspired by the same feelings as his own; we must win! We shall encounter a gallant resistance from a clever enemy who knows no scruples. Let no one allow himself to be deceived by him. If a white flag is shown it has no meaning, unless the troops raising it halt, lay down their arms and hold up their hands. If the enemy gets a chance he will try to mislead us by false orders and signals; everybody must be on his guard against such attempts at deception! Further, if any body of troops is surprised by a volley fired from close by, there must be no hesitation, no turning about, but an immediate dash at the enemy. That is the way to victory and safety. Any retirement is fatal. The one thing the enemy cannot stand against is a hand-to-hand fight with us. We are fighting for the weal and for the lives of our comrades; we are fighting for our flag against an enemy who has forced war on us on the meanest and basest motives, by treachery, by fraud and deceit. Let us be brave; our cause is worthy of it."

On the 13th January Clery's Division moved on to Springfield when the passage of the supply train had been almost completed; the remainder of the troops stood fast.

Warren's and Clery's Troops at Springfield employed the 14th January in closing up on to Spearman's Farm; only the Corps Troops remained at Springfield and near the bridge over the Little Tugela.

The 15th January was a day of general repose.

The Army had taken 5 full days to complete a march of about 22 miles. Putting aside the very unfavourable condition of the weather, which has been already referred to, the blame for this extraordinarily slow rate of progress must be attributed to the unfortunate arrangements for supply and, before all, to the movement of the transport wagons along the same roads as the troops were to use in their march.

Of all the combatant units, the heavy naval guns met with the greatest difficulties on the march through the blockage of the road; though each was drawn by 16 span of oxen, some of these guns, which began the march to Springfield on 10th January, only got to the end of it on the 15th.

Buller's Army, in its first operations away from the railway, had shown clumsiness which augured but ill for the future, and had proved its complete deficiency in that mobility of manœuvre which is an essential preliminary condition to tactical success. As a matter of course there could be no further thought of a surprise of the Boers, on which the whole project was based.

CHAPTER III.

The Passage of the Tugela.

On the 14th January General Buller had made a reconnaissance from Spearman's Hill of the passage of the Tugela at Potgieter's Drift, while General Warren reconnoitred the river at Trichardt's Drift. The country which was to be the scene of the battles fought during the next ten days is traversed by the Tugela in its course from the Drakensberg. The summer rains of the last week had considerably swollen the river, which is very rapid and which quite suddenly becomes a violent torrent whenever there have been storms in the Basutoland mountains. The banks are nearly perpendicular and about 17 to 22 feet high. With a breadth from 55 to 65 yards, and a depth of about 12 feet, the Tugela forms a serious obstacle to movement which even single horsemen can only pass at the drifts which are few in number. South of the river spread rolling downs rising gradually from the Tugela; considerable altitude is only attained north and northeast of Springfield at Spearman's Heights, Zwart Kop, Mount Alice and Spearman's Hill. These mountains come close down to the river, which winds considerably in this quarter. Artillery in position here can cover the passage of the river as far as the left bank; it can, however, afford no support to the further advance of the Infantry owing to the excessive range required to reach the commanding heights across the river.

On the northern bank a sharply defined chain of hills stretches from the Doornkloof to the Drakensberg in the form of a curve slightly concave towards the south. This chain approaches the Tugela closely only at the two most northerly points in the bends of the river. A level country some 2 to 3 miles wide separates the intermediate hills from the river. About 3 miles north-east of Trichardt's Drift the chain of heights making a north-westerly bend forms an obtuse angle, and about 2 miles further on widens out into the plateau of Thaba Myama. The general trend of the heights in this part approximately follows the direction of the valley of the Venterspruit, a tributary stream of the Tugela. A spur of Thaba Myama, called Bastion Hill, runs up fairly close to the Spruit to the south-east of Acton Homes. West of Thaba Myama, similar heights surround Acton Homes on the north and north-west. These heights stretch on right up to the Drakensberg in gentler slopes, and if well defended form, even westward of Acton Homes, a stout barrier against an enemy advancing from the south.

At the obtuse angle where the chain of heights bends to the North-West, lies Spion Kop, a three-cornered table-mountain which considerably overtops not only the neighbouring country, but also the crests near by. From the summit the view extends westward to the mountain barrier formed by the Drakensberg and eastward to beyond the Frere-Ladysmith Railway. No considerable movement on either bank of the Tugela or of the Venter's Spruit, and no encampment North of Spearman's Heights could escape observation from it.

The whole chain of heights from Vaalkrantz to Thaba Myama is absolutely bare; it descends rather precipitously in terraces to the Tugela and Venter's Spruit. The selection of these heights as a defensive position provides for the employment of Artillery up to the maximum ranges.

Infantry, too, has in all directions a good field for distant fire. Only on the limits of the zones of medium and distant Infantry fire (*i.e.*, about 800 to 1,000 yards) in front of the position could an assailant find even temporarily cover from the defender's fire in the numerous dead-angles, hollows and gorges, or behind hillocks and boulders.

In much the same manner the northern slopes run down to the Blaauwbank Spruit on the left bank of which flat country stretches almost up to Ladysmith. The actual crest of the whole chain of mountains is comparatively narrow; the Northern side is hidden from the view and from the direct fire of an assailant operating from the lower-lying ground near the river. The distribution of the troops and the supply of reinforcements could be effected almost undisturbed and absolutely unseen. There was such complete cover for encampments, for the position of troops not engaged, and for held horses, that the Boers could boil their coffee quietly during the most violent cannonade. Many of them found the attractive force of such excellent cover more than they could resist. The want of proportion between the enormous extent of the defensive line—from Thaba Myama to Vaalkrantz, 11 miles—and the small number of Boers, was balanced by the facility afforded for absolutely screened movement within the position.

The whole position from Vaalkrantz to Thaba Myama might be compared to a mighty escarp-wall of which the advanced flanking works were furnished by those two heights and of which Spion Kop forms an elevated central bastion. The Boers could, in such a defensive position, derive the utmost advantage from their method of fighting, while the British would be coping with a task of the utmost difficulty.

The position of the adversaries on the 15th January was the following:—The bulk of the British force, Clery's

Division, Woodgate's Brigade of the Fifth Division and 6 Batteries were halted at Springfield; Lyttelton's and Coke's Brigades, the Mounted Troops, a 15-pr. Field Battery, a Howitzer Field Battery, and 10 naval guns of various calibres had been sent forward to the heights south of Potgieter's Drift. Altogether there were about 22,000 men assembled by Buller on the Upper Tugela. Barton's Brigade and Blagrove's Command continued as previously to furnish a strength of some 5,000 men at Chieveley and Frere.

But little was known of the Boers at the British Headquarters beyond what could be observed with the naked eye; to wit, that they were getting good work put in by Kaffirs at the entrenchments between Vaalkrantz and Spion Kop. The configuration of the country concealed aught else that might be taking place North of the Tugela. No attempt was made by reconnaissances round the flank of the Boer position to gain an insight into the enemy's proceedings. Neither had any news about the Boers come to hand from Ladysmith. The collection of supplies at Springfield was nearing completion.

As has been mentioned, as soon as the Boers recognised the flank movement of the Natal Army, they extended still more towards the West. Their right flank at this time was at Spion Kop, their left occupied Vaalkrantz. They now began to draw over towards Schalk Burger's detachments, which for some time had been on the Upper Tugela, parts of the Commandos which were at Colenso and around Ladysmith. The strength of these heterogeneous forces cannot be stated with any sort of certainty. It may have amounted on the 15th to 2,000, and have risen in the next few days to 7,000. How many rifles these 7,000 Boers actually put into the firing line in the course of the various actions cannot be even approximately fixed under the peculiar circumstances, and more especially on account of the entire absence of fighting discipline in this army of levies.

The Boers directed their special and particular attention to Potgieter's Drift. On that account the bulk of the fighting men was placed on the Brakfontein Heights in the construction of defences on which the greatest energy had been displayed. At Spion Kop and to its west there were, up to the present, only quite weak piquets. The British movements on the Southern bank could be clearly distinguished from the Boer position, and on this account there was a constant supply of information about the enemy without any need for special scouting to acquire it.

The Commander of the British Army in Natal had now to decide as to how he should conduct further operations. Before even beginning the flank march to the left he had expressed and discussed with the subordinate commanders his intention to cross the Tugela at Potgieter's Drift with the Second Division and, if this operation should succeed, to bring the Fifth Division over the river after him in the neighbourhood of Vaalkrantz. Sir Charles Warren had then and there spoken out his misgivings about this plan, and had rightly insisted that it was necessary to cross the river at one and the same moment at several points. By a reconnaissance on the 14th Sir Redvers Buller convinced himself that an advance along the shortest road to Ladysmith, viz., that over Potgieter's Drift, must lead up to a frontal attack against the strongly entrenched heights at Brakfontein, and would amount to piercing the Boer position. The British troops in an advance against this portion of it would have been cramped on both sides by the course of the Tugela, and could have received no sufficient support from their Artillery,* as the only possible

---

* See page 87.

positions for guns were distant some 5,000 or 6,000 yards from the heights held by the Boers. These circumstances induced Buller to give up the idea of crossing at Potgieter's Drift. So it came about that when General Warren, after his return from a survey of the surroundings of the passage at Trichardt's Drift, spoke favourably about them, the General in Chief Command decided to effect a passage at that place and to limit himself to a demonstrative attack at Potgieter's Drift.

This decision originated in a natural anxiety to use the advantages of an enveloping attack to better purpose than they had been at Colenso. For success, however, prompt action was essential. Precious time had already passed unprofitably by. British Cavalry had been on the Upper Tugela since the 10th. If it was impossible to draw up the requisite arrangements on account of deficiencies in the existing resources in maps, all the necessary items of information ought to and could have been sought out at latest on the 11th. Further, if it was definitely considered essential to wait for the arrival of the last Battalion of Coke's Brigade and of the last baggage wagon before beginning to cross the river, the 14th ought to have been fixed as the very latest day on which the Army was to be set in motion again. It is not clear why it was only on that very day that a final decision was come to about the further operations, or why there was a further delay of two days in carrying that decision into effect. That the collection of 16 days' supply was not completely effected cannot be accepted as a sufficient reason for this procrastination. The last Supply-Columns might even have reached Springfield after the beginning of the operations without giving ground for any anxiety lest the army should on this account suffer from want of food. It was quite plain that any delay must turn to the profit of the defender and favour his counter-measures.

As appears from the published despatches, there was no distinct call made on the Garrison of Ladysmith for their co-operation. A specific order—the Fourth Division (White's) had been expressly placed under Buller's Command—would certainly have re-quickened White's energies, severely taxed as they had been by the experiences of the 6th January and by the sufferings of the siege. Lord Roberts also appears to have been of opinion that co-operation between the Garrison and the Relief Force would be desirable. This comes to light in the following sentence which he appended to the reply to Buller's report on his further intentions: "As you have done so much towards ensuring White's safety, it is to be hoped that he will be able to support you by making a vigorous sortie as soon as Warren meets the Enemy." It would have sufficed to pass on this expression of the Commander-in-Chief to the defender of Ladysmith. Buller, however, confined himself to telegraphing to White before his passage of the Tugela that the strong position of the Enemy near Potgieter's Drift rendered a wider sweep essential, and that consequently there would be a postponement of the attack for four or five days. This indecisive sort of communication was not likely to induce White to volunteer his co-operation. Buller could not, therefore, be surprised when he received, on the 16th January, the following not very encouraging answer from Ladysmith:—

"If you have serious doubts about your advance on Ladysmith, inform Roberts and ask for more Troops. If you are thrown back now, Ladysmith will be in a very bad way. If you remain undefeated and capable of attacking as soon as the enemy makes any rearward movement, I believe I can hold this place till 15th February. I have 2,400 men in hospital, and many shaky men on duty. Sickness increases daily. I have, during the last 3 months, lost 230 officers, including killed, wounded not yet recovered, prisoners and sick."

On the 15th January Buller issued his orders for the following day, and summarized them in a confidential memorandum to Sir Charles Warren as follows:—

"1. The Enemy's position opposite Potgieter's Drift appears to me to be too strong to be taken simply by a frontal attack.

"2. I shall, therefore, endeavour to deliver an enveloping attack by moving a detachment over the Tugela at Potgieter's Drift, and thence pushing into the country west of Spion Kop.

"3. You will command this detachment, which will consist of the Eleventh Brigade (of your own Division), your Divisional Artillery, the full strength of Clery's Division, and all the Mounted Troops (except 400 men).

"4. Naturally you will act according to circumstances; my idea, however, is that you should, during the whole operation, persistently refuse your right flank and push forward your left until you reach the open country north of Spion Kop. Once there you are master of the rear of the Potgieter's Drift position, and in my opinion you will make this untenable.

"5. The Fourth Brigade, part of the Tenth Brigade, a 15-pr. Field Battery, a Howitzer Field Battery, and two 4·7-in. Naval Guns remain at Potgieter's Drift. With these I will threaten the position in front of me, and will also make an attempt at crossing at Skiet's Drift so as to draw the enemy away from you as much as possible."

Then follows information about the strength of the Enemy, which Buller puts, far too high, at 7,000 at Potgieter's Drift and 600 at Trichardt's Drift, instructions to take 4 days' supplies, measures for the provision of ammunition, details about the employment of the Engineering Troops, and about arrangements for heliograph and flash-light signalling. Buller concludes:—

> "12. I wish you to begin your advance as soon as possible. . . . As soon as you move off I will begin the passage of the River.*
>
> "13. Send me the Tenth Brigade as soon as you can if you do not detail it as garrison of Springfield, also the eight Naval 12-prs., and all other formations, such as Ammunition Columns, etc., which you do not want to take with you."

General Buller thus divided his Troops into two portions of unequal strength, and placed the stronger, to which was entrusted the execution of the principal task, under the command of his subordinate, Warren, while he contented himself with the *rôle* of a spectator. He left to Warren full freedom of action, and went so far in his own self-effacement, as to indicate merely in general terms, not only the manner of execution, but also the objective of the operations and the time for the commencement. What may have been the views of the General Commanding as to how the plans should be executed, can only be surmised through the medium of a sketch, which was attached to the order, of watering places on the Fairview-Rosalie Farm Road. Furthermore, a conversation, in which Buller intended to explain his intention clearly, made this all the less comprehensible to Warren, because the premise of the General Commanding that the chain of heights forming the Boer position ended at Bastion Hill, and that consequently an envelopment could be effected there, proved to be altogether false. It could, therefore, hardly fail to result that the enterprise was moulded by Warren's independently-formed decisions into grooves in which Buller's

---

* At Potgieter's Drift.

train of thought ran but ill. If he wanted to avoid this result he should, from the very beginning, have given orders precisely determining what Warren was to do, with details as to time and place, or he should have taken the direction into his own hands. He would not make up his mind to that, but tried subsequently, by somewhat unfortunate interference, to acquire an influence over the course of events; it was hardly to be expected that this would serve any good purpose.

The 15th and the morning of the 16th found no change in the situation on either side. The Boers laboured on in strengthening themselves. On the British side the final preparations were made for the further advance. On the morning of the 16th there was an echo of heavy gun-fire from Ladysmith. It was seen that the Creusot gun on Bulwana was hurling shell after shell into the beleaguered town.

On the afternoon of the 16th life was infused into the British Camp on Spearman's Heights. The projected demonstrative movement at Potgieter's Drift was in accordance with orders from General Buller carried out by Lyttelton's Brigade. About 2.30 p.m. the Battalions, accompanied by the Howitzer Field Battery, were set in movement, and after deploying, crossed Mount Alice. As soon as the British Troops appeared on the summit the Boers occupied their positions on the Brakfontein Heights. Apparently only quite a small detachment was pushed forward to the group of hills, situated immediately in front of the drift, called " One Tree Hill," after a single conspicuous tree which stood there.

About 4 p.m. the two 4·7-inch guns on Spearman's Hill and the eight Naval 12-prs. on Mount Alice opened fire on the opposite heights. General Lyttelton, who meanwhile had arrived at the river, had the southern bank occupied by the King's Royal Rifles and the Durham

Light Infantry, and under their covering fire the Rifle Brigade and the Scottish Rifles waded through the river. Although the stream was rather rapid and the depth of the water up to the men's chests, the passage was successfully effected without loss, a cable stretched from bank to bank proving very useful. Arrived on the left bank the Battalions immediately advanced on a broad front against "One Tree Hill." After a few shots the Boers quitted the hill, which was occupied by both British Battalions as a bridge-head. Towards evening the ferry at Potgieter's Drift was set to work again, and in the course of the night the Howitzer Field Battery was transferred to the left bank.

The Naval Guns and the Howitzer Field Battery reopened fire early on the 17th. Every position from Brakfontein to Spion Kop on which any sign of the Boers was discovered, was fired at. After the fire had lasted some time the King's Royal Rifles and the Balloon Section were sent across the river. Both the Battalions already on the left bank were now advanced, in thin skirmishing lines and making careful use of cover, to within about 1,000 yards of the Enemy's positions. The Boers were in occupation of their trenches, but would not allow themselves to be drawn into opening fire. The British Infantry contented itself with what had been done, and at 11 a.m., in spite of the sounds of gun-firing in a westerly direction, withdrew again to "One Tree Hill." And so at the very moment when everything indicated that Warren had now got into action, the Boers were accorded full liberty of movement and enabled to concentrate on the really seriously-menaced position. Buller's object, the distraction of attention from Warren, could, however, only be attained by keeping a firm grip on the Enemy; demonstrative movements could not suffice. It was only the inactivity of the Boers which saved Warren from feeling the consequences of this discontinuance of

H

the action, even before he had completed his passage of the Tugela.

Besides the above-mentioned operations, the 2nd Battalion Dorsets, the 64th Field Battery,* and a Squadron of Bethune's Mounted Infantry were, during the 17th January, sent to Skiet's Drift to carry out the demonstration which Buller had planned there. As this detachment, however, confined itself to closing the drift, its mission was ineffective. The other Battalion of Coke's Brigade, the Middlesex, remained south of Potgieter's Drift.

Late in the afternoon of 16th January, General Warren moved off with his Force. The Mounted Brigade at Spearman's Hill and all other Troops encamped at Hatting's Farm started practically at one and the same time, 5 p.m., along roads which had been specially selected, so that observation by the enemy should be avoided until darkness should conceal the movement. As Dundonald's Brigade moved by quite the shortest road of all, it reached the river first and halting in column of route on the roadside waited for the rest of the Columns. They seem to have encountered serious difficulties on their march, for it was not till 12.30 a.m. that the advanced guard, Woodgate's Brigade with a Squadron of 13th Hussars and the Pontoon Train came up with the rear of the Mounted Troops. As Lord Dundonald could not be found, and as Warren was averse to interfering with his subordinate's arrangements, all the Columns were halted as they stood on the road. Thus it came about that the whole Force spent the remainder of the cold, damp night in column of route, its leading files close by the Tugela; but without having gained any more accurate information as to what was the prospect of affairs across the river.

It was not till 6 a.m., three-quarters of an hour after day-

---

* From Clery's division. The 78th Field Battery was later substituted for it from the Corps Troops.

break of the 17th, that Warren summoned the Commanding Royal Engineer that he might select with him the site for a bridge; after a long search this was found 100 yards above the provisional position occupied close by Trichardt's Farm. The construction of the bridge was to be protected by the deployment of the West Yorks on the right bank of the river, and two Batteries ready for action occupied a position on the heights south of the drift. A patrol of Imperial Light Horse, which crossed to the left bank about 8 a.m., was met by shots from a farm-house situated in front of the drift. Warren immediately ordered the Batteries to open fire, whereupon five Boers left the farm in hot haste. For all that, and though it was bound to draw the Boers' attention to the intended passage, the guns continued their fire for an hour against every spot on the left bank in which Boers could be suspected of lying, and this, too, in spite of the absence of any fire in reply from the Enemy's position. Meanwhile the bridge construction had begun. As the steepness of the banks made it difficult to drive pontoon wagons down to the crossing-place, the pontoons were man-handled down to the water by the Sappers and by an Infantry Battalion detailed to assist them. The West Yorks were ferried across to the left bank while the bridge was being constructed. About 11 a.m. the bridge, 86 yards in length, was finished. Woodgate's Brigade crossed first, and then Hart's Battalions. It was thought that the Third*(Hildyard's) Brigade ought to be held back at first on the South bank as protection to the Guns and the Transport. Dundonald's Mounted Brigade meanwhile rode across during the course of the afternoon.

About midday Sir Charles Warren had to make up his mind as to how he was going to use his troops when they

---

(* *sic.*, should be Second.—TRANS.)

had crossed the river; it was the more difficult to come to a decision on account of the complete absence of reconnaissance. The bulk of the Mounted Troops was still on the right bank. The patrols which had already crossed had gained no insight into the situation of the Boers. At any rate General Warren had not been informed that even at midday he could, with but little trouble, have planted himself firmly on the commanding heights northeast of the bridge, nor that Spion Kop itself was at this moment quite weakly held. Possessing no information about the enemy, Warren did not risk even one attempt to seize, by a rapid dash, the mountain, of which the possession was as indispensable to him for the security of the passage of the Tugela as it was for his advance on Ladysmith. He even restricted himself to the occupation by Woodgate's and Hart's Brigades, about 3.30 p.m., of a position, about 1,600 yards from the river which would cover the passage. About this time, too, the approach of the Artillery to the bridge had been successfully arranged by the construction of ramps, and the guns began to cross the river forthwith.

General Buller, who reached Trichardt's Drift about midday, does not appear to have been pleased with the way things were going on. He refrained, however, almost entirely from interfering with the measures taken by his subordinate commander and only gave a few specific orders to Woodgate's Brigade. In the evening he wrote to Warren as follows:—

"My dear Warren,—Probably I am carrying coals to Newcastle! However, as I am writing personally to you I must ask you to explain to Woodgate, if you haven't already done so, that his advance to-day from Smith's Farm here was all wrong. If we wish to succeed we must, before all things, keep our left flank clear. He was at Smith's Farm. The Yorkshires held a kopje west of it; he advanced in a north-easterly direction, and that was wrong. By doing so he offered his left flank to the enemy. I attach a little plan:—

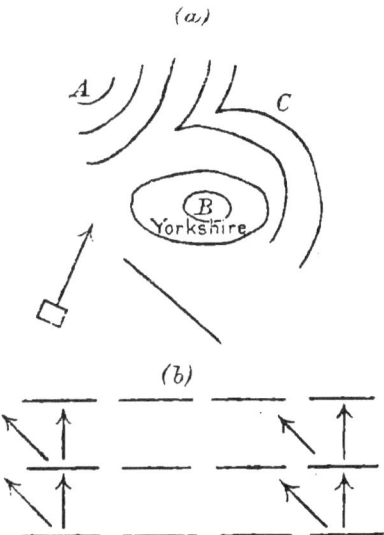

"A was the hill you wanted to take. From B one could see up the kloof C in which you suspected the enemy to be. B was, of course, sufficiently held. But instead of Woodgate advancing on A, which he could easily have done with the occupants of B, he marched in the direction of the arrow, so that he would have exposed his left flank to an enemy posted behind A. That is just what I want to see avoided by all leaders. If a direct advance is closed, the left must be worked round. That would have had the further advantage of being near Venter's Spruit. Advance should be made by échelons to the left. A direct advance may succeed in one line; but if there is any check, the next movement must consist of a half-wheel to the left. In order to manage that, the left flank must be pushed forward and the right follow in échelon. I don't know if I have expressed myself clearly enough. Wynne* will explain it to you again. If you have got round so far that you can swing to the east, you must always endeavour to roll up the enemy's right flank with your own left."

To judge by this the senior leader also failed to grasp that success was principally to be attained by rapidity of action, no matter where or in what form it might be taken; the really important was overlooked in the examination of the incidental. When everything depended on brisk and stirring action, the directing force expended itself in studious and pedantic calculations as to the formation which should be employed; in this situation, however, one formation was as good as another. It was imagined that the success of the advance must be sought in some scientific flank movement, such as might be reminiscent of "Linear Tactics," but the possibility of execution of which appears more than doubtful; while, as a matter of fact, any formation would have been right so long as the movement was the most natural one of marching straight for the heights which were still unoccupied by the Enemy.

While the situation up to shortly after midday, which was still favourable to the British, was being turned to no good account by them, the Boers were not idle in profiting by it. The dilatory advance of Lyttelton's Troops from Potgieter's Drift soon declared itself as an unmistakeable movement of demonstration which could but produce all the smaller impression when it came altogether to an end at 11 a.m. The activity of the British at Trichardt's Drift was accurately observed from the Boer observation posts on Spion Kop. The reports thence, together with what the leader, Schalk Burger, himself saw, left in no doubt whatever at what point alone a serious British advance

---

* Buller's Chief of the Staff.

was to be expected. The situation was so clear that every single Boer was bound to see through it. The remedy called for was so ready to hand that even these men, deliberate and prone to individual action in the fight as they were, grasped at it quickly : a fresh front on the line, Taba Myama—Spion Kop must be presented to meet the British crossing at Trichardt's Drift. So it came about that soon after noon a general drift set in towards the flank which, being concealed by the crest of the heights, was able to work itself out completely unobserved. First in troops, later in detachments of ever increasing strength, the Boers hurried to the threatened flank. On arrival in the position they began at once, as was their practice, to dig rifle-pits and throw up small sangars of stone. Further reinforcements were summoned down from the Besieging Force and employed in the front line on the right flank. About 500 Boers remained behind on the heights of Brakfontein. This then was the sum total of the force which the two British Brigades in front of this flank " occupied."

The following was the distribution of the British Troops on the evening of 17th January :—On their extreme right at Skiet's Drift were 1 Battalion, 1 Squadron of Mounted Infantry, and a Battery. In the centre were 3 Battalions and a Battery on the northern bank of the Tugela in front of Potgieter's Drift, 2 Battalions South of the river, and the Naval Guns on Spearman's Heights. On the left, 2 Brigades of Infantry, the Mounted Troops and the Artillery had crossed the river at Trichardt's Drift and were still in the immediate neighbourhood of the point of passage. One Brigade of Infantry had been left on the right bank for the time being. The Sappers were working at a second bridge by which the transport wagons were to cross. As, in spite of all possible reductions (some of the regimental wagons had been left at Springfield), the total train amounted to 489 wagons, none of which were teamed with fewer than four animals, its immediate transference to the northern bank must have appeared a portentous undertaking in the face of an Enemy who, in his own way, was active. It was of further unfavourable influence on the operations that this park of wagons, large in numbers and awkward in movement, accompanied the Force. The absence of condensed emergency-rations with the Troops was most injurious, for had such been carried by the men, the greatest part of supply wagons could have been left south of the Tugela.

General Warren's investigations on the evening of 17th and morning of 18th pivoted mainly on the selection of a road for his further advance, and in this his thoughts about the transport had great weight. On the morning of the 18th he personally examined the Fairview-Rosalie Road, to such extent at least as was compatible, with due regard to the Enemy; he came to the very natural conclusion that an advance along this road would entail the capture of Spion Kop as a preliminary measure. Knowing that an attack with his right wing did not accord with Buller's intentions, Warren then wanted to examine also the road *viâ* Acton Homes. It does not appear to have been recognised as an essential condition in all these investigations, that in this situation the enemy must, at all events, be defeated before a general advance would be possible, no matter which road were selected, and that every delay would only tend to increase the severity of the unavoidable battle. Woodgate alone of all the subordinate Commanders spoke out for the immediate assault of the heights commanding Trichardt's Drift on the north-east, while Hart wanted to put off the attack till night-time, as he thought it would be too difficult by day. During all these arguments, *pro* and *con*, the precious time for decisive action was slipping away.

Meanwhile, early on the 18th, Hildyard's Brigade crossed the river. The passage of the wagons, which formed a column of no less than 15 miles in length on the march, went on the whole day long. Further, in the forenoon of the 18th Dundonald's Mounted Brigade started off in the direction of Acton Homes " to seek out the enemy." The road leading along the left bank of Venter's Spruit was used for this movement, which accordingly was concealed in the neighbourhood of Thaba Myama by the configuration of the country. When Dundonald reported that he proposed to continue his movement right up to Acton Homes, Warren ordered him to send back 500 mounted men to protect his camp and his oxen which had been sent out to graze on the veldt. Lord Dundonald detailed the Royal Dragoons for this duty and, with the 1,000 Troopers left to him, marched on to Acton Homes, at the same time occupying, with posts, a line of hills so as to maintain secure connection with Warren.

The Boers, however, were fully aware of the importance of the heights at Acton Homes. Over them passed the southern line of retreat of the Free Staters to Oliver's Hoek and the approach to their right flank. They had, therefore, already occupied these heights, though only weakly, and they now sent there 200 more men from the Pretoria Commando and some Free Staters to oppose Dundonald's horsemen. The British noticed this movement in good time. The Advanced Guard, Natal Carabiniers and Imperial Light Horse, rapidly occupied, without attracting attention, a line of hills towards which the Boers were carelessly advancing without having reconnoitred it. When the Boers had arrived within about 200 or 300 yards they were suddenly overwhelmed with rapid fire. The greater number of them went pell-mell back to the heights; 35, however, who had already dismounted, got under cover behind boulders and took up the fight. The

British then pushed more men towards the flanks and round the rear of this small party, and when eleven, including the field cornet, had fallen, the remainder surrendered. The British put their loss at 2 killed and 3 wounded.

The Boers nevertheless continued to hold the surrounding heights; they could in a short time bring up reinforcements there from Ladysmith and from their left flank. Dundonald judged that he was too weak to drive them away without assistance. He had before him a fresh, even if as yet a weak, front; he had not succeeded in gaining the right flank of the Boers. There was a great temptation to make a decided attack on the most sensitive part of the enemy's position before reinforcements could be brought there. But if this was to be, the principal force of the British must be moved in this direction to begin with, and in such a manner as to effect the greatest possible surprise on the enemy; probably they would arrive too late. Before the British Infantry could be on the spot, the quickly-moving Boers could have been reinforced and posted in entrenchments for some time, and this British attack, like any other would fall on a new and strong front. General Warren himself appears, however, to have thought for some time about delivering his decisive attack at this point. At any rate, when he received Dundonald's report that he had got into action with the Boers, he gave orders that Hildyard's Brigade should at 4.30 a.m. on the 19th move to Acton Homes; but he cancelled these orders when reports arrived that the Enemy was being reinforced in his positions round there. Further, the Supply-Column of Dundonald's Brigade, which had been started on the march to Acton Homes, was brought back again.

The whole of Warren's Infantry and Artillery remained for the time being on the Tugela. Moreover, Hart's proposal, to take the Boer position at Spion Kop and on the southern edge of Thaba Myama, was rejected by Warren because, on closer examination, the heights proved to be too difficult for any night enterprise. General Buller has since expressed himself as not pleased with Warren's conduct of affairs, because he did not turn Dundonald's success to advantage so far as to attack the "salient angle of the Boer position," by which apparently is meant Bastion Hill. He even went so far as to think of relieving Warren of his command on this account, but was dissuaded from that course on personal grounds. However, even if he did misjudge the importance of Dundonald's success, it is still easy to understand his annoyance about the slow progress of operations.

On the other hand nobody will deny that there was some justice in Warren's decision to avoid an attack on Acton Homes. The attack here would have been at least as difficult to carry out as it would have been at any other part of the Boer position. But in case of failure here the British Troops would have been in a bad case, more than eight miles distant from their own place of crossing, which was, moreover, commanded by the Enemy.

In consequence of the peculiarity of the topographical conditions of the surrounding country, and of the mobility of the Enemy, any attack by the British was always certain to fall on a fresh front. It was, in fact, unimportant where the attack might be delivered, so long as it was energetically initiated along the whole front at the same time and with every available man. A piercing of the widely extended front of the Boers, which was deficient in depth, held out just as much promise of success as the attempt at envelopment. If an envelopment of the Enemy in this country was the object to be striven for, it must be arranged by manœuvre, as Lord Roberts did almost always later. For such a purpose, however, Buller's Army was wanting in the requisite mobility, for to say nothing of its poverty as regards Mounted Troops, the faulty organisation of its transport made it too immobile for such operations. Attempts at envelopment on the front fighting line were purposeless and were bound to bring about the evils resulting from a dispersion of force.

The Boers had continued to strengthen their position on the 18th. Parts of the Pretoria, Boksburg, and Heidelberg Commandos took position on Thaba Myama, while the Germans and the Heilbronn, Krugersdorp, Winburg, and Senekal Burghers occupied the ground between them and Spion Kop. On the last named were parts of the Vryheid and Carolina Commandos. Several guns were brought up on to Thaba Myama and to the ridge between that and Spion Kop. General Schalk Burger, who was in command of all these combined forces, had moved to the Spion Kop Heights and had fixed his headquarters with the Carolina men.

Nothing of importance had occurred on the right wing of the British on the 18th. General Lyttelton withdrew the Battery which he had sent to Skiet's Drift back to Potgieter's Drift. Under cover of Artillery fire he sent his Infantry out in an advance against the Brakfontein Heights, but on this occasion also avoided committing himself to a real fight.

Up till the morning of the 19th more or less really accurate information about the distribution and the activity of the Boers had reached General Warren's Headquarters. It was known that there were several laagers behind Spion Kop, that the heights running up to Spion Kop from the North-West were also occupied, and that Boers were to be found in the vicinity of Acton Homes. Later it was seen that individual detachments of Boers were busily engaged in making entrenchments on the heights of Thaba Myama. White's heliograph communi-

cated an incorrect report that in the early morning of the
19th from 1,500 to 2,000 Boers had set out on the march
to Acton Homes.

Early on the 19th Warren examined the roads to Acton
Homes, but became convinced that it was impossible for
him to get through on this line either without a fight, and
to that he would not commit himself. So he rested content with the transference, in the very early hours of the
morning, of his Command from the Tugela Valley to the
Venter's Spruit Valley. The movement was conducted
in such a way that the whole of the baggage formed six
columns marching alongside one another, of which the
right flank was protected by the Infantry Brigades. After
the flank movement had been finished, Woodgate's Brigade was on the right wing next to the point of the
crossing, Hart's Brigade was in the centre and Hildyard's
Brigade was on the left of the British. The baggage went
into laager in the Venter's Spruit Valley, about opposite to
the junction with the Thaba stream. Warren wanted to
draw Dundonald's Brigade nearer to himself as he considered it too much exposed to danger where it lay. After
several written explanations, and after a conversation between himself and Dundonald, Warren renounced this
intention; but he crippled the strength of the Brigade by
withdrawing from it Thorneycroft's Mounted Infantry. In
view of the reinforcements which had reached the Boers,
no powerful effect on their right flank could be looked for
from the action of the 600 or 700 mounted men who were
now left at Dundonald's disposal.

On the evening of the 19th Warren assembled his
Brigadiers and the Commanding Officers of Artillery and
Engineers at a council. He then explained that in connection with the further advance, the roads *viâ* Acton
Homes and *viâ* Fairview-Rosalie were under his consideration. He thought, so he said, that he must reject the Acton

Homes Road because the flank march entailed in the valley of the Venter's Spruit was exposed to Boer Artillery fire, and principally because he feared great difficulties in connection with supply. There only remained one day's rations out of the four which he had brought along; there had been no thought given to the organisation of the transport arrangements necessary for the replenishment of the supplies, and no condensed emergency-rations, which would have made the troops independent of their wagons for several days, had been brought at all. Warren rightly judged that the bringing forward of a considerable quantity of supplies entailed in moving further away from the Tugela would be attended with difficulty. Further, Warren appears to have differed from Buller in thinking seriously of the difficult nature of an attack on the extreme right flank of the Boers, and he finally came to the general conclusion that the Fairview-Rosalie Road would have to be opened up by a frontal attack on the heights lying in front of the British position. The Generals and others present agreed in this conclusion, considerations about supply apparently exercising a preponderating influence on them too.

In the same way as Sir Redvers Buller had transferred the Chief Command to Sir Charles Warren on the 15th January, the latter now charged General Clery with the execution of the attack, and for this purpose placed at his disposal Hart's and Woodgate's Brigades, as well as the whole of the Artillery. General Clery was verbally informed that he was to direct his attack against the point where the Fairview-Rosalie Road crosses the heights and against a second point, further west, which apparently lay on the edge of Thaba Myama. In addition, Warren communicated to Clery the following written instructions:—

"I should be glad if you would take care that the Boers are driven, by a series of enveloping attacks, off the ground which overlooks the present position of the Eleventh Brigade. In the early morning an advance must be made as far as the point up to which the Hussars have examined the ground. A line of entrenchments must there be constructed across the slope of the hill.* A portion of the hill which joins this position from the westward can then be occupied. If necessary the Artillery can co-operate in the capture of the western feature and of the higher slopes (of Three Tree Hill). When that is completed I think a Battery can get on to the slope of the western hill (Three Tree Hill) in such a way as to be able to bring the Boer trenches on Spion Kop and on the higher portion of the eastern hill under fire.† Then a further attack can be pushed against the eastern hill while the Artillery advances to the top of the western hill. I think this can be carried out with comparatively small loss, as the Boers can be continuously outflanked."

It must have been clear to General Warren that the attack ordered by him would bring about a hotly-contested engagement on the front of the strong Boer position, which could only be carried through with great exertions and sacrifices. His note to Clery, however, gives no indication of a clear wish that no consideration for the sacrifices to be entailed should operate against the attainment of the object; on the contrary, the fear of heavy casualties is quite apparent in it. How the enveloping movements which had been enjoined could be carried out in this direct frontal attack on the centre of the enemy's position is not clear.

It was doubly important for the execution of the difficult task imposed on General Clery that the Boers should not only be tied down to this position, but also to every posi-

---

* Three Tree Hill is intended.
† The ridge between Spion Kop and Thaba Myama.

tion—Ladysmith, Colenso, Potgieter's Drift, and Acton Homes—in front of which were British troops. The projected operation of piercing the enemy's line could only be made possible of execution by the united exertions of every detachment of the British. At the very least Warren ought to have informed General Buller in sufficiently good time and accurately enough to permit him to arrange for the co-operation of White, Barton, and Lyttelton. Warren, however, confined himself to addressing to the Chief of the General Staff the following note, from which the intention to launch an energetic attack cannot possibly be gathered:—

"I know of only two routes by which we can push northward of the Tugela after Potgieter's Drift,* one by Acton Homes and the other by Fairview-Rosalie. I give up the first because it is too long; the second is too difficult for a considerable number of wagons, unless the enemy is, as a preliminary, completely driven away from it. I am, therefore, taking some special measures which necessitate my remaining at the bivouacs in the Venter's Spruit Valley for two or three days. I will arrange for the taking over of further supplies and will report my progress."

In reply Warren heard from the General in Command that provisions for three days would be forwarded to him.

---

* More accurately "in rear of the Potgieter's (Brakfontein) position."

CHAPTER IV.

THE FIGHT AT THABA MYAMA. EVENTS FROM 20TH TO 22ND JANUARY.

During the night of 19th-20th January a change was made in the Boer Command. Louis Botha had on the 19th received instructions from President Krüger to proceed to the Upper Tugela. Soon after midnight he met the then Commander, Schalk Burger, in the laager of the Carolina Commando, and it was agreed between them that Burger should retain the direction of affairs on the Spion Kop-Vaalkrantz front, while Botha was to take over the Command on the section Thaba Myama-Spion Kop. Early in the morning he rode round the whole position and forthwith devoted himself to ensuring a harmonious and co-ordinated defence, so far as was possible in a general way under all the ruling circumstances. The inactivity of the British Cavalry on the 19th had relieved the Boers of their anxiety about an envelopment of their right wing at Acton Homes, and so all their efforts could be turned to the defence of the position from Thaba Myama to Spion Kop. To this position a Boer detachment, which had been pushed forward to Three Tree Hill, was withdrawn during the night. The number of Boers posted on the south-western edge of Thaba-Myama was subsequently inconsiderable.

Great trouble had been taken in laying out the position from Green Hill to Spion Kop; on the other hand but little had been done west of Green Hill. Nevertheless, in this direction numerous natural defences—rocks, heaps of stones, and so on—made up for the deficiency in artificial works. During the night of 19th-20th yet more was done towards the completion of the defensive arrangements. Kaffirs dug narrow, deep trenches in all directions; as the ground was rocky and only in parts covered with some 20 inches of soil, the labour involved in this was immense. All cover was carefully made to resemble the surroundings, and was difficult to distinguish. In many places the defenders contrived head-cover by laying large stones on the top of the breastworks, a measure which is said to have furnished excellent protection, not only against the effect of the British shrapnel fire, but also against the close-range fire of the attacking Infantry. Only four guns were available for the north-west of Spion Kop. Of these one was placed on the western edge of the Plat Kop and three on the ridge connecting it with Spion Kop. All these guns were withdrawn behind the protecting edge of the slope, so that only the muzzles projected beyond it; the guns were also "dug in" so as to save them from the effects of the enemy's artillery fire. Here and there two suitable emplacements were prepared for each gun 20 yards apart, of which only one was at first occupied. As soon as the enemy got the range of this one, the gun was removed to the second.

On the British side General Clery, who was not aware that Three Tree Hill had been evacuated, wished, before doing anything else, to capture, by an attack at dawn, the advanced position which the Boers were occupying there. He had at his disposal Hart's and Woodgate's Brigades and six Field Batteries; of these he sent forward Woodgate's Brigade at 3 a.m. against Three Tree Hill, while the rest of his Force remained for the time being in their camp on the lower Venter's Spruit. As, in addition to the troops noted above, Hildyard's Brigade was left behind to protect the camp, it will be seen that at first only one-third of the available force was told off for the operation. General Woodgate deployed the whole of his Infantry in line of Battalions for the advance. The South Lancashires and the King's Own (Royal Lancasters) were directed towards the eastern part of Three Tree Hill, while the Lancashire Fusiliers and the York and Lancasters were to move towards the heights lying to the west of the Fairview-Rosalie Road. In this way the Brigadier allowed the whole of his force to pass out of his own control, and consequently deprived himself for good and all of any further influence over the course of the action which ensued. As for the Battalions themselves, each advanced in a formation of great depth on a narrow front.

It has been already said that Three Tree Hill was evacuated during the night; the advance of the Brigade proceeded so far, therefore, without check and without loss. The development of outflanking movements, which Warren had deemed it necessary to order his subordinate to carry out, had, therefore, lost its object. About 6 a.m. three-quarters of an hour after sunrise, Woodgate's right wing occupied the eastern slope of Three Tree Hill, and his left the eastern slopes of the heights opposite Thaba Myama. The advance was now interrupted for the time being. Both Battalions on the right flank began to dig themselves in, according to the instructions received from Warren.

At daybreak, shortly after 5 a.m., Clery had ordered his Artillery to follow up Woodgate's Brigade. Five Batteries were directed on to Three Tree Hill and one, the 78th, on to the extreme eastern edge of the heights. About 7 a.m. they reached their destinations, and with the exception of the 7th and 73rd Field Batteries, which were at first held back, they immediately came into action and opened fire on the Boer positions. As no reply was made to this fire, the British guns were turned on to every point in which fresh-turned soil or contiguous heaps of stones disclosed the existence of the Enemy's entrenchments; and where nothing of this kind was to be seen, every point of ground on which the Boers could be suspected of lying was brought under fire. The British Gunners, whose observation of the fire was supplemented by the record of effect of shots signalled back from the Infantry, succeeded in making good practice. At any rate, the descriptions furnished by those who were fighting with the Boers make it clear that the British guns were correctly laid. If, in spite of the favourable elevations, those for about 2,600 yards, at which the guns were fired, there was but little real effect, the fault lies less in any deficiency in the British artillery material than in the unsatisfactory co-operation of the Infantry with the Batteries. It was clear that, in spite of the experiences at Colenso, the Commanders were still possessed of the mistaken idea that the Artillery fight and the Infantry fight must form two quite distinct phases. As the British Infantry was not for the time being in motion, the Boers had no inducement to leave their covered position, and it resulted that the Artillery fire, which lasted about four hours, effected nothing more than a great waste of ammunition. The moral effect from which so much was always expected was quite trifling, for it is essentially the progeny of material effect. However, according to General Warren's views, " the Artillery alone was to carry on the fire-fight while the Infantry was to settle matters finally with the bayonet alone."

About 10 a.m. the 7th and 73rd Field Batteries, which had been held back till then, were taken up into position near the 78th, and the Artillery fire was continued for an hour more before the Infantry moved forward to the attack.

A glance at the Boer lines of defence should have shown

the British Commander that any attack having its point of departure at Three Tree Hill must strike into a re-entering angle of the Enemy's position, and that it would be under flanking fire during its subsequent progress. It was quite safe to assume that the briskest concentrated fire would break out as soon as ever the British should advance to the attack. The direction of the attack as laid down by Warren was the most unfavourable that could have been devised. An attack further to the West directed on the salient angle of the position at Bastion Hill would have had a far better prospect of success. There was still time for General Warren, who was on Three Tree Hill with Clery, to make the modifications in his orders necessary to effect this purpose. Further, the Mounted Troops and Hart's and Hildyard's Infantry Brigades, which so far had not been brought into the action at all, were available for just such an attack. But the orders as originally issued were adhered to, and General Clery had to get out of the difficulties which confronted him in executing them as best he could.

He decided to direct the attack in a northerly direction, that is, against the southern slopes of Thaba Myama, which were occupied by the Heidelberg and Boksburg men. For such a selection the ground was well adapted, as it provided in this direction much better cover than in the East, where an almost bare slope ran up to the position of the Krugersdorp and Heilbron Burghers. To carry out his purpose Clery brought up his Reserve Brigade, and also put under orders of the Brigadier, General Hart, both the left flank Battalions of Woodgate's Brigade, viz., the Lancashire Fusiliers and the York and Lancasters, and charged him with the execution of the attack. Beginning with Buller, every higher Commander transferred in this sort of way the carrying out of an enterprise, and with that the responsibility, on to the shoulders of his next junior.

Hart's Brigade had left its bivouac about 9 a.m., and had gone forward west of Fairview in a northerly direction. On the way the Connaught Rangers and three Companies of the Inniskillings, a total of eleven Companies, had been diverted away eastward from the Column, already weak for attacking purposes, to furnish protection to the guns on the extreme right flank. The resultant weakening of Hart's Brigade was a consequence of the measures of General Woodgate, who, by simultaneously extending the whole of his Brigade from the very first, had parted with all the force he could dispose of. The troops diverted from Hart's Brigade joined, meanwhile, in the fire-fight which Woodgate's skirmishers had commenced with the Boers opposite them at 1,700 yards and took no part in the decisive stroke.

When the remaining two and a-half Battalions of Hart's Brigade reached Woodgate's left wing, the Troops were told off for the attack. In the leading line were the two already deployed Battalions of Woodgate's Brigade, the Lancashires and the King's Own; in rear of them in second line were the Borders and the Dublin Fusiliers; five Companies of the Inniskillings were to protect the left flank and formed the third line echeloned outwards in its rear. About 11 a.m. everything was ready for the attack.

Meanwhile, except for the fire-fight with the right wing of the British, the Boers had remained absolutely inactive. After a few rounds they had ceased fire from their guns, justly recognising that they must soon get the worst of an artillery duel and that they would then be no longer able to employ their guns in the most important task, viz., the repulse of the impending Infantry attack. The guns remained concealed in their prepared emplacements. Ever since the British had crossed the Tugela the positions had been uninterruptedly occupied by day and by night. The prolonged tension, the extreme pitch of expectation could not but have an effect on the Boers now that the decisive attack was at last about to be launched. Already a certain feeling of uneasiness and insecurity began to be observable here and there in their ranks.

The noise of the bursting shrapnel, the dust and the splinters which were thrown about here and there by the shell which burst on graze, did their work in increasing the impression of danger so well, that those in front who had no stomach for the fight disappeared and sought the cover available further in rear. Nevertheless, the great mass of the defenders stood fast. According to his own account, their commander Botha was quite aware that the strength of the Boer Army lay in its mobility, and he was determined to make the most of this while he "kept his people always on the move, here reducing and there increasing their numbers." This procedure was made all the easier by the configuration of the ground—and by the behaviour of the British who never attacked more than one portion of the position. It was due to this mobility that on the morning of the 20th the hitherto almost unoccupied southern slope of Thaba Myama was furnished out with the requisite garrison.

Meanwhile, the attack commanded by General Hart had reached its high-water mark. The ground across which it had to be delivered is divided into several narrow ridges by the streams running down from Thaba Myama, here and there in ravine-shaped beds; these ridges become narrower and narrower as they approach the heights. The water-courses, some dead angles and boulders offered a certain amount of cover, but cramped the space for deployment so much that on the immediate front of the Brigade only a few rifles could be placed in the firing line with satisfactory effect. Owing to the peculiar configuration the nearer the attack drew on to the heights and the Enemy's position the more cramped became the space for deployment. Both Battalions of Woodgate's Brigade, which were in first line, advanced on a narrow front, only two Companies being deployed and the remaining Companies following 150 yards in rear and covering them. The Battalions in second and third line were hardly extended at all. As the Boer Guns were silent, and as the ground offered cover, the movement went on without interruption. It was only when the first line came within about 1,700 yards of the Enemy that a heavy cross-fire was opened by the Krugersdorp, Heilbronn, Heidelberg, and Boksburg men and the Germans. In spite of this, the attack advanced with hardly any appreciable loss. Rushing from cover to cover in small groups the firing line pushed on to within 800 or 1,000 yards of the enemy, and about 1 p.m. took up the fire-fight. There is no doubt that in this all the disadvantages were, from the very beginning, on the British side.

The Boers were well protected; every rifle could be used in the front line. The distances had been measured to specially prominent points in the foreground, and the moment that the British approached any of these points a more violent and more effective fire was poured into them. The Lancashire Fusiliers mention a white bush near which they suffered particularly severe losses in their advance. The extremely small, almost invisible, targets which the Boers presented were quite unrecognisable by the British soldiers, whose eyes were not trained for shooting at such long ranges; effective practice was out of the question, especially as volleys were chiefly used. It was only as a whole that the Boer position came under fire; at such distances an overwhelming fire of masses was needed for the production of any considerable effect. Accordingly an attempt was made by pushing forward the deeply-formed Troops from the rear to increase the originally weak and now subdued fire-effect of the first line.

But it has already been mentioned that owing to its configuration, the ground in front did not furnish the necessary space for the effective use of many rifles; for instance, it is said that the Lancashires with a total strength of 900 could only find room for 100 rifles in their firing line. The result was that the reinforcements pushed forward from the rear gradually formed a dense crowd, from all the rifles in which it was impossible to obtain combined and sustained fire effect, but, worse still, in which each man embarrassed his neighbour in the proper use of his rifle. Looked at from the Enemy's point of view this crowd presented a very favourable target, which fact, of course, tended to the increase of losses in it. Finally, the attempt to push any more reinforcements from rear to front was given up. The numerous groups in rear squeezed together behind rocks and in gullies into dense, deep swarms incapable of adding to the fire-effect of the leading line.

So it was that while plenty of troops were standing huddled together, useless and idle, the firing line was only able with difficulty to hold its own in face of the always superior and concentrated fire of the Boers. The attack did not succeed during the whole day in bringing the Enemy under a fire even approaching his in volume and effect, for the Commanders did not know how to apply usefully, in increasing the fire, the force which was available, but useless in its existing formation. As this force could not be applied to good purpose in the immediate front, so much of it as was ineffective should have been withdrawn and employed further towards the left against Bastion Hill in such way as might be suggested by the position of the useful features on the ground.

The impossible situation which had thus arisen in Hart's Brigade furnishes another instance of the constant need in the modern fight of independent decisions on the part of leaders of all ranks, and shows how helpless are any troops in the inevitable surprises and unforeseen developments of an Infantry fight, unless all the leaders are endowed with quickness of thought and mobility of mind.

About 2 p.m. the Boer Artillery on Green Hill, which, till then, had remained silent, made an effort to join in the fight. Three Tree Hill was suddenly brought under fire, and the Staff Officers who were standing on the summit had to leave it. No damage whatever was done to the British Batteries, and after a short time the Boer Guns were directed against the Infantry Battalions on the left flank of the British attack. As they were well concealed and protected they were able to remain in action in spite of being under the continuous fire of the British guns.

While these developments were taking place on the southern slopes of Thaba Myama, unexpected success had attended the British further westwards. Dundonald's Brigade, which had till then been in the neighbourhood of Acton Homes, had moved during the forenoon nearer the left flank of the Infantry in accordance with instructions from General Warren, and had halted opposite Bastion Hill. Lord Dundonald, who had been following the progress of Hart's and Woodgate's Brigades, determined early in the afternoon, and the decision was absolutely justified, to contribute something on his own account towards helping them in their attack; as the means to this end he selected the capture of Bastion Hill, for from that position a small detachment of Boers, pushed out in advance of the general line, was taking Hart's left in flank. The South African Light Horse was told off for the enterprise under Colonel Byng, at whose disposal were placed the two Machine Guns of the Brigade. Byng posted two Squadrons and the Machine Guns on a position over against Bastion Hill so as to keep the Boers, who were on the summit, under fire; two other Squadrons, under Major Childe, galloped to the foot of the hill, dismounted in the dead ground there and, protected from the defenders' fire by the steepness of the slopes, climbed up to the top. Arrived there they rushed on the Boers, whom they had taken by surprise, threw them back and about 3 p.m. were masters of this advanced post. But immediately they reached the summit of the hill the South African Light Horse found themselves under heavy fire chiefly from a Boer gun posted on Plat Kop and, although Thorneycroft's Mounted Infantry arrived later on their right, they were compelled, in consequence of their want of numbers, to renounce all the advantage of their success. To make a further advance possible, the co-operation of Hildyard's Brigade and, most important of all, the support of Artillery were essential. As neither was forthcoming the little party could do no more than hold on to what it had won. They dug themselves in as well as they could on the summit of the hill and stayed there in spite of losing their Commander, Major Childe, and several men by artillery fire.

By about 3 p.m. the foremost groups of the British Infantry, after great exertions and with heavy loss, had managed to get within effective rifle range, about 400 yards, of the edge of the heights which the Boers held. The interval which still separated them from the Enemy's position was absolutely bare of cover. Although some portions of the firing line got some cover in the many small hollows in the ground, the situation of the attacking troops under the hot and continuous fire of the Boers was very difficult. The leaders up at the front determined to cut their way out of it with charged bayonets. The Artillery had begun to prepare the way for the assault, and for a quarter of an hour had been keeping up a rapid fire from all the guns. Some sections had already fixed bayonets when Clery stepped in and ordered the cessation of the attack. He reported to Warren that he had now arrived in front of a position which could only be carried by a frontal attack which he, however, considered had no prospect of success, and received the following reply: —

"I am quite of your opinion that a frontal attack is undesirable, and that a flank attack is to be preferred. I should like to hold on to what we have won, if necessary by entrenching ourselves, and to continue the advance to-morrow if it cannot be done in the night. A frontal attack with heavy losses would be a point scored in favour of the Boers."

So about 3.30 p.m. the order was passed up to and along the firing line for the cessation of the attack. General Hart withdrew his detachments as well as he could back into the cover provided by the broken surface of the ground. Portions of the Borders and Lancashire Fusiliers, which had got the furthest forward of all those engaged, had to make the best of their situation in a donga close to the enemy's lines till darkness fell.

However little justified may be the constitutional aversion of the British Commanders to any frontal attack, there is no doubt that in this case Clery was quite right in stepping in to stop the delivery of the assault on the Boers whose fire efficiency was still in no way unabated. The delivery of the assault at this period would have resulted in nothing more or less than a useless sacrifice of troops.

The hours before darkness fell—7.30 p.m.—passed by without any noteworthy incidents. The Infantry fire was kept up by both sides with varying degrees of intensity as long as daylight permitted. The Artillery fire was also maintained; the Boers especially kept the extreme left wing of the British under heavy fire. Hildyard's Brigade which in the course of the afternoon had sent forward to the North detachments of the Queen's and of the East Surreys, to form a support to the Mounted Brigade and to protect the left flank, relieved Hart's most advanced troops when it was dark by the West Yorks, the Mounted Infantry on Bastion Hill by the Queen's; the Brigade also furnished the outposts. The other two Battalions protected the North and North-West of the Camp. The remainder of Warren's troops passed the night in the positions they had taken up during the fight. On the left flank the British posts stood opposite the Boers some 300 or 400 yards distant from them. The British fire lasted almost the whole night through, although it is hardly possible that there could have been any visible target for it. The results of the fight had been obtained with a loss of 329 officers and men.*

The other parts of the Natal Army had remained more or less inactive during the day. General Lyttelton, who had been informed by Warren that he purposed making an attack on Thaba Myama and that a demonstrative attack on the Boer positions opposite Potgieter's Drift would be desirable, sent forward the King's Royal Rifles up to within some 1,600 yards from the Enemy's position about 10 a.m. One Company pushed forward about 100 yards further into a donga and came under fire. Later in the afternoon two of the Machine Guns of the defence joined in the fire-action directed on this Company, whose casualties began to increase, whereon two 4·7-in. Naval Guns and two Howitzers answered the fire. The 64th Field Battery was brought up to within about 2,000 yards of the Enemy and opened fire, as Lyttelton judged, with great effect. About 5.30 p.m. the Rifle Brigade and Scottish Rifles were also moved forward. When darkness fell, however, all the Troops engaged were withdrawn again into the old positions on One Tree Hill. General Lyttelton assumes in his report that it was in consequence of these

---

* See Appendix III.

operations, in which his Brigade lost 2 Officers and 16 Men that the Boers were prevented from supporting the Commados engaged with Warren.

Barton's detachment, the Mounted Infantry of which had carried out a reconnaissance at Robinson's Drift on the 19th, with no very fortunate results, remained almost entirely inactive on the 20th and following days.

As soon as it began to get light on the 21st January, the British discovered that the right wing of the Boers had been withdrawn. In spite of the British outposts being so close to them, they had retired completely unobserved to the real plateau of Thaba Myama. The position which they took up there rested on the right on the commanding heights of Plat Kop, had on its front a gently sloping open field of fire, and was withdrawn, owing to its situation, from the fire of the British Batteries posted on the lower portion of Three Tree Hill. Two Guns under Oberleutnant von Wichmann, of which one had been posted on the Plat Kop on the 20th January, had been removed to a position north of the Acton Homes stream and thence opened fire on the British. In this way the latter were confronted with a fresh and difficult problem. As it could only be solved by a frontal attack, the further advance was given up. Hart's Brigade occupied the position evacuated by the Boers. Warren was disposed to confine further efforts to shaking the Enemy with Artillery fire as much as possible, having regard to the range-power of the guns. The enveloping attack against the Enemy's right wing which Clery recommended was not proceeded with. General Warren himself was disturbed by anxiety about his own left flank after Buller, who had come over again from Spearman's Hill, had told him that the Enemy's right flank had been reinforced by about 2,000 men. This information was confirmed later on by a report from Colonel Kitchener, who commanded the West Yorks, which stated that the Boers at Acton Homes were about to advance against the British left.* Accordingly, at Buller's wish, Warren ordered Clery about 9.30 a.m. to send forward two Batteries to the left flank near Bastion Hill. These subsequently got into action against the Boer's right flank.

So it is probable that the 21st January would have run its course without any action of note if Colonel Kitchener, after a discussion with General Hart, but without the consent of Warren and Clery, had not embarked on a forward movement on the extreme left flank. Warren had appointed him to command the two advanced Battalions of Hildyard's Brigade, the West Yorks and the Queen's, which had moreover been joined in the early morning by four Companies of the East Surreys. Kitchener, about 10 a.m., gave instructions that the four Companies East Surreys should make a forward and enveloping movement by the western slope of Bastion Hill, that two Companies of the Queen's should advance along the crest of Bastion Hill itself, and that further to the right two Companies should push forward from the edge of the plateau. In the intervals between the Columns of assault the remaining Companies of the Queen's and West Yorks were to support the movement by their fire. The assault, which began about 10.30 a.m. and which was launched without any preparatory fire and without any Artillery support, was wrecked as soon as launched. The East Surreys could make no headway whatever in the face of the heavy fire poured on them from Plat Kop, and remained lying down on the western edge of Bastion Hill. Thereupon the Queen's and the West Yorks were halted and withdrawn. Some Companies of the West Yorks had got into a donga and, as had happened the day before with the Lancashire Fusiliers, could only

---

* The movement which Kitchener reported can only have been an incidental affair. According to the statements of Germans who were fighting on the Boer side, the reinforcements which had actually arrived were a long way from having reached the heights mentioned.

effect a retirement when darkness fell. This attack, which had been undertaken entirely on the initiative of a subordinate commander, had lasted just half-an-hour. The two and a-half Battalions which took part in it had lost 8 officers and 110 men.

In the course of the day Warren received further reinforcements, including some Howitzers which were specially useful. Moreover, during the night of the 21st-22nd Coke's Brigade, which had been increased by the arrival of the Somersetshire Light Infantry, was taken across to the left bank of the Tugela on which it was assembled early in the morning of the 22nd. On the evening of the 21st General Lyttelton, of his own accord, sent two Howitzers of the 61st Battery which had hitherto been employed at Potgieter's Drift, and two more reached Warren on the morning of the 22nd. While Coke's Brigade remained along the lower Venter's Spruit on the right flank, two of the Howitzers were brought into position on Three Tree Hill and two on the left flank. They took part in the bombardment of the Boer position, which lasted the whole of the 22nd January.

This day passed by without any final attempt being made to come to a decisive engagement with the Boers and so to clear the road to Ladysmith. General Warren had given up his intention of attacking the right flank of the Boers, and had also quite convinced himself that the Boers were not to be driven out of their positions by means of Artillery fire pure and simple. When Sir Redvers Buller spoke once more in favour of carrying through the attack in the neighbourhood of Bastion Hill, Warren replied that under all the circumstances it was essential that Spion Kop should be taken before the Fairview-Rosalie Road could be thought of as a practicable route for transport. The raising of this objection was altogether justified, for it would have been impossible to march under Spion Kop at a distance of only 2,000 yards from it, so long as that hill was still in the Enemy's hands. Anxiety about the advance of transport was, however, premature at this period, the Boers being still unbeaten. General Buller fell in with the views of his subordinate, and so the centre of gravity of the further operations of the British was transferred to the right wing of Warren's command.

Meanwhile the defender of Ladysmith had once more, in the following heliogram addressed to Buller on the 21st January, offered his co-operation in the forthcoming engagements:—

> "If you will let me know the time fixed for your principal attack, I will make a demonstrative attack here so as to draw away from you as many as possible of the Enemy. My former experiences lead me to hope that I shall be able to draw away a considerable number."

Instead of encouraging White in this laudable intention, Buller answered laconically that he would let White know when the Ladysmith Garrison could most effectively cut in.

No such a communication, however, was ever made.

The Boers kept quiet on the two days after the fight at Thaba Myama and avoided offering any favourable targets to the fire of the British Artillery. The two guns posted on the Acton Homes stream kept the British on the southern edge of Thaba Myama under fire as well as they could, and distributed their shells over the ground in rear of the foremost line so as to endanger the reserves suspected of lying there; the three guns posted between Green Hill and Spion Kop replied at intervals to the fire of the British Batteries.

The effect of the Boer Artillery fire was discounted by many of their shells failing to burst. The Boers also suffered from a continuous scarcity of ammunition, for no sort of communication had been established with the railway at Moddenspruit for the transport thence of the ammunition brought there. The intention ascribed by General Warren to the Boers of making an advance to attack the flank of the British had never been contemplated. On the contrary they, on their part, expected much more, that the British would renew the attack on Plat Kop on the 21st and 22nd. Their suspicion was strengthened on the 22nd by the fire of the two Howitzers which made an extraordinary impression on them and which, in conjunction with the brisk Infantry fire from Bastion Hill, led to the temporary evacuation of Plat Kop. The situation thus created is described by a German who was with the Boers, in the following extract from his diary: "I see how our people are coming away from the position. It is almost enfiladed by the Howitzers which simply blow away the entrenchments. All is lost if the British make an assault now. There's not a man in the trenches. But the 'Vierkleur' is still proudly flying aloft, and this, of course, deceives the British."

Neither of the two Howitzers on Three Tree Hill appears to have produced more than a trifling effect. At any rate the Boers continued to occupy the trenches in front of them; the damage they actually inflicted here was very small in comparison with the tremendous noise of the lyddite shells as they burst, and with the immense displacements of the surface of the ground caused by the explosions; the difference of the effect on the Boers in the two positions is to be explained by the fact that from Three Tree Hill no enfilading of the trenches was possible, and where no material effect was produced, men placed under this Howitzer fire soon got accustomed to it.

The greater part of the Commandos, in which there was constant dread of an attack, passed the nights in their positions even after the 20th. On the same account the guns were always withdrawn from their covered positions at night-fall. The demoralising influence wrought on the defenders' powers of resistance through their being always strung up for a fight was intensified by the absolute breakdown of the commissariat.

As the supply department possessed no means of forwarding supplies from the rail-head at Modder Spruit Station to the troops, and as the customary drawing of rations by the Commandos from the Force besieging Ladysmith had to be suspended on days when there was fighting to be done, the Burghers had to manage as best they could with what was to be found on the farms near the positions, and with what they had with them. Many of them lived for days together on water and biscuits.

As, however, the total loss of the Boers in Killed and Wounded from the 17th to the 21st January did not amount to more than 60 men, they could, in spite of all their hardships, look forward with confidence to the fighting in which they had yet to participate in this neighbourhood.

CHAPTER V.

THE BATTLE OF SPION KOP AND THE RETIREMENT OF THE NATAL ARMY ACROSS THE TUGELA.

At the suggestion of the General Commanding-in-Chief, Warren, before definitely making up his mind to an attack on Spion Kop, assembled a Council of War which was attended by Generals Clery, Hildyard, Woodgate and Coke, the last-named of whom had just arrived on the scene. Warren put it to the Generals—would they prefer an attack on the extreme right flank of the Boers or an advance on Spion Kop? General Clery thereupon expressed himself decidedly against the attack on the extreme right flank of the Enemy, which was sure to be in the end very wearisome and costly in men. The other Generals agreed with him. Warren's plan was accordingly adopted.

The possibility certainly existed that the Boers, whose attention during the last few days had been exclusively directed towards the neighbourhood of Thaba Myama, had only weakly occupied Spion Kop, and that this dominating, roughly cone-shaped eminence might be captured by surprise if energetically attacked. If, however, a decisive success was the object, it would be necessary to combine the rush at or near the centre of the Boer position with a general attack all along the front.

Measures were at first, however, only taken with a view to the seizure of Spion Kop, and this operation was to be

SPION KOP.   TWIN PEAK.   TWIN PEAK.   ONE TREE HILL.   BRAKFONTEIN.

VIEW OF SPION KOP FROM THE SOUTH.

[To face p. 132.

carried out by Coke's Brigade on the night 22nd-23rd January. Coke, however, made it clear that before he could execute his commission he must make an accurate reconnaissance. Further, his Troops, which had just finished a long night-march, were not exactly in a condition to carry out a night-operation. The advance on Spion Kop was accordingly postponed till the night 23rd-24th January.

On the morning of the 23rd when General Buller, as usual, came over to Warren's Headquarters, he found to his astonishment that the situation had undergone no alteration whatever. The Infantry, as on the previous day, stood inactive in the positions taken up on the 20th, and the Artillery had re-opened the usual bombardment of the Boer position. Buller, who clearly suspected that the Spion Kop operation had also been allowed to drop and who, as he said later, "had been dissatisfied with Warren's arrangements ever since the 19th January," now gave full expression to his annoyance: "I observed," he wrote in his report to the Secretary of State for War, "that I had received no further reports and no explanation about the special measures which he, Warren, had in his mind when telegraphing to me on the 19th January; that for four days he had kept his troops continuously exposed to gun and rifle fire on the edge of an almost perpendicular precipice; that this position admitted of no second line; that the supports and reserves were huddled up close behind the firing line in a formation which admitted of no defence, and that a panic or a sudden attack by the Enemy might throw the whole mass in disorder off the heights at any moment. I maintained that the situation was too dangerous to be persisted in any longer, and that Warren must either attack or withdraw his troops."

Buller thereupon reverted to the attack which he wished to have carried out against the Boers' right flank.

Warren in answer to these reproaches pointed to the attack on Spion Kop which he had ordered and which was only postponed. Buller appeared to be satisfied with that. The whole business is illustrative of the peculiar situation in which the General Commanding-in-Chief found himself, in consequence of his having handed over the Command to Warren. Buller himself has said later that he ought to have resumed Command as soon as he found himself no longer *au courant* with what was going on. He justified his action on the grounds of the consideration which he was obliged to show to Warren, who was not only a Divisional Commander, but also his " Second in Command." For all that, since the 22nd four complete Infantry Brigades, two-thirds of the whole Army, had crossed the Tugela, and there is no doubt whatever that Buller ought consequently to have immediately resumed Command and that Warren ought to have gone back to his position of Divisional Commander. This was all the more necessary, because Warren himself, as a result of the increase of his Force, had divided it into two " Wings of Attack," the Rosalie Farm Road forming the boundary between them. The Commanders of these two Wings would have been Warren and Clery, each of whom was provided in the shape of his own staff with the necessary machinery for directing these two bodies.

According to the distribution ordered by Warren the British forces were divided as follows:—

Right Wing, the direction of which was given to General Coke:—

The Royal Dragoons and Thorneycroft's Mounted Infantry on the extreme right flank, south of Spion Kop.

Two Battalions of the Eleventh and one and a-half Battalion of the Fifth Brigade under General Woodgate on the eastern edge of Three Tree Hill.

Four Field Batteries and two Howitzers on Three Tree Hill.

A Field Company Royal Engineers on the Spion Kop stream.

In second line the Tenth Brigade* under Colonel Hill on Venter's Spruit.

Left Wing, under General Clery:—

Two Battalions of the Fifth and two Battalions of the Eleventh Brigade, under General Hart, on the southern edge of Thaba Myama.

Left of this, near Bastion Hill and in camp on Venter's Spruit, the Second Brigade (Hildyard's) complete.

On the right bank of Venter's Spruit, for the protection of the western side of the camp, five Companies of the Fifth Brigade.

North-west of the camp, on Venter's Spruit, the Mounted Brigade less Thorneycroft's Mounted Infantry.

South-west and west of Bastion Hill two Howitzers and two Field Batteries.

At Buller's suggestion, General Woodgate was entrusted with the direction of the attack on Spion Kop in place of General Coke, who had not completely recovered from a broken leg. Buller gave him Lieut.-Colonel A'Court, of his own Staff, as Intelligence Officer. As General Coke continued to be in command of the right Wing of Attack, although he was not leading the attack on Spion Kop, the matter of command was not exactly simplified by this interference on the part of the General Commanding-in-Chief.

General White had reported to Buller on the 22nd that on that day there had been great activity and stir in the Boer camps. Towards sunset about 500 Boers had left to

---

* On the 23rd January, this brigade was joined by a Battalion of Imperial Light Infantry (Colonial troops).

reinforce the main laager at Clydesdale Farm. He, General White, would open fire at daybreak so as to induce them to come back again.

To this message Buller replied with a description of the situation on the Upper Tugela. Warren had been standing for two days in the position he had taken up within about 1,300 yards of the Enemy's position which, being above them, could not be seen into by the British; the approach to them lay over bare slopes; it was impossible to get guns up into Warren's position in consequence of the steepness of the slopes. The Boer position had been swept by the fire of Howitzers and low-trajectory Guns posted in rear of the Infantry line; the Boers replied from Creusots and other Guns; the British had the best of this Artillery duel, because they enfiladed the Boers' trenches and because the Boers' fire was rather ineffective; on the next day an attack would be made on the salient left flank of the Enemy's position, on Spion Kop, from the British position opposite Potgieter's Drift (?).

The last and decisive attempt at an attack on the left bank of the Tugela was thus only incidentally mentioned; nothing whatever was said about any co-operation by the Garrison of Ladysmith. Consequently the inactivity of White during the subsequent operations, if it cannot be excused, can be at least, to some extent, explained.

Meanwhile preparations were being made for the attack. General Warren and his subordinate Leaders keenly reconnoitred the ground in front of Spion Kop. There was also a discussion of details between Warren, Coke and Woodgate. In the course of the afternoon the various Commanders concerned issued their orders.

Warren's orders ran:—

"Three Tree Hill, 23rd January, 1900, 2 p.m.

"1. To-night an attack will be made on Spion Kop with $2\frac{1}{2}$ battalions under General Woodgate.

"2. This attack will be supported by the Troops on Three Tree Hill under arrangements to be made by the General Officer Commanding the right Wing of Attack. If firing is heard during the night from the direction of Spion Kop, the Artillery on Three Tree Hill will fire star-shell and open fire on the ground in rear of the Enemy's position to prevent the advance of reinforcements. At daybreak the Infantry will open fire on the same points.

"3. It rests with the General Officer Commanding 'Left Wing of Attack' to open fire on the Enemy in his front in order to detain him there if firing commences on Spion Kop.

"4. An Officer from the Staff of each Wing of Attack will report himself to the General Commanding at midnight on Three Tree Hill.

"5. All Troops are to be acquainted with the above instructions. Fire is only to be opened by order of the Battalion Commanders.

"6. Countersign Waterloo.

"7. As soon as fighting begins, constant reports are to be made by lamp-signalling or heliograph or orderlies to the General Commanding at Three Tree Hill.

"8. The distribution of the Troops into right and left 'Wings of Attack' is only to be regarded as a purely tactical measure. For administrative purposes the old distribution of the Second and Fifth Divisions holds good, and Casualty Lists are to be made out accordingly.

"9. General Talbot Coke will assume temporary Command of the Fifth Division, and will appoint his own Staff.

"10. The Imperial Light Infantry has joined to-day and will be under the orders of the General Officer Commanding Right 'Wing of Attack.'"

In accordance with the above, General Coke, as Commander of the Right "Wing of Attack," issued the following Operation Order :—

"23rd January.

"1. The General in Command has determined to capture Spion Kop.

"2. The operation will be conducted by General Woodgate. He will dispose for this purpose of two Battalions of his own Brigade, which will be joined by about 110 men of Thorneycroft's Mounted Infantry and a half Field Company Royal Engineers.

"3. Rendezvous at 7 p.m. immediately east of the Royal Engineers' Camp. The Troops are to form up under cover.

"4. Every man is to carry 150 rounds. The General Officers Commanding Tenth and Eleventh Brigades will allot 3 mules to each Battalion during the course of this afternoon. The ammunition to be carried by these mules will be supplied by the Battalions concerned. The Troops are to carry a full day's rations. All horses will be left at the Royal Engineers' Camp. The mules will follow at the rear of the Column. Entrenching equipment is to be carried by the Troops.

"5. The Officer Commanding Royal Dragoons will arrange for the occupation of all native kraals on the route, and also for that of Wright's Farm. All inhabitants are to remain indoors.

"6. The Troops will, of course, carry their water-bottles filled, and attention is to be drawn to the fact that it may be difficult to replenish them. The Battalions are to arrange, as far as possible, that a supply of water shall be available in rear in biscuit boxes* loaded on mules or otherwise.

"7. The General Officer Commanding Eleventh Brigade will arrange that the Volunteer Ambulance Corps and the Brigade Bearer Company provide stretcher-parties. No ambulance wagon is to advance beyond the Royal Engineers' Camp before daylight."

---

* A biscuit box contains about 35 galls. of water.

Lastly, General Woodgate issued the following Operation Orders:—

"23rd January, 3.40 p.m.

"1. The General Commanding has decided to capture Spion Kop to-night.

"2. For this purpose the following detachments will be formed:—

>6 Companies of the 2nd Battalion King's Own (Royal Lancaster).
>2nd Battalion Lancashire Fusiliers.
>180 men Thorneycroft's Mounted Infantry.
>Half the 17th Field Company Royal Engineers.

"3. The troops will parade at 7 p.m. at White's Farm,* 800 yards north-east of the Pontoon Bridge.

"4. Reserve ammunition will be carried on the mules provided by the Tenth Brigade.

"5. A full day's ration will be carried. Wagons with cloaks, water-carts, and Machine Guns are to advance as soon as they can do so without being observed.

"6. The South Lancashire Battalion will furnish 6 mules, 3 to each battalion, for water supply.

"7. For the transport of water in waterproof leather bags (Pakals), mules are to be employed. †

"8. 20 picks and 20 shovels are to be carried.

"9. Countersign Waterloo."

The above orders are typical of the method of compilation of British orders. They contain a mass of orders about details which could perfectly well have been entrusted to the care of junior Commanders. But we look in vain for that essential reference to any support to the Attacking Column which should have been furnished by other Troops under Warren's Command; the measures pre-

---

* Wright's Farm is no doubt meant. The order as to the place of assembly was subsequently in accordance with instructions from General Coke, altered to "a point north of White's Farm."

† The waterproof leather bags (Pakals) proved to be unpractical. Consequently ships' biscuit-boxes were substituted for them later on.

scribed in his own, the first-quoted, Orders with regard to support by long-range fire can hardly be considered as fulfilling all requirements; neither is there any mention of an adequate supply of entrenching equipment; nor, most important of all, of any assistance to be furnished by the Artillery in close support, or even an indication that such was to be expected in the course of the fight. These omissions were to be bitterly avenged.

It fell in with the idea that Woodgate's attack alone was to deal the decisive blow, that General Clery's Troops should for the present remain altogether inactive. They were in part withdrawn from the edge of the heights, which they had till now occupied, nearer to Three Tree Hill and Venter's Spruit. This movement gave the Boers a free hand to transfer the troops from their right wing to the decisive point.

Spion Kop, the scene of the fighting which was now to begin, rises like a tower above the mountainous ridges joining it from the East and North-West, and commands them and the country in the North-East towards Blaauwbank Spruit and in the South-West as far as the Tugela. The ridge joining from the East rises in the Twin Peaks to an altitude which approaches that of Spion Kop.

The summit of Spion Kop is, as it were, strewn with boulders of all sizes, in the spaces between which grows short, coarse grass. Where there is any soil it is shallow. In plan the surface of the summit may be compared to an equilateral triangle with its apex on the North and its base on the South. It is not absolutely flat, but slopes gently downwards from the South towards the centre, and from near that point rises again towards the edge on the northern side.

From this elevated edge the mountain slopes steeply towards the valley of the Blaauwbank in several terraces. The result of this configuration is that the field of fire from

THE SUMMIT OF SPION KOP.

To face p. 140.

the centre of the plateau is limited towards the North by the edge of the mountain, and that it is quite impossible for rifles placed at the centre to produce any effect whatever on the northern slope. So unless the British advanced right up to the northern edge, the Boers could come up to it in absolute security. The slopes in all other directions, and specially that on the South towards the Tugela, fall away steeply from the summit. On the south-western angle the ascent is made easier by several terraces which combine to form a chain of high points stretching along the East of the Spion Kop stream towards Trichardt's Drift. The lowest of these terraces which lies north-east of Wright's Farm is called Height A, the second lowest, which extends to the foot of Spion Kop, Height B, and the third lowest, which, however, forms only a narrow projection on the south-western slope of Spion Kop, was called by the British, after some trees standing on it, Four Tree Spur.

The Royal Engineers' bivouac, where the British Troops assembled, is situated about $2\frac{1}{2}$ miles north-east of Wright's Farm at the point of junction of a small stream which rises in Three Tree Hill with the Spion Kop stream. A good road leads to it. At the junction of the streams there is a ford from which a road gradually rises up to Height B. The summit of Spion Kop is reached thence by a zig-zag path, subsequently improved during the action, which, winding about between stones and boulders, is in some parts quite steep, in others almost level. The ascent from the Royal Engineers' bivouac to the summit can be made by any one walking independently and unencumbered in an hour and ten minutes. By night and during the action, when ascent along the zig-zag path was made difficult by the stream of wounded men coming down and by other hindrances of all sorts, almost an hour and a-half to two hours were needed.

The movements of their Enemy up to this time had created a conviction in the Boers that a serious attack was only to be looked for on their right, *i.e.*, in the vicinity of Thaba Myama and the Green Hill. In full confidence that their mobility would enable them to reinforce in good time any point suddenly threatened by an unforeseen attack, they had occupied only weakly the other portions of their extended position. So it came about that on Spion Kop, which had been included in the line of defence since 15th January, there remained only a small detachment of the Vryheid Commando. Moreover, no great attention had been paid to the artificial strengthening of the mountain for defence. It is true that the construction of two lines of shelter-trenches, one behind the other, had been begun; the work, however, had soon been stopped again.

Either as the outcome of the suspicions aroused by the British reconnaissance of the ground in front of Spion Kop on the 23rd or, as was so often the case with the Boers, by a pure chance, some of Krantz's German Corps were sent to reinforce the Garrison of Spion Kop, which was thus brought up to a strength of about 100 men. A Krupp Gun was to have been hauled up on to the mountain on the 24th. During the night, 23rd-24th, some of the Germans made cover for the Gun which was expected, while the rest of them, with 50 or 60 men of the Vryheid Commando, kept watch in a long shelter-trench which lay a few paces in rear of the south-western edge. Half the men were on the look-out while the remainder slept in the trench. No further measures for security were taken, and in any case no picquets were pushed out beyond the immediate neighbourhood of the trench.

An English doctor who went through the war with a Boer ambulance wrote on the 23rd January as follows about the spirits of the Boer Army on the Upper Tugela:—

"There is great excitement everywhere. If matters go on like this for a few days longer the Boers will up-stick and away. Matters are just on the balance. Leaders and men are looking more anxious than they did at the retreat from Weenen.* As the entrenchments are not at all shell-proof, and principally because it is difficult to retire from them, the Boers do not like them. I really believe the British will get through in the end. The uncertainty of the issue, combined with the exertions of fighting during the last two days, have had a great effect on the Boers."

In the twilight of the 23rd January, about 7 p.m., the Troops detailed for the capture of Spion Kop assembled in the ravine near the Royal Engineers' bivouac. There the men received detailed instructions as to what they were to do. Talking and smoking on the march were forbidden; all noise was to be avoided as much as possible. On coming across the Enemy everybody was to throw himself flat on the ground without making any reply to the fire which might be expected, and then, on the command of the Officers, there was to be a rush with the bayonet at the Enemy's position. All the Officers, including General Woodgate, had provided themselves with rifles.

About 8.30 p.m. General Woodgate's Column moved off, General Coke commanding the right "Wing of Attack," of which Command it still formed a part, inspected it as it passed him. An hour later he sent two Companies of the Connaught Rangers after it, with instructions to prepare and entrench a rallying-point in case of a reverse, about two-thirds of the way up to Spion Kop.

Lieut.-Colonel Thorneycroft had, as far as possible, reconnoitred the route by day and had fixed landmarks and guiding-points so as to be able to pick it out again in the dark. He now headed the Column accompanied by two of his own Officers and men. The detachment of his own

---

* *See* p. 42 Waters' Translation "War in South Africa."

Regiment followed him, dismounted, in file; behind it came General Woodgate with his Staff, then the Lancashires, the Royal Engineers, and in rear six Companies of the King's Own (Royal Lancasters). The Infantry moved in column of fours, five mules loaded with spades were led alongside the half-company Royal Engineers, of which the men themselves carried a large quantity of entrenching tools.

At the foot of the mountain where Height B joins Spion Kop the Column halted and closed up. About 10 p.m. the real ascent began. The night was dark and rainy. A light breeze blowing from the direction of the mountain prevented the Boers from hearing anything whatever of the unavoidable noise, the clatter of arms and equipment, or the rolling of dislodged stones. About 11 p.m. the moon rose; in spite of this the march along the rough path was extremely trying and very slow progress was made. Halts for rest were frequently necessary, and during them the men sat down and many fell asleep forthwith. It was found that the Royal Engineers were over-loaded; some of the entrenching tools had to be left behind.

Towards morning when the British were nearing the summit a mist arose and concealed their approach to the very last. The head of the Column had reached the top about 3 a.m. Thorneycroft formed his men up in line. The Lancashire Fusiliers formed line in rear of Thorneycroft's men. Bayonets were fixed. The line advanced in silence. Suddenly they were challenged by a loud "Halt! who goes there?" They were in front of the Vryheiders' shelter-trench. In accordance with the instructions, everybody threw himself down on the ground. The Boers opened a brisk fire into the darkness. As soon as Thorneycroft judged that the moment had arrived when there must be a pause for re-loading magazines, he gave the order for the charge. This was entirely successful.

The Boers cleared from their position neck and crop; one of them, not quick enough in leaving the trench, was pinned down. A second trench was also carried by storm. Shortly before 4 a.m. the British were in possession of the height. The fight had only cost them ten men in Killed and Wounded.

To announce to the rest of the British Troops the success thus gained, General Woodgate called for three cheers. This was the signal for the British Artillery to open fire. The Guns had been laid the previous evening, and all arrangements had been made with lanterns and clinometers for continued night firing on to the reverse slope of Spion Kop.

The question now arose, How was Woodgate to derive full profit for his easily gained success in the attack? It would have been impossible for the British Leaders to form in their own minds anything like a satisfactory picture of the general topography of Spion Kop from the available maps, which were extremely rough. In any case, however, it is certain that on a table mountain such as Spion Kop there can only exist two practicable fire positions, viz., one curved outwards towards the Enemy and another, on the opposite edge, whence the surface of the plateau would be commanded by fire. The northern edge only ought to have been thought of as a position for the British, who wanted to wedge themselves, as it were, into the Boer position.

But even now no instructions were given for a thoroughly useful reconnaissance. The sentries of the picquets were only pushed a short distance forward. Consequently Woodgate, who was still unaware that the northern edge was not more than some 150 to 250 yards in front of him, decided to entrench himself at the very same points which his Troops had carried by storm. There the men began to dig a line of shelter-trenches which ran from about the centre of the western side of the plateau towards

L

the south-eastern angle, and which extended for a length of about 400 yards. There was an elevated bit of ground in rear of the centre, which was also entrenched. But no really serviceable protection was provided. The disinclination of the British soldiers to spade-work, their great fatigue, the want of entrenching tools,* the shallowness of the soil covering the plateau, all these considerations combined to make the work severe and only to a very small degree satisfactory. So it came about that quite unserviceable trenches of only about 3 ft. 4 in. to 4 ft. in height and some 12 in. to 18 in. in depth were made. The countless stones lying about, which the Boers understood how to use to good purpose in making parapets or sangars, were not sufficiently turned to account. Further, the British had not yet learned from their Enemy how to make embrasure-like head-cover† to protect themselves against shrapnel or close-range Infantry fire.

When daylight gradually dawned the conviction spread, as was inevitable, that the whole line of defence was faulty. Some parts of the trenches lay only some 150 yards from the northern edge where the field of fire ceased. The steep ascents from the north, the north-west, and the north-east could not possibly be brought under fire. On the other hand the British trenches lay open to the flanking fire of the Boers, especially from the neighbourhood of the Twin Peaks.

For the defence of the entrenchments the Troops were so distributed that the Lancashire Fusiliers occupied the extreme right flank. Then on their left came Thorneycroft's Mounted Infantry and the King's Own (Royal Lancasters). With a strength of about 1,500 rifles it was impossible to find places for all the Troops in the trenches, although the

---

* The British infantry had not taken their small entrenching implements into the field with them. The tools provided by the Royal Engineers' field company were insufficient.

† See page 114.

men were crowded into them at close intervals. Some of the Troops were therefore taken back further to the rear. General Woodgate sent away half a section of the Engineers to improve the path up the mountain side.

The Boer Garrison of Spion Kop had completely abandoned the hill; not one of them remained even on that portion of the northern area which had not been occupied by the British. Vryheiders and Germans had rushed down the slope and had alarmed the Boer Commandos laagered down below. The news immediately produced almost indescribable confusion. It seemed that the whole line of defence would be untenable if the British continued to hold the hill.

The two Leaders of the Boer forces on the Upper Tugela, Schalk Burger and Louis Botha, were both present near Spion Kop, and justly appreciating the gravity of the situation, proceeded at once to institute energetic counter-measures. Schalk Burger sent 90 men of the Carolina Commando, under Prinsloo, to occupy the north-eastern edge of the plateau, and 50 Heidelbergers, under Marais, to take post West of the Twin Peaks. While these measures were more of a nature to hold in check the British advance, Botha immediately formed the decision to drive the British out of the position, which was of such importance to them, by means of a counter-attack. He sent for all the available men from the Commandos of which he had the direction, and as the various parties arrived he despatched them up the hill with orders to attack the British. Botha, moreover, took steps to ensure that, having regard to their resources in that arm, a proportionately large force of Artillery should be placed in readiness to support the attack. A Krupp Gun and a Maxim-Nordenfeldt Gun which were near Green Hill were swung round on to Spion Kop, a Krupp Gun was taken north of Spion Kop into the valley of the Blaauwbank Spruit, another Krupp Gun and a large calibre Maxim-Nordenfeldt were taken to the vicinity of the Twin Peaks; two more 7·5 centimetre Creusot Guns were sent for from the extreme right wing, but they did not reach Green Hill till several hours later. All these guns were completely concealed from the British Artillery, and some of them to such an extent that only indirect fire could be used from them against Spion Kop. Observations of effect were signalled back to them by heliograph posted on the edge of the heights.

The first parties of the Boers reached the edge of the plateau about 7 a.m., coming in small groups from the North-West, North and North-East. Nothing occurred for some time as neither of the adversaries could see the other on account of the impenetrable mist. Only just at those points where the Boers came, at a few paces' distance, in touch with the British picquets the fighting opened even in the mist. A German present in the Boer ranks writes: "When it was light it was found that we had formed a thin skirmishing line, in which there were hardly more than 200 or 250 rifles on the north-western, northern and north-eastern edges. We suddenly saw the British standing and kneeling in thick swarms about 300 yards to our front. They fired some volleys and then charged with the bayonet, but when about 100 or 150 yards from us they were thrown back, and several groups of them then tried to rush separate points in our line, without, however, gaining any success."

Meanwhile the British Batteries maintained their fire without interruption. When at about 7 a.m. the fog began to lift off Spion Kop, Woodgate and his subordinate Commanders became aware of the faulty position of their entrenchments. An immediate effort was made to correct the fault by pushing forward the picquets to the northern edge. This brought about the collisions in the fog already referred to in which the Boers say that they tore the rifles from the hands of several British soldiers as they were in the act of firing. The Boers, however, had already planted their feet firmly on the edge and drove the British back without much trouble. Even when stronger parties were sent forward the advantage remained with the Boers.

To quote further from our authority: "After their onslaughts had come to grief the British rushed back and formed a firing line which stretched in a gentle curve right across the plateau at about its centre. A steady fire-fight opened. At first both sides shot so wildly that one's senses were almost paralysed by the quite too awful din." About 8 a.m. the sun dispersed the fog and the Boer guns began to overwhelm the British position on Spion Kop with shot and shell. The Boer Artillery, without any hesitation, opened fire over the heads of their own riflemen, and kept it up, the shell frequently bursting only 30 to 100 yards in front of the Boers' firing line without ever doing them any harm. The effect from the beginning was very good, which is not surprising in view of the concentration of fire, the crowded, exposed and ill-protected formation of the British, who consequently presented a very favourable target, and the position of the Boer Guns, in which they were quite secure from any injury.

Lieut.-Colonel Thorneycroft wrote in his report: "The Boer shrapnel fire was very accurate, the bursting of the shell was well-timed and swept the whole length of the plateau." The splinters of stone thrown about by the shell bursting on graze or falling blind increased the effect.

Lieut-Colonel A'Court had left Spion Kop between 7 and 8 a.m. to make his report about the situation on the hill. He reached Warren on Three Tree Hill about 9 a.m., and as he spoke in a very sanguine way about the prospects of the Spion Kop enterprise—he said he thought the summit could be held against any Enemy till the Day of Judgment—Warren turned his own attention to some technical instructions about path-making and water-supply about which he had concerned himself when he had ridden over early in the morning to the foot of the mountain. Nothing whatever was done towards the support of the Troops, in addition to the rather ineffective Artillery fire, except that six Companies of the Connaught Rangers were posted on the eastern spur of Three Tree Hill to open very long-range fire on the extreme right flank of the Boers.

The British Artillery was neither able to silence the well-concealed and protected Boer Guns, nor to join effectually in the Infantry combat. Insufficient range-power and anxiety about firing over the heads of their own Troops prevented it from producing any great effect on the decisive point. So some of the Batteries, at any rate, directed their fire, as they had during the preceding days, against the Boer positions on Green Hill and Thaba Myama in the vain hope that they would keep the Commandos there from moving away towards the scene of the fighting. Even the fire of the heavy guns posted on the southern bank of the Tugela was ineffective on account of the great distance from Spion Kop.

In spite of all this, nobody on Three Tree Hill seems during the early forenoon to have thought of the situation as doubtful. The blow was, therefore, all the more staggering when shortly before 10 a.m. the following heliogram from Colonel Crofton reached the General commanding: " Reinforce at once or all is lost. General dead."* " What has happened?" was anxiously asked in Warren's Staff. They were not to remain long in a state of uncertainty.

The originally favourable situation of the British Troops on Spion Kop had gradually taken a more and more un-

---

* General Woodgate had been mortally wounded and did not die till some days later.

favourable turn. The groups pushed out from the shelter-trenches towards the northern edge had never been able to produce any serious fire-effect against the Boer marksmen. They lay crowded together under cover of boulders and heaps of stone 100 yards, 50 yards, and even less from the Boers. As soon as a man showed himself a hot fire was opened. This fire often began even before the man had got his head up above the cover and when only his khaki helmet was to be seen—an example of the necessity for carefully matching in colour the clothing and equipment of Infantry with the surroundings of the field of action; the soft, low Boer hat and its indistinguishable colour proved far more serviceable.

As every one of the frequent attempts to rush the edge of the plateau had failed, the British leaders tried to overcome the difficulties by pushing still more reinforcements to the front from the reserves which had been held back in the shelter-trenches. But it was impossible to restore the balance. The Boers, creeping forward under cover of the boulders, first one by one, then in larger parties, gradually gained ground. One who was in the fight writes about this creeping forward: "From most points on the extreme edge (I lay on the north-west edge) it was impossible to clearly see the British soldiers lying on the ground. So most of us began to push forward a foot or so at a time, the men next one another firing and creeping by turns. In the course of an hour we were able to creep forward 100 yards, some more, some less. At last the low earth heaps thrown up by the British could be seen almost without raising oneself. The two firing lines were now only separated by a level space on which lay but few boulders; on to this the Boers did not advance."

Gradually, too, the reinforcements sent for by Botha came along and climbed the steep slopes which gave them cover from the British fire. The Pretoria Commando, which was the first to arrive, strengthened the Carolina Commando, on whose right the Boksburg men posted themselves. Moving forward on the western edge they came under the British Artillery fire and had to be withdrawn. Germans, who had formed part of the Garrison of the hill, joined themselves to the Carolina Commando. On the extreme right Free Staters from Senekal and Winburg were engaged under General Cronje.

The frontal and flanking fire of the Boers caused bigger and bigger gaps in the British ranks. General Woodgate was mortally wounded soon after the fight began, and so was Colonel Blomfield, of the Lancashire Fusiliers. The command devolved on Colonel Crofton, of the King's Own. He ordered his Signalling Officer to heliograph to Warren the news of Woodgate's death and the request for reinforcements. So owing to a misunderstanding on the part of an apparently overwrought signaller, the message was despatched which, as has been mentioned, created alarm.

Shortly before the receipt of Crofton's message, Warren had ordered General Coke to send a Battalion up the hill, and the Imperial Light Infantry had accordingly been despatched. General Coke was now instructed to send yet another Battalion. The Middlesex were accordingly moved off about 10 a.m., and the Dorsets soon followed. When they had started, Coke asked to be allowed to proceed himself to the hill where the greater part of his "Wing of Attack," in all five Battalions, and Thorneycroft's Mounted Infantry were assembled. He began the ascent after 11 a.m.

After Warren had seen to the reinforcement of the troops on Spion Kop, he replied by heliograph to Crofton: "I am sending two Battalions. The Imperial Light Infantry is already on its way up the hill. You must hold out to the last. No surrender."

On the 24th January General Buller had not crossed the Tugela, as had been his daily practice, but had posted himself near a signalling station on Spearman's Hill. As all messages from Spion Kop to Warren's Headquarters had to be transmitted* through this station, Buller became acquainted with Crofton's message. At the same time a rearward movement of the British Troops on Spion Kop was observed. As a result, Buller had grave misgivings as to whether the direction of the fight up there was in proper hands, and he accordingly heliographed the following message to Warren: "If you do not transfer the Command on the summit to some really good hard-fighting man you will lose the hill. I propose Thorneycroft." Warren accepted this suggestion as an order and passed it on to Spion Kop in the form: "With the approval of the General Commanding-in-Chief I appoint Lieut.-Colonel Thorneycroft to the Chief Command on the summit with the local rank of Brigadier-General."

He omitted to make General Coke, who did not start on his way to Spion Kop till 11 a.m., aware of this order, and to this must be ascribed the distressing confusion which subsequently supervened in the direction and command at Spion Kop.

Originally about 1,500 men had reached the summit of Spion Kop; an additional 1,000 were on their way up there. Suitably distributed, these 2,500 were more than sufficient to continue to hold the narrow front on Spion Kop, if only support were furnished to the Troops engaged there, in some other direction or manner. When two more Battalions were pushed up, not only was there no use for them, but they tended to increase the existing confusion. There resulted a crowding of men on to a narrow front and a consequent increase in the fire-effect produced by the

---

* In order to get better cover for it the signalling station at Spion Kop had been established on the southern slope.

Boers. In this way the saucer-shaped formation of Spion Kop exercised under the existing conditions, as fatal a power of attraction as did the St. Hubert Farm on the 18th August, 1870, during the Battle of Gravelotte. There, too, more than 40 Companies were finally assembled in the most limited space, could not manage in any way to develop their force, and so got repeatedly into such critical situations that the Leaders misguidedly kept sending yet more reinforcements to their assistance. It is perfectly comprehensible that local Commanders under the stress of fighting, which is inflicting heavy losses on their own Troops, will call for support, but this should not lead away those conducting operations into the adoption of measures of which they ought to recognise the futility.

If the desire was to furnish direct support to the Troops on Spion Kop, it would have been more to the point to do so by sending forward some guns, as was done in a similar situation at Spicheren on the 6th August, 1870; on that occasion the Infantry on the narrow plateau of the Rotherberg could not be induced to stand fast and firm until the Brandenburg Batteries dashed up into action on the top of the hill. In the same way it could not fail to have made a great impression on the Boers had their ranks been suddenly rent by an unlooked-for storm of shrapnel. It is perfectly true that no mean difficulties had to be surmounted. A young Subaltern of Artillery entrusted with the investigation had declared that it was impossible to get guns up on to Spion Kop; but considering that the Boers always managed, by hook or by crook, to get their clumsy "Long Toms" on to the top of the highest mountains, this "impossible" is rather unconvincing. It is also a proof that the British themselves were not thoroughly convinced of the "impossibility," that later on during the engagement, guns were actually got up on to Spion Kop even in darkness, and that Lord Dundonald volunteered to bring some of his own Machine Guns up there. The Boer Gunners were hourly expecting their baptism of fire from British guns in action on the hill-top, and were clearly of opinion that once the guns should be in position there, the issue of the fight would be decided in favour of the British by them.

The most effective, though doubtless only partial, support would have been furnished to the Troops hard put to it on Spion Kop, by attacks in all available strength and with the utmost energy on all the other portions of the Boer front. As the attention of the Boers was exclusively directed to Spion Kop, and as a large part of their Forces was assembled there, such measures would not only have taken the strain off the Troops engaged there, but would in all probability have enabled the still available $2\frac{1}{2}$ Brigades of Infantry to gain a complete success in their own attack. In any case even a demonstrative attack would have sufficed at least to divert the Boers from directing flanking fire on to Spion Kop.

Meanwhile, the Boers had gained further advantages on Spion Kop. They pressed nearer and nearer on to the British parties thrown out in advance of the entrenchments and shot them down almost at the muzzles of their rifles. Thanks to his highly developed and independent initiative, and his superior shooting power, each individual Boer was able, in the absence of any centralised control or decentralised direction of the fight, to seize every opportunity for using his own rifle to good effect; on the other hand the rigorously exercised fire-control to which the British soldiers had been accustomed at all field-days in peace-time was perforce absent on this occasion owing to the overpowering din of battle, the impossibility of seeing the ground in the front, and the ever-increasing casualties among those who should apply it. The Troops found themselves suddenly confronted in a critical situation with the task of having to produce fire-effect in the absence of any guidance, and they lacked the power to think and act for themselves necessary for its achievement. The Boers' fire swept the open space lying between the foremost groups of the British and their entrenchments so that it was almost impossible to reinforce the former from the latter. Scattered groups constantly ebbed back to the entrenchments, and yet Thorneycroft and Crofton, by their own personal efforts, succeeded in many instances in bringing the men forward again. Shortly before noon, however, the whole right flank and the centre melted back into the shelter-trenches. Only a part of the King's Own (Royal Lancaster) on the left wing still stuck to their forward position.

The Boers, now in undisputed possession of the edge of the hill, successfully endeavoured to make the situation of the British in their originally defective entrenchments unendurable; they poured in a hot rifle fire at the closest ranges, and kept up a ceaseless Artillery fire on them. Gradually the crowded trenches were filled up with Killed and Wounded. Yet as far as could be managed by the exertions of the officers still in action, the Boer fire was answered. Beyond the reach of such exertions the men lay inactive in the trenches, not venturing to show themselves in any way. General Coke, who at this time was climbing up the mountain, was met by the flow of an unbroken stream of fugitives who were coming away from the front on all sorts of pretexts.

The sufferings of the troops on Spion Kop were intensified by parching thirst. The sun was burning hot by now; it was only 14 days since the majority of the troops engaged had come off a long sea-voyage, and they were still subject to the so-called "artificial thirst" which, according to English accounts, is an after effect of long sea-voyages or of prolonged subsistence on preserved foods. It was found to be impossible to maintain the supply of water to the forward line. Although large quantities of water had been brought up to the south-western edge, and though there was even on the summit a spring, of which, however, the supply was soon temporarily exhausted, there were no means of getting the water up to the firing line. On the other hand there was no want of ammunition the whole day long; most of the British did not venture to fire any more.

About midday when Lieut.-Colonel Thorneycroft had to be informed of his appointment to the Command of the Troops on Spion Kop, he too was lying wounded in the firing line. The orderly bringing Warren's heliograph message to him was killed while trying to reach him. A few minutes later Lieutenant Rose, of Thorneycroft's Mounted Infantry, crawled towards his Commanding Officer and shouted to him, "Sir Charles Warren has heliographed that you are to take Command. You are a General." He added that the right flank was hard pressed and that he had seen reinforcements advancing against it.

Thorneycroft was soon to find occasion to prove himself the "really fighting man" General Buller thought him to be. Suddenly on the right flank of the British there was a fluttering of white cloths. The Boers came forward out of their concealment and were on the point of witnessing just such a laying down of arms in the open as had occurred at Nicholson's Nek.* Already some of the British were standing "Hands up." Struggling to his feet and raising himself to the full of his impressive stature, Thorneycroft, with the spirit of a hero, shouted to the Boers: "I'm in command here. I'll have no talk about surrender." He then withdrew the most seriously menaced part of the British firing line out of the trenches, but could not prevent about 180 Lancashire Fusiliers being taken by the Boers.

---

* *See* p. 40 Waters' Translation "War in South Africa."

Meanwhile, the leading portion of Coke's Brigade had arrived. Some of the Imperial Light Infantry reinforced the King's Own (Royal Lancasters); the Middlesex were sent off to the hard-pressed right flank. Led by Thorneycroft in an irresistible charge, some of this Battalion with the Lancashire Fusiliers and the Mounted Infantry once more took possession of the trenches which had just been abandoned; the Boers scrambling over them regained the edge of the plateau, but had to abandon their prisoners.

Shortly before 1 p.m. General Coke, commanding the Tenth Brigade* reached the top of the south-western slope of Spion Kop. As he remained just below the plateau, and as he knew as little about Thorneycroft's appointment to command as Thorneycroft knew of his arrival, Thorneycroft continued to direct affairs on the summit. No understanding was arrived at between them. Coke acquired the impression that too many Troops had already been sent on to the hill. He therefore kept back all Troops reaching the south-western corner to form a reserve. The first to arrive were the Dorsets and some of the Imperial Light Infantry, and these were later joined by the Scottish Rifles and Bethune's Mounted Infantry from Lyttelton's brigade. At the urgent request, however, of Colonel Hill, commanding the Middlesex, for reinforcements on the right flank, the remainder of the Imperial Light Infantry were soon afterwards sent forward. Immediately after the abortive surrender of the British in that quarter, the Boers had begun to push round on the eastern and south-eastern slopes of the hill and threatened to envelop the right flank.

About 12.50 p.m. Coke sent the following report to General Warren through an intermediate station which had only just been established half-way up the hill: " I am

---

* General Coke was still suffering from the effects of a broken leg, and on this account had only been able to make the ascent very slowly.

now on the slope of Spion Kop close to the plateau. I am informed that the Troops are lying closely packed on the summit. They are holding out, although exposed to shrapnel fire and suffering heavy losses. I have not allowed any more reinforcements to advance into the foremost line. The Troops engaged know that succour is ready at hand. Ammunition is being pushed up."

This was the first message received by Warren since the heliogram sent by Crofton's instruction, though he had several times applied to Thorneycroft for a report on the situation. But as the last named had been all day long in the firing line, no request of this kind had reached him. Warren, therefore, now addressed himself to Coke, who about 1.30 p.m. amplified his report of 12.50 p.m. with a further message that the situation was very serious and that if the Artillery did not succeed in silencing the Enemy's guns, the troops would not be able to hold out for a second day.

Even before these reports came to hand Warren had recognised the necessity of supporting the defenders of Spion Kop with Artillery. For this purpose he did not make use of the Batteries then on the spot, but despatched an order to No. 4 Mountain Battery to come across the river and advance to Spion Kop; this Battery had only landed in Natal a short time before and had marched out of Frere in the early morning of the 24th January *en route* for the Upper Tugela. Warren also ordered that some Naval Guns, which Buller had placed at his disposal, should be taken up the hill. He further ordered that the Field Company should prepare the path up the hill for the ascent of the guns.

Meanwhile, it was quite certain from the moment they were issued that these measures could not fulfil their purpose on the 24th. Warren's other orders were to the effect that an abundance of sandbags, cartridges, provisions and water should be got up on to the top of the hill.

For some time there had been no more idea on the part of the Boers of genuine offensive movement. They contented themselves with shooting at the British on the plateau. About 1 p.m. the intensity of the fire was at its greatest. According to Botha's account there were altogether five Guns and two Maxim-Nordenfeldts in action as well as the men with rifles. Some of these latter began to fail in ammunition, for no arrangements of any kind had been made in connection with a further supply. It was only on the flanks, along the western and south-eastern slopes, that Botha still hoped to come to grips with the British. On the south-eastern slope efforts were still made, although with insufficient forces, to hem in the British right flank. On the western slope " Fighting-General " Cronje, who was in command there, was required to direct his fire on the British moving to and from the south-western corner. He roundly refused to comply with the order as it would result in his drawing on himself the fire of the British Artillery.

In the ranks of the Boers, side by side with a display of manly resolution and firmness, there were instances here and there of faint-heartedness, not to say of cowardice. The need of a strong restraining discipline made itself distinctly felt. When Botha during the afternoon rode away from the positions on and north-west of Spion Kop he found a great number of men who had withdrawn from the fight, and it needed all his influence to bring them up to the front again.

On the 23rd January General Lyttelton had sent back the King's Royal Rifles across the Tugela by Potgieter's Drift, there to relieve Coke's Brigade, which had moved off to join Warren's Troops. With his remaining three Battalions and the 64th Field Battery he made, at daybreak, his fourth demonstrative attack on the Brakfontein Heights. The leading two Battalions (one each of the Rifle Brigade and the Durham Light Infantry) advanced to within rifle-shot of the Boer shelter-trenches and began a fire-fight with the occupants. General Buller, however, who did not wish for any serious engagement in this quarter, directed the withdrawal of the Brigade at 8 a.m.

About 10 a.m. Lyttelton received from Warren a request for support, and soon afterwards there followed a heliogram bearing no personal signature and couched thus : " We are holding the whole of the edge of the height up here, but are being heavily attacked from your side (*i.e.*, from the East). Help us. Spion Kop."

Thereupon Lyttelton sent the Scottish Rifles also back across the Tugela and ordered them and Bethune's Mounted Infantry and the King's Royal Rifles to march by a Kaffir drift in the direction of Spion Kop. The crossing of the river was begun by the Mounted Infantry at 11.45 a.m., by the Scottish Rifles at 12.30 p.m. and by the King's Royal Rifles at 1 p.m. During the passage of the two first units General Lyttelton noticed the arrival of considerable reinforcements at Spion Kop. He therefore justly considered that the despatch thither of further reinforcements was unnecessary, if not actually harmful, and he accordingly gave to his last Battalion, the King's Royal Rifles, instructions to direct their march on the Twin Peaks.

Bethune's Mounted Infantry and the Scottish Rifles, moving by the path already used by Woodgate, reached the plateau of Spion Kop after 3 p.m. While Bethune's two Squadrons* were held back in reserve by General Coke, the Scottish Rifles were little by little pushed up

---

* There is no mention anywhere of where the horses were left. It is, however, probable, that they remained at the foot of Spion Kop.

M

in support of the front line; they were principally engaged on the right flank.

The King's Royal Rifles, after crossing the drift, first marched a good distance down stream, and when they drew the Enemy's fire, wheeled to the left and took the direction of the Twin Peaks. The Battalion was divided into two half-battalions, each of which deployed two half-companies in the firing line, while the remaining two half-companies followed in support; a third Company of each half-battalion was echeloned on the left and right respectively, and the fourth formed the Half-battalion Reserve. Thus formed and under fire of the Boers the Battalion began the ascent, which proceeded very slowly on account of the very steep slope, whose peculiar contour, however, gave the assailants a good deal of cover. In order to be able to aim at all effectively, the Boers had to crawl a long way out along their rocky glacis, and there they came under the fire of the second line of the British directed over the heads of the first line. About 5 p.m. the first line of the British came close up to the edge of the hill.

After a somewhat protracted fire-fight the right half-battalion fixed swords and took by storm the portion of the Twin Peaks immediately in their front. The left half-battalion supported the charge with their fire and then rushed the other half of the kopje. This well-planned and energetically-executed attack on the apparently strongest part of the Boer position thus ended in complete success. The Boers left their positions in haste, taking with them both the guns which had been posted in this vicinity, and which, by their flanking fire, had inflicted so much damage on the Troops on Spion Kop.

General Lyttelton had hardly given orders for the advance of the King's Royal Rifles when it struck him that their isolated attack was hazardous. He was strengthened in this opinion by a report from his Staff Officer, who had been to Spion Kop and who now said that the attack of the King's Royal Rifles had no prospects of success. Accordingly about 2.30 p.m. he issued orders that the Battalion should retire and, as it continued to advance, repeated them. It appears that the Commanding Officer only heard of the second message conveying the orders, which was transmitted partly by heliograph and partly by flag. About 5 p.m., shortly before the Enemy's position was taken, he sent the following perfectly apposite reply: "If I can recall the leading sections I will do so. But it is difficult to get a message to them. The hill is terribly steep." When he had taken The Twin Peaks, the Commanding Officer reported that he would hold it unless he received instructions to the contrary. Thereupon he received two orders to retire, the second of which called his attention to the published intentions of the General Commanding-in-Chief. So when darkness fell the Battalion began its retirement, and crossing the Tugela returned to Spearman's Hill. Shortly before it moved off Colonel Buchanan-Riddell was killed.

The success of this Battalion produced no small impression on the Boers, and its immediate result was a great improvement in the harassing situation of the troops fighting on Spion Kop. General Botha fully recognised the importance of keeping a firm hold on the Twin Peaks from whose heights his position on Spion Kop could be taken in rear. He despatched all his reserves to the threatened point under his Staff Officer Edwards; but there was only a very small party of them available. General Cronje, who has already been referred to, refused to send to the front a party of his Burghers who were lying about doing nothing under cover of a line of boulders; he said it was too late and that the Burghers would soon have to go down the hill again, and that Botha himself had better take over the Commando, Free Stater though it was. It appears that Schalk Burger, too, was languid in his direction of the defence of the southern front. So it was really a slice of luck for the Boers that only a single battalion made the attack on the Twin Peaks and that it was prevented, by superior orders, from turning its success to advantage. The result was that the Boer's left wing could now quite well remain near the hill which had been captured.

On Spion Kop there had been but little change in the grouping of the combatants. Boers and British still lay in front of one another at closest possible range, but still no decisive issue was arrived at. This indecisive ebb and flow of the struggle when almost grip to grip is a frequently presented feature of this war; it traverses the hitherto generally held opinion that the modern Infantry fight, when once the combatants are at quite close quarters, will be quickly settled one way or another.

With the exception of the Dorsets, all the reserves held back by General Coke had gradually been absorbed in the firing line; but these supports, which, moreover, generally reached the firing line reduced in strength, could not give a forward impetus to the firing line; they only sufficed to steady the balance.

In this fighting at close quarters the Boers had certain advantages; they found better cover behind boulders and at the sharply defined edge of the plateau, than the British had in their defective entrenchments; and they hardly suffered at all from Artillery fire. Besides this, they knew how to snatch moments of repose in the course of even the heaviest fighting; generally only a part of their men were firing in the foremost line while the remainder, retiring into dead angles and behind large masses of rock, drank their coffee in perfect comfort. The result was that the Boers always had men in fresh trim available for the repulse of any rush forward made by the British. On the call, "There come the Khakis," everybody able to use a rifle reappeared in the firing line. A German officer thus describes the fight at this period: "Taking it all round, our irregular firing line was better sheltered than the British; besides which we could generally catch them obliquely as they were in a central position. The stupidity of the British soldiers also added to their disadvantages. To me it is more than doubtful whether the Burghers would have held out if the Artillery had not hailed shrapnel and pom-pom shells over our heads into the Enemy. The British rifle-fire was constantly weakening, but when the firing line was reinforced it burst out again, to faint away once more. Sometimes the British, sent forward from the rear-most sections, could be actually seen as they advanced into the firing line; sometimes when they crawled along the ground they reached the front without being seen at all. Although many of them gradually fell asleep, the fire of the Boers never entirely ceased; they waited for the moment when a British helmet should be seen somewhere, to overwhelm it with fire from all sides, so they soon ceased to appear. A few weak attempts of isolated groups to rush forward in a bayonet charge were crushed from the very outset. At the same time our line was getting thinner every minute the afternoon advanced; we had lost not a few of our men, and many unscathed men even crept back to the rear."

The difficulties of the situation of the British on Spion Kop are clearly reflected in the reports which Coke and Thorneycroft sent to Warren during the afternoon. First, Thorneycroft reported about 2 p.m.:—

> "I have held out to the utmost with the Troops which were up here when fighting began. Some of the Middlesex have now arrived. I am told that the Dorsets are coming too; but the truth is we are not strong enough to hold such an extended line. The

> Enemy's guns north-west of us are smothering the whole plateau. They have got some guns on the east too. Cannot you bring Heavy Artillery to bear on the guns in the north-west? What reinforcements can you send to hold the hill till to-morrow morning? We want water badly. We have many Killed and Wounded. If you really want to hold the hill through the night you must send more Infantry and get at the Enemy's guns."

This report first passed about 3 p.m. through General Coke's hands, he having moved higher up the hill up to the signalling station just under the summit. He had not (as Thorneycroft had) received all his impressions actually in the thick of the fight, and did not, any more than previously, agree with the idea of bringing up more Infantry, so added the following to the message just quoted:—

> "I have seen this report and have ordered the Scottish Rifles and the King's Royal Rifles* to strengthen the firing line. The Middlesex, Dorsets and Imperial Light Infantry Battalions have already gone up. 120 men of Bethune's Mounted Infantry have also gone forward as reinforcements. It seems that we are now holding our own."

Soon after this, General Coke went up the hill as far as Four Tree Spur, and about 3.30 p.m. sent thence the following report about the situation:—

> "We are suffering heavily under shrapnel fire on our left front, coming from the direction of Three Tree Hill. We are on the point of sweeping the Boers off the hill. The necessary reinforcements have been sent forward. The Scottish Rifles have just reached the summit. Casualties are heavy. We want more doctors, food, and especially water. †

---

* Coke was mistaken here. He did not have the King's Royal Rifles under his orders.

† This report only came to General Warren's hands about 7.30 p.m.

When this message had been despatched, General Coke, accompanied by Colonel Morris, C.S.O. to General Warren, who had come over to him some time before, went right up to the summit and made a survey of the situation. On the right flank he met Colonel Hill, Commanding the Middlesex, and Colonel Coke, Commanding the Scottish Rifles, who were together at the moment. Colonel Hill had previously sent a written report to Coke in which he expressed his opinion that there were already enough Troops in the firing line and that they ought to hold out till darkness fell and should then entrench themselves better. Coke approved of this scheme and, in ignorance of Thorneycroft's appointment, believing Hill to be the Senior Officer in Command, charged him with its execution.

It appears that Coke subsequently lost this confident frame of mind; at any rate, about 5.50 p.m. he sent a fresh report to Warren in which he expressed himself in distinctly less favourable terms about the prospect:—

"The situation is as follows—The troops originally sent up are still in their positions. They have suffered heavy losses. Many Killed and Wounded are still lying in the shelter-trenches. The Artillery fire has been and still is very severe. Is there any certainty that our guns will be able to silence the Enemy's if I hold the position till morning? Failing that, to-day's experiences will be repeated. I have kept Bethune's Mounted Infantry and the Dorsets quite fresh for the protection of a withdrawal. If I stop I will endeavour to employ these Troops in getting food and water forward to the firing line.

"The situation is extremely critical. To attack and capture the kopje in my front, I must advance several hundred yards in the face of a numerous and well-entrenched enemy. My position there in front of the (Boers') quick-firing guns would be even less favourable.

"Please give me orders, and if you wish me to withdraw, cover my withdrawal from Connaught Hill."*

In this was expressed for the first time the thought of retreating, although as yet only in a conditional form. The situation was described in exactly the same terms in a report sent at 6.30 p.m. by Thorneycroft, who still believed himself to be the only responsible commander on the hill:—

"The Troops which marched up here last night (Lancashire Fusiliers, King's Own and Thorneycroft's Mounted Infantry) are completely exhausted. They have no water. Ammunition is running short. In my opinion it is impossible to continue to hold this position, even with the reinforcements which have arrived, as long as the Enemy's Artillery are able to keep up their fire on the hill. The Enemy has got three long-range guns, three of shorter range, and several Maxim-Nordenfeldts, which have commanded the whole plateau since 8 a.m. I have not been able to ascertain the casualties, but they have been very severe, especially in the Regiments which came up last night. I request orders as to what I am to do. The Enemy is now (6.30 p.m.) keeping up a severe fire (rifle, shrapnel, and pom-pom) on both our flanks, while our front is always under a hot rifle fire. The only thing I can do is to hold the position. If my losses go on increasing on the same scale, I shall hardly be able to hold out through the night. Plenty of stretcher-bearers and as much water as possible should be sent up here. The situation is very serious."

This report never reached Warren at all. The transmission of news between the Commanders on the hill and Warren's Staff was defective. From 3.40 p.m. onwards no news was received from the scene of the fighting, and this

---

* South-eastern spur of Three Tree Hill.

was not due to any failing on the part of those responsible for supplying information. Coke and Thorneycroft sent plenty of reports, and Warren, too, took great trouble about keeping up the connection with the Troops engaged by sending up Colonel Morris and, late in the afternoon, Lieutenant Winston Churchill. The fault lay far more in the insufficiency of the signalling arrangements. To be sheltered from the Enemy's fire, the heliograph instrument had to be fixed on the southern slope of Spion Kop, whence, on account of the intervening heights, communication with Warren's Headquarters on Three Tree Hill was only possible by making the circuit of Spearman's Hill, and during the afternoon heliographing was interrupted owing to the light being bad; all of which shows how inherently unreliable and subject to accidents such means of communication are, and that to ensure the transmission of information, every available description of supplementary and up-to-date apparatus must be employed, even in the thick of the fight. The small trouble of laying the necessary wires for the establishment of telephonic and telegraphic communication would have been amply repaid.

Warren has been reproached by an English authority for not having gone up to Spion Kop himself during the course of the evening. True it is that, as a rule, it is not the business of the General in Command to go into the foremost fighting line and there to issue his orders; such a proceeding would be opposed to the opinion prevailing in the British Army, that subordinate Leaders should be allowed full liberty of action in carrying out their orders, an opinion which, with all the weight of a fixed principle, found such remarkable expression in the demeanour of Buller and Warren. But it is debateable whether on this occasion a departure from the rule was not demanded on the score of expediency. At any rate, there was no necessity for Warren to remain always on Three Tree Hill, especially as there was no intention of throwing the troops placed there into the fight that day. Consequently he could, without any cause for misgiving, have been represented temporarily there by one of his Brigadiers.

As during the whole day no attack on a broad front was even initiated against the centre and right flank of the Boers, so as to draw them away from Spion Kop and thereby to lead up to an issue favourable to the British Troops, Spion Kop itself had certainly become the one and only decisive point in the field. The single issue of the heavy fighting had pivoted on the maintenance of a firm grasp at that point. If that grasp were maintained, the neglect to attack the other portions of the Boers' front could be repaired on the following day, and for such an attack the possession of so commanding a point as Spion Kop would be invaluable.

In order that the possession of the hill should be assured, it was specially necessary that Warren himself should go, even if only for a short space of time, and investigate the situation on the spot. He would in this way have certainly been able to find out the state of confusion which ruled in the spheres of command and direction, and he could have applied the remedies. Uninfluenced by the impressions produced in the immediate fighting-line, to which Coke and especially Thorneycroft had been subjected for hours together, he could have reviewed the situation with greater calmness of judgment than was possible for either of these Officèrs. His wishes, if clearly and decisively expressed, must certainly have had an effect on Leaders and Troops. Perhaps Warren might then even have convinced himself that nothing was to be gained by an unsophisticated crowding of Troops on to Spion Kop, that the road to victory did not lie over that hill, but, given a firm hold there, that it ran through the front of the Boer lines in which it formed a salient.

As a matter of fact Warren never went up to Spion Kop; he only sought, as he had previously, to influence the course of events by means of instructions to his subordinates, the despatch of reinforcements and other similar unimportant measures, mostly of a technical nature. About 6.30 p.m. he asked Coke if, in the event of the remainder of the Troops being withdrawn out of the zone of fire, the summit could be held by two Battalions. Soon after that, at Buller's suggestion, he gave orders that Colonel Sim was to go up to Spion Kop with half a Company of Engineers, a large working-party, the two Naval 12-prs. and the Mountain Battery which had just arrived. The Engineers were to help in getting the guns up the hill, as well as to improve the entrenchments on the hill itself and to prepare covered positions. Besides that Warren gave Sim a written order for Thorneycroft in which he distinctly demanded—for the first time—that Spion Kop should be held. Finally, he took two more Battalions of Hildyard's Brigade on the right wing, the East Surreys and the Devons, evidently in order to have at hand more Troops for the reinforcement of those on Spion Kop.

As darkness fell the fire on Spion Kop gradually died down. Late in the evening a fresh attempt made by a small party of Boers to take the southern slope and envelop the right wing of the Scottish Rifles was repelled by them without much trouble. Here and there a shot still rang out, but generally speaking the fight came to an end soon after sunset, 7 p.m. The exhaustion of both sides after the heavy fighting, which had lasted ten hours and a half, claimed its due.

The time had now arrived for the British Leaders to acquaint themselves clearly with the situation of their Troops, and to decide what further measures should be undertaken. Those Troops which had first reached the hill hardly possessed any further value for fighting purposes. In an absolute tangle of Units, reduced in force by serious losses, robbed of a great number of their Officers, they needed time and repose before they could be got into fighting trim again. Even the Scottish Rifles, the Imperial Light Infantry, and the Middlesex, which had joined the fight later, required some rest and to be sorted out again into proper formations, before they could be considered as perfectly ready for further action. Only the Dorsets and Bethune's Mounted Infantry, which Coke had held back in reserve, were as good as fresh. The numbers of Killed and Wounded lying thick on the limited area occupied by the British seriously hampered the movement and employment of the Troops on the plateau; the sight of so much suffering tended to demoralize them.

Of the measures taken for the improvement of their situation; of the bringing up of water, and food, and ammunition to the south-western slope of the mountain; of the forward movement of Mountain and Naval Guns, and of the Engineers, the Troops and their Leaders knew hardly anything. All contact with the Enemy had been lost owing to the complete exhaustion of the Troops and the absence of reliable direction; consequently it was not noticed that the Enemy's situation also had meanwhile undergone a complete alteration.

In the belief that the fight would have to be renewed the following morning, all the Commanding Officers were convinced that the Troops would not stand the test a second time. The idea of deliverance from an insupportable situation by a night-attack suggested itself; Troops kept in hand for such a purpose were quite handy and fresh; the Boers' dread of night fighting was well known; but nobody appears to have felt the energy within himself to carry out the idea.*

---

* The idea of a night-attack is expressed only in a report from General Lyttelton's Brigade-Major.

Consequently all the Commanding Officers present on Spion Kop came, after a short discussion, to the unanimous decision that withdrawal was inevitable. That no single attempt was made to gain possession of the hill for good and all may be partly explained by the peculiar concatenation of adverse circumstances. General Coke, after his conversation with Colonel Hill,* had gone half-way down the hill-side, and Colonel Hill, who, as far as General Coke knew, was the Senior Officer present on the hill, was left to see to the execution of the measures decided on for the maintenance of the position. The Commanding Officer of the Scottish Rifles, who took part in the discussion among the Commanding Officers, was aware of this arrangement, and consequently a search was made for Hill before any decision was come to among them; but he could not be found. General Coke, by reason of the unfavourable selection he had made for his own resting-place, was not in a position to have any influence on the decisions of the Commanding Officers on the hill, but he might have prevented their execution. Just at the critical moment, about 9 p.m., however, he was called away by a lamp-signal message from Warren's Headquarters to go and make a personal report there. He tried to ascertain the degree of importance to be attached to this order, but as the oil of the lamp was burned out, there was no possibility of picking up connection again with Headquarters, and Coke consequently felt he must comply; which he did, leaving his Staff Officer, Captain Phillipps, behind at the signal station to attend to any question which might arise about details, etc.

In this way it came about that Thorneycroft's decision to evacuate the hill was put into execution. As early as 7 p.m. a beginning was made of the collection of the Killed

---

* See page 167.

and Wounded, and preparations were made for marching off. Soon after that the Column moved off, the Middlesex leading and the Scottish Rifles, who were to protect the withdrawal, closing up the rear. When the leading Company approached, it was met by Colonel Hill, who was opposed to the decision to evacuate the plateau. There arose an animated discussion, in the course of which Colonel Hill could not take his stand as the superior of Lieut.-Colonel Thorneycroft because, according to a peculiarity of the British regulations regarding seniority, although Hill was himself, as a Colonel, senior to Thorneycroft, the last-named held the "local rank of a Brigadier-General." Thorneycroft closed the argument with the assertion that he was in Command and took all responsibility. The Brigade-Major of Coke's brigade, who was close to the signal station, made a second attempt to stop the continuance of the withdrawal; about 11.30 p.m. he had been awakened from sleep by the noise of Troops on the march, and recognised that the withdrawal was in process of execution; he immediately ran out the following order: "To the Commanding Officers of the Dorsets, Middlesex, Scottish Rifles and Imperial Light Infantry. There is no authority issuing from Major-General Coke or from Sir Charles Warren for the withdrawal. General Coke was called away by Sir Charles Warren shortly before 10 p.m. When he quitted the fighting-line about 6 p.m. the Troops were holding their positions; he went away thence to make the report that he could maintain the position. Somebody or other has, without any authority, given an order for withdrawal and a heavy responsibility lies at that person's door. Were the General here he would order the immediate re-occupation of the position."

Captain Phillipps succeeded in retaining half-way up the hill-side some of the Dorsets and Scottish Rifles; but when morning broke and neither support or orders arrived these Troops also withdrew.

Meanwhile Thorneycroft had continued the withdrawal of the bulk of the Troops and would not allow himself to be dissuaded from his determination, when he came across Sim's column and with it Lieutenant Winston Churchill bearing a message from Warren which could only have been despatched with the intention of keeping hold on Spion Kop. Sim also delivered his written message from Warren in which the intention of retaining Spion Kop was clear; but neither message made any impression on Thorneycroft, who said it was too late to cancel the decision which he had made. About 2 a.m. the withdrawal of the bulk of the Troops under Thorneycroft was finished, and about 2.30 a.m. Thorneycroft reached Warren on Three Tree Hill where, just about the same time, a report was received from Captain Phillipps concerning the evacuation of Spion Kop.

Meanwhile an event had occurred on the Boer side which proved the existence of a like state of exhaustion and of war-weariness. The Boers, too, had completely surrendered Spion Kop just about the same time as the British had done the same thing. General Botha, who, unlike Warren, had always remained near the scene of the fighting during the battle, had late in the evening gone to the Chief Laager, which was fixed north-east of Spion Kop. He expressed his conviction that the British would give up the hill again in consequence of their heavy losses; but for all that, as may well be understood, he was uneasy about the issue of the fighting and especially about the fate of the left flank, and he sent several messages to General Burger enjoining him to hold out. About midnight one of the messengers returned with the news, personally vouched for by Commandant Prinsloo, that Burger had retired and that Spion Kop itself was almost completely evacuated.

The men, too, posted there, though not belonging to Commandos under Burger's orders, impelled by excessive fatigue, by hunger or by fear, had stolen away one by one or in groups from the scene of the fighting and, finally, hardly a single Boer remained on the hill. They considered themselves the more justified in this because, as early even as during the pauses in the fighting in the course of the afternoon, there had been discussions going on in the various shelter-places about the possibility of retirement. Even if they had wished to, the Leaders were quite powerless to keep their men up at the front. The process of the evacuation of the hill is thus described by the German on whose authority several quotations have already been made: " The day gradually reached its close without anybody knowing what was going on or that any change had taken place. We were all still expecting some great effort on the part of the Enemy which would sweep us down off the plateau. With that there was a growing scarcity of ammunition, and some of the guns made longish pauses in their firing. Hope of victory was very faint. The sun sank, and a quarter of an hour later it was dark. Firing ceased and the Boers, in spite of their orders to remain on the plateau, sneaked away to refresh themselves in the laager. I do not believe that there were four (untouched) Boers left on the hill an hour after sunset. Finally, I was left all alone and I followed the example of the others, for I couldn't keep awake any longer and I didn't want to be captured."

An extremely critical situation had been thus brought about, for if the hill were not occupied again the whole position would be broken and the result of the battle must be unfavourable to the Boer Army. And the development of this situation was in no way due to circumstances over which the Enemy exercised any direct control, but to such as were altogether attributable to the conditions prevailing in the innermost organism of the Boer Forces.

Botha, however, did not allow himself to be disconcerted by this unlooked-for catastrophe. He scraped together all the Forces he could reach and thus succeeded in bringing some 450 men up to the hill shortly before daybreak. When they advanced over the edge of the height in the early dawn, they found to their immense surprise that the hill had been abandoned by the British, and saw that they themselves were the masters of the bitterly-contested battlefield.

The issue of the fight at Spion Kop was a result of the complete physical and moral exhaustion of the Troops on both sides. The greater endurance and energy of his direction and the pre-eminent will-power of a single man had grasped a victory for the Boers—a proof of the power in War of a Leader's personality. It was simply and solely to the qualities for Command possessed by Botha, that the thanks of the Boers were due for the fortunate issue of the Spion Kop fight.

As already mentioned, General Warren heard of the evacuation of Spion Kop about 2.30 a.m. Although he could understand from Captain Phillipps' report that the lower slopes of the hill were not yet abandoned he, unlike Botha, forthwith gave up his cause as lost and did not make the slightest effort to improve the situation. He immediately addressed the following report to General Buller:—

> "Colonel Thorneycroft has given up his position on Spion Kop on his own responsibility. The troops are retiring. Can you come at once and decide what is to be done? A decision must be arrived at immediately."

Owing to interruption of telegraphic communication

this message had to be taken by a mounted orderly, and so was not delivered into Buller's hands till 5 a.m. He at once went over to Warren, reaching him at 6 o'clock, and now at last he took over personal Command.

Although he did not agree with the evacuation of Spion Kop, although the retirement had been initiated under no compulsion and carried out without interruption by the Enemy, and although not one-half of Warren's Troops had taken part in the fighting on the 24th, he immediately decided on a withdrawal across the Tugela. This movement was immediately set afoot, but it lasted three full days on account of the enormous train of transport which had been imprudently hauled across the river.

Either by reason of their dulness or from fear of the superior numbers of British troops left posted close by Three Tree Hill, the Boers let slip the chance of harassing the British as they were withdrawing across the river under their very eyes. They believed that they had fulfilled their duty by simply repulsing the attack, and they confined themselves to holding the summit of Spion Kop. What profit would not a somewhat more active adversary have made out of this situation!

While on Thaba Myama and at the Green Hill there was the customary firing of snap-shots in all directions, the Boers during the midday and afternoon of the 25th allowed a sort of tacit truce to prevail at the decisive point— Spion Kop. The British profited by this, not only in burying their dead on Spion Kop, but also in initiating in complete security a sufficiently perilous retirement in the face of a victorious Enemy posted on a commanding position. A few shells which plunged harmlessly into the ground near the bridge furnished the only proofs of Boer objection to such proceedings. Buller reported about the conduct of the withdrawal:—

"On the 25th I began the withdrawal commencing

with the ox and heavy mule transport. This was concluded on the 26th. The loaded ox-wagons were drawn across the ford with double spans at the rate of about 8 per hour. The mule-wagons went across by the pontoon-bridge, but all the mules had to be outspanned and the wagons to be man-handled across. On account of the darkness of the night it was impossible to use the ford during seven hours; on the other hand, the pontoon-bridge was in use night and day. Besides the Machine Guns, the 6 Field Batteries and the 4 Howitzers there crossed the bridge :— 232 ox-wagons, 98 ten-span, 107 six-span, and 52 four-span mule-wagons, a total of 489 vehicles. In addition to the foregoing, the ambulances crossed to and fro carrying over the sick and wounded."

"At 2 p.m. on the 26th all the ox-wagons were across the river. To them succeeded till 11.30 p.m. the (light) mule-draught vehicles, and then the bridge was clear for Troops. On the 27th, about 4 a.m., all the Troops had crossed. At 8 a.m. the pontoon-bridge was dismantled and the whole operation finished. At 10 a.m. all the Troops had reached their fresh camp.

"Everything passed off without delay, which reflects credit on the Staff. I must make special mention of Major Irwin, R.E., and of his Pontoon Troop, who were absolutely indefatigable."

Buller closes his report about the defeat with the words :—

"Thus ended an undertaking which I believed was certain of success. We have had serious casualties and have lost many whom we can ill spare. On the other hand, we have inflicted on the Enemy losses quite as severe as our own. He is thoroughly disheartened, while our troops, I am happy and proud to say, are in splendid condition."

On the 27th January the British Troops were back again in their old bivouacs at Spearman's Hill, Hatting's Farm, and Springfield. Only Lyttelton's Brigade still held on, at the heights of One Tree Hill, to the north bank of the Tugela.

The casualties of the British in the engagements from the 17th to 24th January were proportionately heavy. They amounted in Killed, Wounded and Missing to a total of 1,742, and were more than 20 per cent. in several of the Units.*

The Boers are said to have lost in the engagements on the Upper Tugela, from the 19th to the 31st January (inclusive), 98 Killed, 231 Wounded, and 50 Captured, of whom, according to Botha's report, 50 (according to other reports 70), were Killed and 120 Wounded at Spion Kop.

A report submitted by Lord Roberts to the Secretary of State for War presents the whole course of events on the Tugela in a very keen and true light. It runs:—

> "1. My Lord,—I have the honour to bring to the notice of your Lordship certain reports in which Sir Redvers Buller describes the passage of the Tugela on the 17th and 18th January, 1900, the capture and evacuation of the position at Spion Kop on the 23rd and 24th, as well as some engagements of minor importance which took place between the 19th and 24th January on the right or eastern line of advance.
>
> "2. The plan of the operations is not very clearly described in the report itself; but it may be gathered from it and from the documents annexed to it that the original intention was to cross the Tugela at or near Trichardt's Drift and thence, following the road leading behind Fair View and Acton Homes, to gain the open plain lying north of Spion Kop; the Boer position opposite Potgieter's Drift being too strong for a frontal attack. The whole force, with the exception of one Brigade, was placed under Sir

---

* *See* Appendix III.

A BRITISH COLUMN CROSSING THE TUGELA.

[*To face p.* 180.

Charles Warren's orders. On the day after the passage of the Tugela he seems to have held a Council of War with his Generals and senior Staff Officers, and to have come to the decision that the outflanking movement mentioned in Sir Redvers Buller's secret instructions was impracticable in view of the inadequate supply arrangements.

"He subsequently determined on making the advance along the shorter route which leads in a north-easterly direction and which branches off at a point east (?) of Three Tree Hill. The choice of this route, however, involved the capture and occupation of Spion Kop.

"It is not, however, clear from the reports that the occupation of Spion Kop would have been essential had the direction for the march laid down by Sir Redvers Buller been taken. As, however, Sir Charles Warren considered impracticable the wide outflanking movement which was recommended to, if not enjoined on him, he ought forthwith to have reported to Sir Redvers Buller the measures he proposed to undertake. It is not clear whether he did this or not; justice towards Sir Charles Warren, however, demands that it should be stated that Sir Redvers Buller was throughout fully informed of all that took place. He was constantly present during the operations, and he on several occasions gave advice to his subordinate, and on the day after the withdrawal from Spion Kop personally resumed the Chief Command.

"3. In his remarks on Sir Charles Warren's report Sir Redvers Buller is very hard on the manner in which Sir Charles Warren carried out the instructions received by him. Without any acquaintance with the *terrain* or with the existing conditions it is difficult to say whether the delay, the selection of a faulty direction, and the deficiencies in leadership, of which Sir Redvers Buller complains, could have been altogether avoided. If, however, it was his opinion that his instructions were being incorrectly carried out, it was, as I judge, his manifest duty to interfere as soon as he had reason to believe the success of the operations was endangered. Sir Redvers Buller also admits that. His reasons for not interfering can hardly be deemed relevant. An undertaking of the greatest importance was being carried out, and no personal considerations should have restrained the General Commanding-in-Chief from insisting that the affair should be brought to its conclusion in such a way as in his opinion would secure the desired objective with the least possible sacrifice.

"4. As regards the withdrawal from Spion Kop, which was taken, after hardly any opposition, early on the 24th and which, however, had subsequently to be held the whole day long under an extremely heavy fire and the holding of which would have exercised a decisive influence in the Relief of Ladysmith, I regret that I cannot share the view of Sir Redvers Buller that Lieut.-Colonel Thorneycroft exercised a wise self-restraint when he gave the order for the withdrawal of the Troops. Even allowing that the necessary arrangements had not been made so that the position should be reinforced during the night, that its defences should be repaired and that Artillery should be brought up, in which respect the report of Sir Charles Warren does not differ so very much from the contrary opinion of Sir Redvers Buller, allowing further that the Senior Officer present on the summit might have been earlier informed by Sir Charles Warren of the instructions he had issued regarding the reinforcement and support of the Troops, I am still of the opinion that it was an inexcusable fault on the part of Lieut.-Colonel Thorneycroft to take on himself the responsibility and the right of Command. Even if the Enemy's fire had not entirely ceased during the night it would not have been hazardous, and even allowing that, in consequence of failure in oil, the lamp-signalling communication was temporarily interrupted, some understanding could have been arrived at between Lieut.-Colonel Thorneycroft and General Coke, or Sir Charles Warren by means of a messenger in the course of two or at most three hours. It appears that General Coke left Spion Kop at 9.30 p.m. for a consultation with Sir Charles Warren. Up to that time there had been no thought of withdrawal.* Immediately General Coke had gone, Lieut.-Colonel Thorneycroft, without reference to higher authority, issued an order which upset the whole plan of attack, and which rendered useless the sacrifices which had already been incurred in its execution.

"On the other hand, it is no more than justice to record that it would seem that Lieut.-Colonel Thorneycroft bore himself most gallantly the whole day long, and that it was doubtless owing in a large degree to his efforts and to his example that the Troops held on so long to the heights before the withdrawal was ordered.

"5. The conduct of Captain Phillipps, Brigade Major Tenth Brigade, in the difficult situation merits high recognition. He did his best to remedy the fault which had been committed, but it was too late. Signalling communication was not restored till 2.30 a.m. on the 25th. By this time it would have been impossible for the Naval Guns to reach the summit of the hill before day-break. General Coke did not return, and Lieut.-Colonel Thorneycroft could not be found. Moreover, the greater part of the troops had already begun to march off; even the fatigue-party with the half-company of Engineers had turned back.

"6. It is regrettable that Sir Charles Warren did not himself go up to Spion Kop even in the course of the afternoon or evening, especially as he knew

---

* Not quite accurate. The decisive consultation beween Thorneycroft, Crofton, and Caoke took place before 9.30 p.m.

that the situation there was very critical and that the loss of the position implied the failure of the operations. The result was that he had to summon General Coke to his Headquarters in the evening in order to acquaint himself with the course of events. Consequently the Command on Spion Kop fell to Lieut.-Colonel Thorneycroft. But General Coke was in no way aware of this. Sir Charles Warren at the suggestion of General Buller had ordered Thorneycroft to assume Command on the summit, at the same time appointing him a temporary Brigadier-General. This order, however, was not brought to the notice of General Coke who, till he went away at 9.30 p.m., understood that the command would devolve on Colonel Hill as the Senior Officer after General Woodgate had been wounded. Omissions and mistakes of this kind, though possibly unimportant in themselves, may exercise a considerable influence on the course of events. I think that Sir Redvers Buller is justified in his observation that there was a manifest want of organisation and system which very seriously prejudiced the defence.

"7. The attempt to relieve Ladysmith, which is described in the despatch, was well conceived. I agree with Sir Redvers Buller that it ought to have succeeded. Its failure may to some extent be ascribed to the difficulties of the *terrain* and to the commanding position taken up by the Enemy; also in all probability to the mistakes made by Sir Charles Warren and to his want of talent for direction. But whatever may have been Sir Charles Warren's shortcomings, the want of success must also be ascribed to the disinclination of the General Commanding-in-Chief to exercise his authority and to keep matters in the right groove, and also to the unjustifiable and uncalled for assumption of the responsible control by an Officer of junior rank.

"8. The gratifying feature in these reports is the

admirable bearing of the Troops during the whole course of the operations."

Lieut.-Colonel Thorneycroft adduces the following reasons in explanation and excuse of his fatal decision : —

" 1. The superiority of the Boer Artillery which, on account of the positions it occupied, could not be brought under the fire of the British Artillery from its lower-lying position in the neighbourhood of the camp, or from any other place.

" 2. His ignorance of the steps which were taken during the course of the day to support him with other guns than those of the Mountain Battery. He did not believe that this Battery would be able to maintain itself under the longer-ranging fire of the Boer guns and the close-range rifle fire.

" 3. The absolute want of water.

" 4. The difficulty of making entrenchments and cover, which should be of practical use against Artillery fire, with the few available spades, and having regard to the rocky nature of the ground on the summit.

" 5. The impossibility of holding the heights so long as the Boer Artillery was not silenced, ' which could never have happened.' "

PART II.

THE THIRD ATTEMPT AT RELIEF (VAALKRANZ).

CHAPTER VI.

THE THIRD ATTEMPT.

The physical and moral strain of the preceding days had told on the troops of the Natal Army, and they were able in consequence to thoroughly enjoy several days of complete repose which, thanks to the inactivity of the Boers, succeeded the retirement across the Tugela. Of the whole Army only Lyttelton's Brigade, which continued to occupy One Tree Hill, was in the immediate front of the enemy; the other Brigades, which were encamped south of Spearman's Hill, were quite out of touch with him.

Thanks to the ample provision of good food, the baneful impressions produced by the futile sacrifices in the recent fighting disappeared quickly.

As the General Commanding-in-Chief had been completely in the background during the recent engagements, the Army did not consider him, but his subordinate leaders, responsible for the failures, and it continued to look to him as its Chief with undiminished confidence. He announced that he intended to make a fresh attempt at the relief, and that he believed that he had now found "the key" of the Boer position.

The gaps created in the British ranks during the recent fighting were filled up by reinforcements which arrived in the very nick of time. In addition to about 1,200-1,500 reservists for the Infantry, the Army received 2 Squadrons 14th Hussars, a Battery of Royal Horse Artillery, half a company of Royal Garrison Artillery with 2 5-in. guns: a total of about 2,400 men and 8 guns, so that Buller's force stood once more at its original strength of 26,000 to 27,000 men.

In succession to General Woodgate, mortally wounded, General Wynne took over command of the Eleventh Brigade, and was replaced as Chief of the Staff by Colonel Miles. The mounted troops were divided into two brigades: the First Brigade, of which Colonel Burn-Murdoch, Royal Dragoons, took command, was composed of the three cavalry regiments now present; while the Mounted Infantry, under their old commander, Lord Dundonald, formed the Second Brigade. The 13th Hussars and the Royal Dragoons each furnished one troop as divisional cavalry. Further, the Fourth Brigade (Lyttelton's) was taken out of the Fifth Division (Warren's), being replaced there by Coke's Brigade, and being for the present left independent of the organisation of any division.

On the Boer side, too, the repose after the heavy fighting was very welcome. Manifest as were the advantages to be gained thereby, this loosely-organised and uncontrollable levy of militia could never have borne the strain which is thrown on troops garnering with all their energies the fruits of victory in a vigorous pursuit.

It was not till the 28th January, by which day the last

British detachments had disappeared from their ken on the right bank of the Tugela, that the Boer leaders were summoned to a Council of War to decide how the success gained four days previously should be turned to advantage. Botha's proposal to follow up over the Tugela with the right wing found no supporters. The only measure decided on was to send a fairly strong patrol over the river at Trichardt's Drift to pick up information about the further intentions of the British.

While the Natal Army was being reinforced the number of their opponents was diminishing. Parts of the Commandos investing Ladysmith which had been brought down to the Upper Tugela went back again. It appears that furloughs were once more granted. General Botha himself went to Pretoria at the end of January for a few days.

The occasions on which the British Commander displayed the set purpose of winning a victory were few, but his tenacity in regard to a plan when it was once formed was great. Even now the intention of effecting the Relief of Ladysmith by an advance across the Upper Tugela was not renounced before hazarding for a second time the chances of a fight. The pertinacity of the British Commander was expressed in an exchange of views which took place between him and General White immediately after the failure at Spion Kop. Buller closed his very first communication to White about the capture and evacuation of Spion Kop with the words:—

> "I am going back *viâ* Potgieter's Drift and intend to try again to reach you straight; but I fear that my force is not strong enough."

To this White answered on the 27th:—

> "I have only to-day received your despatch of the 25th. In this war we must expect to suffer heavy losses and be ready to chance them. If you make

another attempt to relieve us and fail, the fate of Ladysmith is sealed. Is not the Seventh Division available as a reinforcement for you? I could feed my men for another month, but not all my horses, and my troops could do nothing in the open field without guns. My resources in medicines and bandages are almost exhausted. The daily number of deaths amounts already to from eight to ten.

"I put the question to you and the Government whether I should not abandon Ladysmith and attempt a junction with you in the open field. I believe that I could bring 7,000 men and 36 guns into action.

"If you would make all preparations for a battle and would draw off the enemy—let us say during the afternoon of a day to be agreed on between us—I would attack the same evening and do my best to effect a junction with you. The attack from here would make a great impression; I fear, however, that my people are weak and to some extent demoralised.

"The fall of Ladysmith would produce a bad impression, especially in India. I am deeply concerned at the gravity of the situation and feel sure that you will inform the authorities accordingly. Runners report that the Boers suffered heavy losses on the 24th, and that they were very discouraged by your artillery fire. If we stick to them we can effect a junction, but it is a desperate proposal which I am making. It involves the sacrifice of my sick and wounded, of my Naval Guns, and of the rolling stock of the railway. I could not maintain myself for more than two or three days in the open field. If political considerations demand it, or if there exists a prospect of sufficient reinforcements for our relief, I will hold out here to the last."

However, if Buller's first communication may appear to have been to a certain extent composed under the influence of the failure, his answer to White's report brings his optimism and the quick change in his spirits clearly to light:—

"We had awful luck on the 24th. I had got two Naval Guns and a Battery half-way up Spion Kop when the troops evacuated it. If we had had the good fortune to have had among all the colonels up there one really useful soldier, we would have been in Ladysmith in four days.

"As it is, our situation is in no way improved. Some regiments have suffered severely. On the other hand the Boers have had great losses and are shaken. For a whole week they had to occupy their shelter trenches at a range of 900 yards to 1,300 yards from us, and our Artillery did its duty. We have lost 1,400 men; I estimate their losses as at least 1,000 men.

"The question arises whether I can relieve you in a one-day battle. At this moment they, the Boers, are holding the position north of Potgieter's Drift. I believe there is no doubt about that: on the other hand they are holding the position Acton Homes-Spion Kop on my left flank. Perhaps they will not stay there; but if they do I doubt whether I can get to the Roodepoort position, which I hear, moreover, is strongly entrenched.

"I intend to attack the Potgieter's position about Wednesday (31st January). If I succeed we can then carry out simultaneous attacks, you on Lancers' Hill and I on Roodepoort. This holds out the earliest prospect of success. Be assured I will leave nothing untried.

"I had already written this when I received your despatch. I also am of opinion that a dash through can only be the last desperate effort. I will try to attack the position, and after that we will see what is to happen.

"Some old Boers told our doctors on Spion Kop

that 16,000 men were in front of me, and that 4,000 only had been left at Ladysmith. I cannot be sure that that is accurate, but runners also say that the bulk of the Boers are here. Lord Roberts informs me that he cannot strengthen me, but that if you hold out till the end of February he can by that date reach Bloemfontein and will have relieved Kimberley. According to his view this will automatically relieve the pressure on Ladysmith. I doubt this anticipation of Roberts; I believe I had better act for myself and that as quickly as I can. What do you think about it?"

Besides being noteworthy on account of the opposition to Lord Roberts' judgment which it implies, this declaration of Buller's opinion is remarkable as regards his views on the subject of co-operation between the besieged troops and the Relief Force. He does not propose that White should engage the Boers investing Ladysmith during the decisive battle, but that he should defer action until the line of investment itself should be attacked. Thus the investing troops would not be hindered from taking part in the fighting on the Tugela; but everything depended on the result of that fighting, for the decisive issue lay there. If Buller were victorious on the Tugela, to which result White could contribute largely by keeping the investing troops pinned down to their line, the relief of Ladysmith must ensue.

White answered again on 28th January:—

"Thanks for your telegram of to-day. The loss of Spion Kop is most regrettable. I think it would be better that you should confine yourself to bombarding the enemy and advancing step by step, possibly by sapping, than that you should commit yourself to a last decisive attack. According to information which I consider reliable, the Boers are discouraged by the superiority of your armament and cannot stand up against it.

"Keep them therefore in their trenches and bombard them as hard as you can! I do not believe they will stand it long. I rely on your sticking to the Boers and not allowing them to turn on me with all their force. By sacrificing many of my horses, I can hold out for another six weeks, and in that time, while you are bombarding the Boer positions and Lord Roberts is advancing, the Free Staters are sure to disperse. I think the estimate about the enemy's strength here and in front of you is correct; but here his guns are protected by barbed-wire entanglements and mines. The Boers can get here from the Potgieter's position in an hour and a half,* and in that lies their great strength. You must not let them leave you to throw their full strength on me."

White, relying on the always unreliable information provided by runners, thus concurred in Buller's unjustifiable opinion of the impression which the fighting at Spion Kop had made on the Boers. As regards further operations and the methods to be pursued in relieving Ladysmith, however, his views more closely resembled those of Lord Roberts, who telegraphed on the 28th that if Buller did not feel absolutely certain of success he had better wait for the effect of his (Lord Roberts') movements in the western theatre of operations. Lord Roberts said he purposed to begin his advance on the 5th February, and expressed the hope that even this much would draw away some of the Enemy's force from the Natal theatre of operations to the Free State.

The War Office also felt called upon to take part in these discussions from London, and proposed that White might make a sortie and effect a junction with Buller; but gave up the idea when Buller, thus differing from White in opinion, declared that it was out of the question. The War Office

---

* The distance from the line of investment was about nine miles.

then asked Buller, through Roberts, whether there was a position in Natal which could be made impregnable with a garrison of 10,000 men. Roberts, in transmitting the inquiry, allowed it to be seen that he considered the line of the Tugela to be such as was suggested. He also closed the telegram, dated 18th January, with the words : " If you do not think that you have a reasonable prospect of success you would, in my opinion, do better for a number of reasons always to act on the defensive behind the Tugela until the operations which I am now arranging meet with the success which I hope for from them."

Buller declined the suggestion, observing that to carry it out a strong force of artillery would be needed as well as 16,000 men, and that he could not express his approval of the proposal in any way. Unmoved by any argument he held much more to the necessity for a fresh attempt at Relief. According, however, to what he said later before the War Inquiry Commission, he admits the correctness of the governing idea of Lord Roberts' operations, and sees that his own operations were of secondary importance towards the final issue of the War ; but he still thought Lord Roberts' estimate of the time needed was all wrong for, according to his view, Lord Roberts could only reach Bloemfontein on the 7th March at earliest.* He held that by defensive operations behind the Tugela, he would not have been able to prevent the Free Staters from withdrawing to their homes or from resisting the advance of the principal army, and that the Transvaalers would have been able to continue the siege of Ladysmith even after the capture of Bloemfontein. Giving weight to such considerations he thought that the only possibility of saving Ladysmith lay in continuing to attack the Enemy until he should succeed in either

---

* Lord Roberts entered Bloemfontein 13th March.

gradually wiping him completely out or in forcing him to a decisive battle in which he hoped to annihilate him. From a fighting point of view Buller's correct reasoning about the subject must command unqualified approval.

On the 29th January he expounded his plan in greater detail in a telegram to Roberts:—

> "My plans for my next attempt to relieve Ladysmith are founded on crossing the Tugela at three points and turning the flank of the Spion Kop position on the east by using a drift which has only just been found.* The discovery of this drift completely alters the situation, for it enables me to reach a position† which I had previously considered unapproachable. I am only waiting for the arrival of the Horse Artillery Battery from India, after which I hope to be able to make a successful attack at 4 p.m. on Wednesday.‡ The daily loss in dead at Ladysmith now amounts to eight or ten. Bandages and medicines are running out, so delay is no longer permissible.
>
> "This time I feel quite certain of success. The enemy is, in my opinion, very disheartened by the severe lessons of the last few weeks, while we are all in good spirits. It is always risky to prophesy, but so far as my exertions can, humanly speaking, conduce to the desired end, I think I can promise you that I shall in no case make any useless sacrifice of troops."

Buller's confidence of victory seems to have made an impression on Lord Roberts; at any rate he withdrew his opposition to the carrying out of a further attempt at Relief, and on the 30th January reported to the War Office: "Buller proposes another attempt at Relief, in which I am convinced that he will be successful."

---

* Munger's Drift.
† Presumably the Vaalkranz Heights are intended.
‡ 31st January, 1900.

The unfavourable and rainy weather during the last few days of January caused Buller to postpone the attack. Roberts announced his concurrence. Delays had arisen in the Free State too, and the situation in the western theatre of the war would develop all the more favourably, the longer the Enemy should be pinned down to Natal.

On the 4th February Buller described his situation as follows in his reply to a despatch which had remained unanswered for some time on account of the exchange of telegrams:—

"Ladysmith is in a bad case. White himself keeps up his spirits, but some of his subordinates are beginning to despair. According to his own calculations he still has a strength of 7,000 men; he has a daily death-rate of from eight to ten men, and according to his latest report he has 2,400 men in hospital. They are already eating horse flesh there as nothing else is left. He expects to be attacked this week by superior forces, and even though he may profess to be in good spirits, I doubt myself if he really is. He has asked me to keep the Enemy away from him, but I can only manage this by a further advance. I am going to try to get through the mountains to-morrow. My people are full of confidence. Most of my officers when I explained my views to them last night, seemed to believe in a success, and I hope for one too. If I can get through I shall reach a plain about 3½ miles in breadth and 15 miles in length. The Enemy will be occupying the heights on both sides and will also take up a strong position on the edge (of the plain). I shall probably encounter great difficulties about water supply. Such is the situation.

"I do not believe that an invasion of the Free State will have any real influence on our circumstances here. As far as I can learn the Transvaalers will not go into the Free State, and they are our principal opponents here. You ask how you can help me. The only real help would be another division, and that, as I know quite well, you cannot spare."

While this exchange of opinions was proceeding between the two principal British Headquarters, the preparations for the ensuing attempt at Relief were being pushed forward.

In addition to Pontoon Bridge No. 1, which had been in use for some time, a second, viz., No. 2, was thrown two miles further down stream. From 27th January work had been carried on at a road about two miles in length along which heavy guns could be moved on to the Zwart Kop. This was ready on the 27th January, on which date a beginning was forthwith made of getting six naval 12-prs., two guns of the 64th Field Battery, the Mountain Battery, and the two 5-in. Fortress-Guns on to that hill, which had been fixed on as the main Artillery position. With the assistance of wire cables, and in spite of the difficulties which were increased by the recent heavy fall of rain, fourteen guns were successfully taken up on to the summit. But the two 5-in. guns could only be brought as far as a position on a spur of the eastern slope, as it proved impossible to get them on to the summit itself. The guns were almost completely hidden, but it had been impossible to conceal from the Boers the work which had been going on for several days on Zwart Kop.

On the 3rd February Wynne's Brigade moved from near Spearman's Farm to Potgieter's Drift and relieved Lyttelton's Brigade in its position at One Tree Hill; the last-named brigade moved into a fresh bivouac situated north-west of Zwart Kop near No. 2 Pontoon Bridge, which was not hidden from the Enemy's view. The next day the whole of Clery's Division joined it there.

On the 3rd February, too, there was a Council of War at Buller's Headquarters, at which he stated his intentions. These were to make a demonstrative attack on the Brakfontein Heights from near Potgieter's Drift, and while this was being delivered to construct a fresh pontoon bridge over the Tugela. As soon as this work should be completed the troops advancing towards Brakfontein were to be withdrawn and, crossing the river by the new Pontoon Bridge No. 3, were to make an enveloping attack on what was believed to be the left flank of the Boers at Vaalkranz. Buller intended after that to bring forward his artillery on to Vaalkranz, and, supported by it, to push to the north through the gap between Vaalkranz and Doornkloof. To provide against the probability that the last named also would be included in the Boer's defensive line, the right flank was to be protected by the occupation of its "lower slopes." It was thus proposed to push over the Tugela range and reach the level country lying between the Brakfontein Heights and the lines of investment round Ladysmith. The principal object in view seems to have been to accomplish this end, and there was at least no expression of any thought about using the penetration of their position, once it should be effected, as a preliminary to fighting the Boers in a country more favourable to the attack.

The practicability of Buller's plan must from the very first appear open to doubt by reason of the *terrain*. The plain between One Tree Hill and the Brakfontein Heights, the easternmost big bend of the Tugela and the hilly ground, including Vaalkranz, which slopes down to the river here, are not only all commanded by the Brakfontein Heights, but also by Spion Kop, and moreover are flanked by Doornkloof, which is of almost the same altitude. Every artillery position north of Spearman's Heights is either taken in flank from both sides or, if its front faces the north-east or north-west, is taken in reverse from one side or other. Infantry advancing to the attack here is similarly situated. Vaalkranz itself, which was believed, on the strength of a farmer's description, to be a favourable artillery position, is a narrow ridge running from north-west to south-east, which could only be accorded a passing thought in connection with artillery action in a north-easterly direction. But even then, the position of the guns would be flanked from the Brakfontein Heights and the southern portion of Doornkloof. The British Commander must also have been misinformed about the nature of the ground between Vaalkranz and Doornkloof. According to other reliable reports, furnished by Germans who were engaged here, the lower slopes and spurs of Doornkloof run quite close up to Vaalkranz and do not leave any open gap here at all, but only a narrow ravine in which flows a stream. Of the possibility of the British breaking through in this quarter, a German officer recorded the following opinion in his diary : " If the British pierce our line here they will come on a ravine, be taken on both flanks and come to utter grief."

Thus, if the Boers occupied Doornkloof and the heights surrounding Vaalkranz on the north and east in good time, the Vaalkranz operations were altogether devoid of purpose or prospects. Considering their own quickness and the British slowness of movement, they could not fail in this. Perhaps Buller's intention could have been realised if the right flank had been secured by the capture of Doornkloof, steep and rugged though it was, and if no northerly movement had been made till that was effected. There was, however, a desire to avoid the difficulties and sacrifices involved in the capture, and so the occupation of the " lower slope " was decided on : in whatever direction further advance was made this was a mere compromise.

In the course of the 3rd February the following written order was published :—

" Spearman's Camp, 3rd February, 1900.
" 1. The General Commanding intends to attack

BRAKFONTEIN HEIGHT. VAALKRANTZ. DOORNKLOOF.

VAALKRANTZ.

[To face p. 198.

the extreme left flank of the Enemy's position, and to attempt to carry the Heights of Vaalkranz.

"2. The operation will begin with a demonstrative attack on the Brakfontein position. This will be carried out by both Brigade Divisions of Field Artillery and the 61st (Howitzer) Field Battery covered by the Eleventh Brigade (Fifth Division).

"3. During this demonstrative attack the Fourth Brigade supported by the Second Division, all under command of General Clery, will take up a suitable position east of No. 2 Pontoon Bridge with the general idea of making the Enemy believe that a passage of the river to the left bank will be made by this bridge. The four guns of the 64th Field Battery* are placed under General Clery's orders.

"4. After the artillery fire has lasted long enough to make the enemy occupy his shelter trenches, the left Battery will limber up, cross the river by No 2 Pontoon Bridge, back into its new position to cover the construction of No. 3 Pontoon Bridge at Munger's Drift. At the same time the Fourth Brigade will advance so as to cover this movement; the fourteen guns on Zwart Kop and the two 5-in. guns on the slopes will open fire on Vaalkranz and the Boer trenches.

"5. As soon as No. 3 Pontoon Bridge is ready, the remaining five Field Batteries will retire in succession. They will follow one another, beginning from the left flank, at intervals of 10 minutes, and under command of Colonel Parsons will advance simultaneously into position for the support of the infantry attack on Vaalkranz. Colonel Parsons will report himself to General Clery.

"6. After sufficient artillery-preparation the Fourth

---

* This Battery joined the Second Division in the place of the 78th Field Battery, which had been transferred to the Corps Troops. Two guns were on Zwart Kop.

Brigade, supported by the Second Division, will attack Vaalkranz under the orders of General Clery.

"7. As soon as the hill is carried, the artillery will advance on to it and open fire on the shelter trenches on Brakfontein, making use of every chance which offers to enfilade them. Colonel Parsons will take care that two Batteries shall constantly keep a look-out towards the heights on the right flank.

"8. The First Cavalry Brigade is, if possible, to advance into the plain *viâ* Vaalkranz, and the Horse Artillery Battery is to be brought into action against any suitable target that presents itself.

"9. The Second Cavalry Brigade is to secure the right flank and the rear during the whole course of the operations.

"10. The Officer Commanding Royal Artillery will direct the action of the fourteen Guns on Zwart Kop and of the two 5-in. Guns posted below them. His task will be to prevent the enemy from bringing any reinforcements from the right towards the rear;[*] further, to fire on all localities from which rifle-fire is directed on our infantry when it advances and to subdue the fire of every gun which the enemy brings into action.

"The Royal Scots Fusiliers will be under the orders of the Officer Commanding Royal Artillery.[†]

"11. The Naval Guns on Signal Hill and on the plateau below it, will take part in the engagement with a view to subduing the fire of the Enemy's Guns, to the prevention of any movements of the Enemy from his right to his left flank, and to the direction of fire on all shelter trenches whence fire is directed on our attacking columns.

"12. The Officer Commanding the Pontoon Troop will arrange to construct No. 3 Pontoon Bridge as

---

[*] Apparently this means any movement from Doornkloof (Colenso) towards the point of British attack.

[†] Detached from Barton's Brigade.

early as possible. The construction will be covered by the Fourth Brigade, four guns of the 64th Field Battery and the Field Battery referred to in para. 4 above.

"13. The Officer Commanding the Tenth Brigade is responsible for the security of the Camp at Spearman's Hill and of the kopjes near Potgieter's.

"14. The 61st (Howitzer) Field Battery will advance for action from the kopjes,* and will move to the right under instructions from the Officer Commanding the Field Artillery into a position to be selected by him, from which Kranzkloof, Doornkloof, and the shelter-trenches at Brakfontein can be brought under fire.

"15. The Natal Signalling Officer, in conjunction with the Officer Commanding the Telegraph Section Royal Engineers, will arrange for the establishment and maintenance of connection between Signal Hill, Zwart Kop, the kopjes,† and General Clery's Staff, as well as between Signal Hill and the plateau on which the two 12-prs. are placed,‡ and between Zwart Kop and the two 5-in. guns.

"16. The Balloon will be sent up in order to furnish information to all Batteries of which the fire-effect can be observed.

"17. The General Officer Commanding Fifth Division will superintend the execution of the instructions contained in paras. 2 and 3 above, and as soon as he thinks he can do so without risk, will send the whole of the Eleventh Brigade, or a portion of it, to the right flank to support the Second Division.

"18. The General Commanding-in-Chief will be found at the commencement of the action on the heights on which the two 5-in. Guns are posted."

---

* One Tree Hill.
† One Tree Hill.
‡ Apparently Mount Alice.

The instructions conveyed in this order are manifestly too far-reaching; without any notice being taken of the Enemy or of his intentions, the course of the development of the action was anticipated in minute detail, instead of the orders being limited to simply giving the correct direction for the movements of the troops towards the Enemy and to stating how and when their action should commence. Everything subsequent to that would be the concern of those leading in the fight and would have to be arranged on the foundation of such situations as might arise, but which could not possibly be foreseen.

The operation was to be carried out on the 5th February, but no mention was made of this in the long order quoted. On the 4th February, a Sunday, the movements of the British consisted of the Second Division moving from its camp, south of Spearman's Heights, up to the Tugela, and taking up its position near Lyttelton's Brigade, close by No. 2 Pontoon Bridge.

During the first days of February the weather had suddenly changed and cleared up, but it had become quite exceptionally hot.

In expectation of an early and favourable issue, the spirits of the British troops had risen still higher. It is noteworthy that on the 3rd February, two days before the heavy fighting which was to be expected, one part of the Army held a large athletic sports meeting.

Although no British movement north of Spearman's Heights could escape their view, and although there could be no possible doubt as to the importance of the recent movements of troops, the Boers were in no sort of hurry to initiate countermeasures. It is true that their phlegmatic habit would never lead one to expect prompt action on their part, but on the other hand their recent successes increased their confidence in their own powers. Everyone of them was firmly convinced that if the British should advance again they would be repulsed as easily as they had been at Colenso and Spion Kop. There was a general feeling among them that the Boers were the finest soldiers in the world, and they were by no means minded to pay any attention to the suggestions of their European mentors or to fall in with their proposals.

Trusting to their luck they had only posted an utterly inadequate force to hold the section between Spion Kop and Doornkloof, which had now become the most important in the line of the Tugela. Spion Kop was occupied and several Commandos of Free-Staters, under Prinsloo, were on the Brakfontein Heights; but on the left flank, west of Doornkloof, there were only 490 Johannesburgers, of whom only 95, under Viljoen, occupied Vaalkranz itself, while the remainder were distributed under Assistant Commandant Du Preez, south of Vaalkranz, on both sides of the Doornkloof stream. At first there were six Guns in this part of the field, viz., two Krupp Guns and two Maxim-Nordenfeldts near Twin Peaks, one Krupp Gun on the Brakfontein Heights, and a Maxim-Nordenfeldt on Vaalkranz. The number of the Boers is said to have risen during the fight which ensued to 5,000 or 6,000, but at first there were certainly not more than 2,000 rifles in action. Since Botha's departure, General Schalk Burger had been in absolute command.

The British Troops were posted as follows early on the 5th February:—The two Mounted Brigades had left their camp at Spearman's Farm at daybreak and were now on the north-west of Zwart Kop. Dundonald's Brigade had detached strong parties to watch Skiet's Drift and Trichardt's Drift. On Zwart Kop and its slope, where Colonel Nutt was in command, sixteen Guns of various calibres, under escort of the Royal Scots Fusiliers, were posted in concealed positions. North-west of Zwart Kop, near No. 2 Pontoon Bridge and under General Clery's command, were the Second, Fourth, and Fifth Brigades with four Guns of the 64th Field Battery. On the left bank the Eleventh Brigade, with six Field Guns, a Howitzer Field Battery, and two Naval 12-prs., were posted on the heights north of Potgieter's Drift. The Tenth Brigade protected the camp at Spearman's Farm and the heights to the north of it. Besides this four Naval Guns were in position on the left wing at Mount Alice. The General Commanding-in-Chief selected as his own position the plateau at Zwart Kop on which the 5-in. Guns were placed, and later on, when the Second Division moved to the north-east of this hill, he went there too.

At 6 a.m. Wynne's Brigade advanced from One Tree Hill towards the Brakfontein Heights on a broad front; the battalions of the South Lancashire and York and Lancaster Regiments were in the foremost line in deep formation with ranks in widely-extended skirmishing order; the King's Own (Royal Lancaster) followed as supports in a similar formation. The Lancashire Fusiliers, which had suffered the most severely of all at Spion Kop, remained in reserve at One Tree Hill. The advance was conducted with great deliberation and caution and hardly drew any fire from the Boers.

An hour later the seven Batteries were taken a few hundred yards north of One Tree Hill right out into the open plain, and thence, supported by the Naval Guns on One Tree Hill and Spearman's Heights, they began to shell the Boer position. Not a gun or a Boer was to be seen and so, in accordance with the usual practice, those points were fired at in which the presence of Boers was suspected. Although by this time ample proof had been given of the futility of shelling an unoccupied position of which even the site had not been accurately ascertained, the customary procedure was still rigorously followed.

The occupants of the shelter-trenches on the Brakfontein Heights had been instructed not to open fire until the Enemy should have approached within 400 yards. This measure, which was quite at variance with the usual procedure in the defence, was in every way suitable to the circumstances, for, bearing in mind the previous activity of the British in the plain near Potgieter's, the assumption was justified that nothing more serious than another demonstrative attack had to be dealt with. But even more was involved in the assailants being forced to come to closer quarters with their obstinately silent foe, for the further the attack should be pushed home the more difficult would it be to break it off later on.

Besides all this the experiences of Colenso and Spion Kop justified the belief that their superior marksmanship would enable the Boers to ward off even a real attack if the assailant were allowed to come within close range. Possibly, too, there was some idea of subjecting him to the ordeal of a "fire-surprise," which had already been practised so successfully by the Boers on several occasions.

In this scheme, however, they were disappointed, for the British were still more than a thousand yards from the position when a single shot was fired and immediately all the Boers posted on the Brakfontein Heights accepted this as the signal to open fire. The British continued to advance for some time longer and then opened fire in reply.

Thus it happened that a fire-fight at long ranges—the very thing which should have been avoided—was brought about, which clearly shows that marksmanship and instinctive talent for the use of ground cannot of themselves make useful soldiers; for that there is unquestionably the further need of an iron discipline, which can only be obtained by soldierly training and drill, and of a mental grasp of all the requirements of the fire-fight which can only be developed by constant instruction in battlefield-musketry.

The Boer Artillery, too, was silent at first, and it was not till 10.30 a.m. that the five guns on the Twin Peaks and on the Brakfontein Heights opened fire on the British Artillery, which was, in number of guns, five times their superior. Protected by their position from the action of the Naval guns, which were the most effective that the British had and beyond the range* of the Field Batteries, the Boers were able to gain and maintain the upper hand. As may be learned from English sources of information, the accuracy and briskness of their fire made an impression. If the ammunition, etc., had not been so inferior, the effect on the Field Batteries, which were standing right in the open fully exposed in front of the Boer guns, must have been annihilating. As a matter of fact, however, the British artillery lost only 2 officers and 8 men.

Meanwhile, soon after the opening of the artillery action, Lyttelton's Brigade had moved off to the ground between Munger's Drift and Zwart Kop. Soon afterwards Hildyard's Brigade followed, as also later Hart's Brigade, to cover the construction of the bridge. On account of the excessive force of the current at Munger's Drift which had been originally selected as the site of the construction, the bridge was not laid at that point, but further downstream just north-east of Zwart Kop. The work on it began at 8.30 a.m. and was finished at 11.15 a.m. While it was proceeding individual Boers crept down under cover of the high-standing mealie-crop from the Doornkloof

---

* For range of the British guns, *see* (Vol. xxxii., page 22).

Range Table of Boer guns :—

	Extreme Range.	Extreme Range for Time-fuze Shrapnel, &c.
7·5 cm. Creuzot	11,000 yards	11,000 yards
7·5 cm. Krupp	6,600 yards	3,850 yards
Maxim-Nordenfeldt	2,750 yards	—

The last-named gun could with necessary expedients be laid up to 4,400 yards; at ranges beyond the limit of the time-fuze, Shrapnel shell was fired with percussion fuzes.

stream to within 600 or 800 yards from the site of the bridge and opened a brisk fire on the Engineers' working parties. Hildyard's Brigade, which had been told off to protect them, confined its efforts to replying to this fire from the right bank, but the Boers, unchecked by this, caused several casualties among the working parties. The troops entrusted with the duty of covering the construction should have made it their business to prevent this sniping at the working parties by pushing a party across the river to the left bank.

Although in order to carry out successfully the principal task of the day, viz., the passage of the Tugela and the capture of Vaalkranz, it was before all things necessary that the bulk of the Boer forces should be kept for as long as possible away from this portion of the field, no sooner was the construction of the bridge completed than the withdrawal of Wynne's troops was ordered. The demonstrative attack was quite distinct as regards the time of its execution from the principal action, and was thus, to all intents and purposes, deprived of any such value, always questionable enough, as it might possess; the period allotted to it corresponded, as it appeared, exactly with that prescribed for the conventional form of such manœuvres in peace-time; the rather purposeless and purely rule-of-thumb procedure of the troops engaged in it might have been suggested by reminiscences of old-time barrack-square drills. At any rate an English eye-witness mentions that he was reminded by the demonstrative attack of the well-regulated course of a day at manœuvres on Salisbury Plain.

Really to ensure the success of the fresh attempt to master the line of the Tugela, the river should certainly have been crossed at several points, and from all of these determined attacks should have been made so as to render it impossible for the enemy to concentrate his forces against the point selected as that of the principal passage. There was certainly no object in only pretending to cross at one place, and in actually crossing, with serious intention to attack, at one other. It was impossible to pre-determine with safety at what point it would be best to pierce the enemy's line, except by the light of the experiences of the attacks made from all the points of passage. Once that point should be determined, it would be for the reserves to apply there the pressure needed for the penetration of the line.

At Vaalkranz the Boers were helped in the matter of concentrating their forces towards the decisive point, not only by reason of the set time-table procedure of the demonstrative attack and of the manner in which it was carried out, but also by reason of the inconsiderable distance between the two points of passage.

First of all the six Batteries limbered up under the accelerated fire of the Boer guns, the seventh, *i.e.*, the 63rd having already been withdrawn across the Tugela at 9.30 a.m.; they retired by Batteries from the left flank to behind One Tree Hill at intervals of 10 minutes from 12 noon till 1 p.m., and then were taken to No. 2 Pontoon Bridge that they might get into action again north of Zwart Kop. The last Battery to retire, the 78th, was the only one to suffer from the fire of the Boers; an ammunition wagon, of which the team had been shot, had to be manhandled out of action.

When the Artillery had all retired, the Infantry withdrew in good order to the rear of One Tree Hill, where it arrived at 1.30 p.m. In spite of the increased intensity of the fire directed on them by the Boers, their losses were quite insignificant, being altogether only 23 men; this was attributable to the great ranges at which the action was carried on.

As soon as the leading Field Batteries had come into

position north of Zwart Kop fronting north-east, a little after 1 p.m., they and the guns on Zwart Kop itself opened an extremely heavy fire on Vaalkranz. Viljoen, who was directing the defence there, describes this bombardment as the severest he was under during the whole war. A third of the small garrison was placed out of action even before the attack on the hill began. After the Artillery had been firing for about an hour Buller allowed Lyttelton's Brigade to advance. But he kept back the King's Royal Rifles on the right bank, so that at first only the Durham Light Infantry, the Rifle Brigade, and the Scottish Rifles, shortly afterwards followed by the Devons (from Hildyard's Brigade), crossed the river. The Durham Light Infantry was given by Lyttelton the direction of the southern peak of Vaalkranz, the Rifle Brigade that of Munger's Farm.

The passage of the bridge, which was accomplished at the double in small groups, and the further advance came under the fire of Du Preez' men posted in the mealie-crops and in the dongas south of Vaalkranz, which took them partly in flank. To avoid this the troops in rear, on leaving the bridge, moved in file about 100 yards along the river-bed under cover of the steep banks and then deployed to the right; this resulted in their immediately coming under a heavy frontal fire from Vaalkranz and under heavy fire on their right flank from the vicinity of the Doornkloof stream. The guns on Vaalkranz and the Brakfontein Heights joined in; the leading companies were almost swept back into the river bed, but the deployment was successfully effected on a second attempt, and both battalions, on broad fronts and in open formations, were soon able to begin their forward movement. About 4 p.m. the Durham Light Infantry reached a hollow at the foot of Vaalkranz. The Rifle Brigade, though under a hot fire from the east, maintained their prescribed direction, believing that Hildyard's Brigade was following and that it would account for the enemy on the flank. After a short pause to regain their breath the Durham Light Infantry climbed up Vaalkranz and about 4.30 p.m. fixed bayonets and drove off the few Boers who still held on to the southern edge. In this attack the Durham Light Infantry lost 2 officers and 35 men. Soon afterwards the Rifle Brigade also reached the heights.

The whole attack appears to have been carried out by the British Infantry without any fire preparation. That in spite of this it succeeded is attributable to the small number of those in the defence, to the formation of the ground—for the steep slopes of Vaalkranz could not be adequately swept by fire from the summit—and principally to the powerful combination of fire effect produced by some seventy British guns on the defenders who were occupying a restricted area.

As for the Boers, Viljoen had been stunned at the critical moment by the explosion of a lyddite-shell which burst close by him; the remnants of his little force retired in haste in a northerly direction. As the British, however, did not follow far, the Boers were able to establish themselves on the northern edge and even succeeded at the instigation of Viljoen, who had recovered his senses, in withdrawing too at the last moment the Maxim-Nordenfelt gun, the safety of which was very severely compromised. Of the 95 men who had been posted on Vaalkranz, 29 were killed and 24 wounded; 6 unwounded prisoners fell into the hands of the British.

The question now arose how to profit by this initial success. The Durham Light Infantry and the Rifle Brigade, as a reserve to which the Scottish Rifles had meanwhile moved forward, followed up the Enemy to the ridge of Vaalkranz which lies roughly at its centre. A further advance was precluded by the Artillery fire of the Boers on the Brakfontein Heights and by respect for the

Enemy on the right flank. It was perfectly plain that the first thing to do was to effect his removal thence; but this was checked by Buller himself. So far he had carried out his plan step by step, but now he seemed suddenly to think that his intentions could not be executed. He countermanded Hildyard's advance and that of the Cavalry. Hildyard had to recall the Devons who, acting on a perfectly correct impulse, had turned against the Enemy who were threatening the right flank of Lyttelton's Brigade; they now took up a position near Munger's Farm. Buller only allowed the King's Royal Rifles to follow up Lyttelton in consequence of the urgent appeal made to him by the latter. The whole operation which had just begun so favourably came to a standstill. What moved Buller to this sudden alteration of his intentions has not been explained. The story goes that he said "We have done enough," and there was an end of it.

And so, even in the manner of their execution, the Vaalkranz operations produced the impression of a carefully cut-and-dried sham fight. Because it did not develop in all its features exactly according to the programme of the General in Command, he lost all confidence in its success and gave it up almost before it had been begun. In contradiction to the expression of his intentions to Lord Roberts,* Buller even made out subsequently, in a despatch to the War Office, that the fight at Vaalkranz never was a seriously-intended effort.

Making allowances for the limited space available in the position he had carried, Lyttelton established himself there as well as he could under the heavy fire which the Boers kept up well into the night. Stones, boulders, various inequalities of the ground furnished cover of one sort or another. The eastern slope of Vaalkranz could

---

* *See* page 194.

not be occupied by reason of the Boer's heavy fire. The foremost line of the British, the Durham Light Infantry on the left, the Rifle Brigade on the right, took up during the evening a position facing north-eastwards and lay down on the ridge of the hill itself and on the western slope; in second line there were, on the right, the Scottish Rifles and a half-battalion King's Royal Rifles, and on the left, on the western slope of Vaalkranz, the other half-battalion of the last-named; the Devons were in a donga which ran along the southern foot of Vaalkranz and at Munger's Farm. The rest of Buller's troops occupied bivouacs on the positions they had reached during the day.

When night fell Lyttelton arranged the entrenchment of the position. What with the weariness of the troops, the want of every kind of entrenching tools, and the rocky nature of the soil, it needed all the energetic efforts of the officers to induce the men to do any work at all.

As at Spion Kop, the results in the way of protection were pitiable and unsatisfactory. The suggestion of a night-attack which was conveyed to Buller from one quarter was summarily rejected by him.

The Boers spent the night in bringing on to Doornkloof a 15-cm. and a 7·5-cm. Creusot gun which had been sent down from Ladysmith. Further, 2 more 7·5 cm. Creusots brought from Spion Kop and the Maxim-Nordenfeldt rescued from Vaalkranz were placed in position at Kranzkloof. Botha, who had just returned from a journey to Pretoria, arrived from Ladysmith and Lucas Meyer from Colenso, both bringing with them reinforcements by the arrival of which the numbers of the Boers were brought up, as has been mentioned, to 5,000 or 6,000. The number of their guns now amounted to ten. But for all this, the situation of the Boers, after the loss of Vaalkranz, was regarded as very serious; they were, however, determined to hold on to the heights which they still occupied north and east of Vaalkranz, and it was an advantage to them that the position they henceforth occupied was partly withdrawn from the effect of the British artillery fire.

On the morning of the 6th February a condition of absolute helplessness prevailed at British Headquarters. The hopeful spirit which Buller had expressed in his telegram had changed to the exact opposite when the difficulties of breaking through had been more clearly recognised the day before. Buller asked Lyttelton what he thought of the possibility of advancing with one brigade between Vaalkranz and the Tugela against that part of the mountain which was still occupied by the Boers. Lyttelton rightly spoke out against any such enterprise, for the advance of the brigade would be taken in flank from the Brakfontein Heights. Consequently Buller's Infantry remained stationary on the 6th February.

It was rightly considered injudicious to bring forward the Artillery on to Vaalkranz,* but on the other hand the Field Batteries were pushed forward so that they could bring their fire to bear on the northern portion of that hill. All day long the whole of the Artillery kept up an extremely heavy fire which was directed principally against the ravine between Vaalkranz and Kranzkloof, as well as on the northern slope of the former. According to eye-witnesses the British frequently fired at heights which were not occupied at all, and consequently the effect was not great. A German officer writing on this occasion in his journal about the uselessness of artillery fire unless combined with simultaneous action by the infantry, made the apposite remark: "The British have pinned all their hopes on the guns and that is the principal cause of their discomfiture."

The Boers replied to the British cannonade. The

---

* *See* page 198.

"Long Tom" on Doornkloof, which was principally used against the Troops in close formation on the right bank of the Tugela and against Zwart Kop, was temporarily overpowered by the British heavy guns owing to a well-aimed shell blowing up the Boer ammunition-supply and thus putting the gun out of action for several hours. The Boers' light guns were directed against Lyttelton's Brigade. Although the Boer Artillery was posted quite as advantageously as it had been at Spion Kop, the effect was not nearly so good for the British Infantry on this occasion was not so closely bunched together and consequently did not offer such favourable targets. Further, the damage actually inflicted by "Long Tom" bore no proportion to the report of its discharge.

In the course of the day the British Engineers dismantled No. 2 Pontoon Bridge, and with the material thus made available, constructed a fresh bridge, No 4, opposite the southern end of Vaalkranz.

About 4 p.m. the indecisive fight which was going on between the two Artilleries was reanimated by a Boer surprise attack. A veldt fire had broken out on Vaalkranz in consequence of the shell bursting there; under cover of the smoke which clung to the ground, a party of Boers crept forward to within about 700 yards of Lyttelton's left flank and suddenly opened a hot fire on the Durham Light Infantry lying there. The British line, completely taken by surprise, was thrown into confusion, the Boers charged and drove off the Durham Light Infantry. At this critical moment the four companies King's Royal Rifles which were posted in reserve in rear of the left flank made a counter-attack, and their advance, energetically carried out, caused the Boers to turn about; from this time onwards Lyttelton's Brigade held undisputed possession of their position. Only the artillery cannonade and the occasional long-range musketry fire of the Boers continued.

At 5 p.m. the leading Troops of Hildyard's Brigade, to which had been attached the Connaught Rangers from Hart's Brigade, began to cross the river, not however to make good the attack on Doornkloof, which had been broken off on the 5th, but to relieve Lyttelton. As the Boer fire died down at nightfall it was possible for the relief to be carried out without casualty, the West Yorks, East Surrey, and Queen's going into the foremost line, while the Connaught Rangers were placed on the right and the Devons on the left of the second line.

Hildyard's Troops, quite fresh as they were, immediately set to work to improve the entrenchments on Vaalkranz, and during the night succeeded in materially strengthening them. It was certainly to this work that the Brigade could primarily attribute the smallness of its casualty list on the following day. The flanking and reverse fire to which the British on Vaalkranz were exposed necessitated the construction of many traverses and parados, in consequence of which some parts of the entrenchments assumed the form of quadrilateral chests.

Lyttelton's Brigade went back across the Tugela and about 9 p.m. reached its camp north of Zwart Kop. During the two days' fighting it had only lost 225 men.

Buller, during the course of the 6th February, made the following report to Lord Roberts:—

"After an engagement which lasted the whole of yesterday and which, for all that, was attended by only trifling casualties, I have pierced the Enemy's line and now hold a height which cuts his position in two, and which opens my way to the plain of Ladysmith if I can advance. Once there I shall be 10 miles from White, while the Enemy holds only one position between us in which he can offer any resistance. But in order that I may be able to bring forward my Artillery and stores into this plain I must throw back the Enemy either on my right or on my left flank, a proceeding which will cost me 2,000 or 3,000 men. While I have every hope of success I am not quite certain of it. The question arises to what extent such losses in men may influence your plans and whether you consider the Relief of Ladysmith worth this price. It is the only possible way of liberating White; if I do not adopt it I know of no other."

In this expression of his views Buller considerably exaggerated the value of the results of the engagement so far as it had gone, and on the other hand was doubtful about the final success of his operation. Whereupon Roberts, who originally had been in favour of the adoption by the Natal Army of a waiting policy, now took up the train of thought originally pursued by Buller and represented it energetically and conclusively to the very man who had first expounded it. His answer contained the first indication of the really decisive issue—the defeat of the Boer forces covering the investment :—

"Ladysmith must be relieved, even if at the cost of the losses you expect. I would persevere in spite of all. I hope that the Enemy will be so severely punished that you may be able to draw White's Troops towards you. Tell your Troops that the Honour of the Empire is in their hands, and that I have not the least doubt of their success."

In spite of this energetic exhortation and in spite of the assumption by the Commander-in-Chief of the responsibility, Buller could come to no decision on the 7th. He neither advanced to the attack with the troops which, not having been as yet engaged, were still fresh, more than two-thirds of his Army, nor did he withdraw Hildyard's Brigade from its perilous situation on Vaalkranz, though the only reason for its retention there lay in a subsequent attack on Doornkloof or Brakfontein. All that happened was that during this day, too, both adversaries kept up a cannonade which brought about no particular results. Further, as regards the British, Wynne's Brigade was withdrawn across the Tugela and was replaced on One Tree Hill by the Somerset Light Infantry Battalion.

Buller had Vaalkranz reconnoitred again by Warren to ascertain its value as an artillery position, while he himself tried from the right bank of the Tugela to get some insight into the state of affairs on the other bank. Through these investigations everybody acquired the conviction that fundamental errors had arisen in the formation of opinions regarding the lie of the land.

Thereupon Buller assembled a Council of War at 4 p.m., and there placed before his Generals the telegram he had received from Lord Roberts, asking them what measures should be next taken. Of all those present only Hart spoke out in favour of the continuation of the attack and professed his readiness to take the Brakfontein Heights with his own Brigade. Warren said he could only agree to a withdrawal on the presumption that Buller had already thought of another point at which to make an attack, whereon the latter replied that he now thought that an attack on Hlangwane and the passage of the Tugela below Colenso, followed by an advance towards Bulwana, held out more abundant prospects of success than a continuance in the present direction of the attack. He added that he had during December* gone carefully into the question of operations on the line of which he now spoke, and that he had then recognised that it entailed long drawn-out fighting in the bush and in very difficult country, but

---

* Buller had at this time thought that an offensive movement East of the Railway in the direction of Hlangwane had no prospect of success, because his troops were not practised in wood-fighting. He himself spoke later on this subject in these words : "I did not think my people were up to wood-fighting, which is a difficult class of operation, calling for a great deal of individual determination : the men lose touch with their officers, and so require a lot of special training before they can do any good at wood-fighting."

that the men had now made such immense progress in their training for battle that he considered an attempt in this direction could be thought of.

All the Generals agreed with these proposals, but with the premise that they knew nothing about the new direction of the attack. Buller immediately decided to give up the Vaalkranz operations. At 7 p.m. orders were issued for the withdrawal of the whole of the Natal Army to Springfield, and Warren was instructed to carry out the movement while the General Commanding-in-Chief went on in advance to Springfield and thence to Chieveley.

The baggage was first moved away: this, strange to relate, had been brought forward into the low ground on the Tugela and even into the zone of the enemy's fire. At 9 p.m. Hildyard's Brigade, hardly at all molested by the enemy, was taken back on to the right bank, and the dismantling of the bridges went on till about midnight.

On the 8th February, about 5 a.m., the Second, Fourth, and Fifth Brigades and the Field Artillery began their retirement under Lyttelton. On the 9th these Troops reached the camp at Spearman's Farm, on the 10th Pretorius' Farm, and on the 11th Chieveley. On the 8th February parts of Coke's Brigade, of Warren's Division, held the heights of One Tree Hill and covered the withdrawal of the heavy artillery. In the course of the afternoon these, the last Troops of Warren's Division and both the Mounted Brigades, followed on to the camp at Spearman's Farm. On the 10th, as soon as the transport, which totalled up to 600 wagons, had left the camp, Warren marched to Springfield where he left the York and Lancasters, the Imperial Light Infantry, the First Cavalry Brigade, the Battery Royal Horse Artillery, and two Naval 12-prs., all under the command of Colonel Burn-Murdoch, for the protection of the left flank against any Boers who might be remaining on the Upper Tugela, and on the 12th reached Chieveley with the rest of his troops.

The Boers as usual made no attempt to profit by their success, although, for instance, the isolation of a party left behind as rear-guard on One Tree Hill on the 8th February and the passage of a large number of transport wagons over the Little Tugela, each furnished them with ample opportunity for inflicting damage on their opponent.

They fired a couple of harmless shells at Lyttelton's force as it was going away, and on the 8th they assembled the now inevitable Council of War at which Botha very reasonably proposed that they should push forward against the British right flank, take Zwart Kop and cut off the retreat to Chieveley; but Burger, who was the responsible Commandant on the Tugela, could not make up his mind to any such action, and the decision was postponed until the 10th when a second Council of War was to assemble with Joubert as president; by that time, of course, the opportunity had passed for making any profit out of the situation.

Such was the course of events in the rashly undertaken and as suddenly renounced operations at Vaalkranz, and the issue was, so far as concerns material damage to the British, not severe after all. The loss in killed,* wounded, and missing amounted altogether to 20 officers and 354 men, and of these casualties about a quarter fell to the share of the Durham Light Infantry. The Boers suffered the loss of only 60 men. But worse than the loss in men was the prejudicial moral effect of their repeated failure on the British; later events however proved that owing to their strict training in peace-time they were sufficiently possessed of grit and spirit to make it possible, after a short interval, for them to be led once more against their adversaries.

---

* *See* Appendix III.

With the exception of Burn-Murdoch's and Blagrove's* forces, the whole of the Natal Army lay concentrated on and after the 12th February at Chieveley. Its distribution was so far modified that Barton's Brigade, which had previously been independent, formed part of Warren's Division in place of Lyttelton's Brigade, that Wynne's Brigade, also of Warren's Division, received from Blagrove's force the Reserve Rifles in exchange for the Lancashire Fusiliers, and that Lyttelton's Brigade went back to the Second Division. General Lyttelton himself took over the Command of the Second Division in place of General Clery who had fallen ill, and was succeeded in his brigade-command by Colonel Norcott, commanding 1st Battalion Rifle Brigade.

---

* *See* Appendix I.

PART III.

THE FINAL ATTEMPT AT THE RELIEF, EAST AND NORTH OF COLENSO.

---o---

CHAPTER VII.

THE ENGAGEMENTS SOUTH OF THE TUGELA.

After the failure at Vaalkranz, Buller gave the Troops in Chieveley Camp several days' repose. Rations were issued on a fresh scale and the men were to some extent provided with new clothing and boots.

Lord Roberts had by now collected all the recently-arrived reinforcements in Camp at Modder River Station and hoped that his advance through the Orange Free State would draw thither some part of the Boer forces engaged in Natal.

The reports and despatches which Buller sent to Lord Roberts about this time, betray a depression of spirits which throws his previous optimism altogether into the shade. On the 9th February he telegraphed to Lord Roberts:—

> "The occurrences of the last three weeks have proved to me that I have considerably over-estimated the powers of the Ladysmith Garrison. I do not feel

that I am strong enough to effect the relief of Ladysmith unless I am given more Troops. If you could reinforce me and if White can hold out long enough it might be possible, but with my own Troops it is out of the question. I will go on attacking the Enemy, for this draws him away from Ladysmith; but the prospects of success are insignificant. Can you send me the other half-Battery of the 5 in. Guns? I have got two here, but would like to have the whole Battery at my disposal."

In another telegram he says:—

"Even if I am strongly reinforced the fate of Ladysmith is, in my opinion, only a question of days. Wherever I turn I come on the Enemy in force superior to my own. They do in six hours and seven miles what takes me three days and 26 miles.

"When I reported in December that I would make the attempt to relieve Ladysmith, the Fifth Division had just arrived at the Cape, and the Sixth and Seventh Divisions were expected there; two days after that you were appointed to the Command, and you ordered that all Troops subsequently arriving were to be employed in Cape Colony. I understood from you that you calculated on being in possession of Bloemfontein at the end of February, and on thus removing pressure from Ladysmith.

"I hope your calculation is correct, but I must admit that I consider it very risky to base on it all hope of the Relief of Ladysmith. I am doing all I can, and I certainly believe that I retain the full confidence of all those who are with me, and they know the difficulties I have to contend with. If, however, there is any idea that somebody else could do better, I would rather be sacrificed than have the loss of Ladysmith on my shoulders. I should like you to forward this to the Secretary of State for War."

Lord Roberts replied from Modder River on the 10th February in a long telegram in which he reviewed once more the whole course of the Campaign up to the date of his arrival, and then continued:—

"As for your remarks about the Sixth and Seventh Divisions, it is true that if you had retained the Chief Command, you could have made use of them in Natal, but they were actually sent out for employment in Cape Colony. You knew this and never asked for them as reinforcements. You knew White's position in the middle of January and his inability to afford you material assistance, and I also informed you in detail on the 26th January of my intentions, which consisted of assembling here in the West of Cape Colony all available men for a big offensive stroke.

"With all these considerations before me, I had no grounds, since the date I first assumed the Chief Command till yesterday, for supposing that you considered reinforcements essential for the Relief of Ladysmith. To strengthen you would mean giving up the whole plan of operations which I explained to you on the 26th January, and in the prosecution of which I see the best prospects of our success both in Natal and in the north of Cape Colony. Moreover, great difficulties and delay in the conduct of the Campaign would be involved, and a rising of the disaffected Dutch population in Cape Colony, which is weakly garrisoned, would not be improbable. I must therefore request you to confine yourself to the defensive in a strong position until such time as I can see whether my advance brings about the success I hope for. Our little Army cannot last out long under the repeated heavy casualties entailed in fighting on the Tugela for no definite result. I will gladly meet your wishes as regards the half-Battery of 5 in. Guns, but more I cannot do."

Meanwhile Lord Roberts appears to have formed some doubt about the capacities of the Commander of the Natal Army, for he telegraphed to him on the 12th February:—

"Referring to your telegram of the 9th in which you say that if you are not reinforced the fate of Ladysmith is, in your opinion, merely a question of days, I should like to hear the opinion of your Second-in-Command on this point. The question is of such importance to our position in South Africa that I should like to know whether Sir Charles Warren shares your views."

Warren, whose views were to all intents and purposes the same as Buller's, proposed to continue attacking the Boers, "but so to arrange it that the chances of losing men may be as small as possible." Agreeing with Lord Roberts he, too, was most hopeful about the advance on Bloemfontein, and expected much from the issue of a Proclamation, after that town should be taken, declaring the Orange Free State to be British territory. This he considered would make the Free State Boers withdraw for fear of losing their farms. Finally, he advised that sapping should be employed in attacking the Boers north of the Tugela.

In this answer Lord Roberts could, however, find no clear and decided expression of Warren's preference for the defensive or for a renewal of the attack; the latter, however, was not only desirable, in view of the necessity for the early Relief of Ladysmith, but was also quite practicable with the Forces at hand for it. Meanwhile public opinion in England and in a more subdued way, of course, in Buller's Army, too, began to clamour with increasing vehemence for another attempt at Relief. That Buller did not entirely shut his eyes to this is indicated in his telegram to Lord Roberts, dated 12th February:—

"I know that Ladysmith is in danger, but I feel myself too weak to relieve it. Do not, however, condemn me to entirely defensive action which would give the Boers a free hand to turn with all their force against Ladysmith. General White has telegraphed to me: 'The nearer you establish yourself to Ladysmith the better are our prospects.' I think that is quite correct and hope that you will not insist on my resting inactive and leaving Ladysmith alone. During the recent operations the Boers have lost two men for every one of ours, and for the last three weeks our attacks have caused the cessation of the bombardment of Ladysmith. As I have said before, I shall do all I can, and you may rely on it that I shall not sacrifice my Troops uselessly."

In this exchange of views can be clearly seen the quick and frequent variation of the spirits of the Commander of the Natal Army who after some days of the deepest depression would see everything in a rosy light again. He hankered to try his luck once more, and yet could come to no clear decision as to how the attempt should be made; all he begged was not to be left on the defensive.

From Lord Roberts' answer, however, it is plain that all he wanted was a definite and final decision should be made—

"My reason for telling you to remain on the defensive is to be found in your own statements that you are too weak to relieve Ladysmith without reinforcements, and that the fall of Ladysmith is only a question of days. As, however, I have no reinforcements to send to Natal, any operations of the success of which you are not absolutely confident, seem to me to be only a useless waste of force. You should wait and see whether my advance into the Free State will draw away forces from your front and so simplify your task. I do not require that you should remain absolutely inactive all the time, provided that you keep clear of complications which result in heavy losses. Harass the Enemy as much as you can. I leave you liberty of action and rely on your assurance that you will not sacrifice the Troops uselessly."

This communication from Lord Roberts, combined with White's message of the 8th February, which has already been mentioned, confirmed Buller in his decision to make yet another attempt at the Relief. This time he proposed to advance below Colenso with the intention of first of all seizing the important position of Hlangwane, whence he would be able to flank the whole Boer position of Colenso. If he once occupied this hill, his passage of the Tugela would be assured, and the whole of this section of the river would be dominated by the British Artillery.

After the British withdrawal, the Boers had remained inactive in their laagers on the Upper Tugela. Their Chief Commandant, General Joubert, had, from the very beginning, looked on the whole War as a misfortune which was sure in the long run to result in the ruin of his Nation. He still hoped for an amicable agreement with the British, and all through the campaign he had tried to act towards them with such forbearance that an understanding with them should be easy to arrive at. Even after the successful fighting at Vaalkranz he proposed to Presidents Kruger and Steyn to come to terms with their powerful adversary; he considered that moment propitious as the situation could hardly be more favourable for the united Republics. He himself, however, did not wish to take more British territory than that which had already been occupied under the necessities of the campaign. But there was no need for the employment of such arguments to hold back the Burghers in their strong positions on the Tugela; on personal, and every other ground, they were by no means anxious to attack. After the British withdrawal they gave themselves up with complete unconcern to their quiet, undisturbed laager life, hoping that Buller would also give up trying to attack them any more now he had so often failed.

The fighting strength of the Boers dwindled away to an alarming extent, through the custom of furloughs to visit their homes. There was an old tradition, which had its origin in the Kaffir wars, that after three months in the field every Burgher was entitled to 14 days' leave of absence. Originally this arrangement involved no risks, for substitutes were always forthcoming for those who might go away, and now many of them, weary of their laager life, seized on it as an excuse to pester their leaders with applications for leave of absence. Nobody was possessed of adequate penal powers, and so it frequently happened that those whose applications for leave had been refused, stole away by night for good and all. The Government was under no delusion as to the danger thus involved, but could not rise to the height of energetic measures, as it was feared that they would excite discontent among the Burghers; these desertions, however, caused considerably greater loss of strength in the Commandos than had all the casualties during the recent fighting. At this period there were scarcely two-thirds of the original number of the Burghers on Commando in Natal in the Field, and the fighting strength consequently did not amount to more than some 10,000 or 11,000 men.

The Commander-in-Chief, General Joubert, was investing Ladysmith with about 4,000 men; Louis Botha was on the Upper Tugela with about 5,000, and Lucas Meyer held the positions north of Colenso and Hlangwane with some 2,000 more.

Joubert had entrusted Louis Botha with the Chief Command of all the Commandos on the Tugela, but he had refrained from bringing this appointment to the knowledge of Lucas Meyer who had so far held an independent Command at Colenso. Taking this into consideration, Botha abstained for the present from proceeding in person to the Colenso position to take over the Chief Command, because he did not wish to offend Lucas Meyer who was a much older man and whose assistant he had been in former times. Thus it came about that Meyer, who was of no great capacity and who was not an active man, was left in command on the very flank which was now the more important.

This confusion of command and direction led later on to several omissions and false measures, which could not well have occurred under the undivided control of the energetic Botha.

It was intended that if the British should advance east of Colenso, they should be forced to carry the strong position of Hlangwane, Plat Kop, Green Hill, Monte Christo.

Till the 14th February there were in this position only some 1,800 men with two Guns. On the right flank parts of the Wakkerstrom Commando held Hlangwane, from which, as far as Monte Christo, parts of the Standerton, Bethel, Middelburg, Swaziland and Krugersdorp Commandos prolonged the line of defence. A Krupp Gun and a Maxim-Nordenfeldt were placed on Hlangwane in covered emplacements constructed of stones, faced with sandbags to afford protection against splinters, and completely concealed from the Enemy's view. Shelter-trenches laid out just as cleverly and as completely concealed were dug for groups of six to twelve men on the forward slopes, head cover against shrapnel being furnished by suitably placed blocks of stone. The Boers passed the nights in their trenches; they had also constructed a quantity of rough shelters with the aid of planks and sheets of corrugated iron looted from the houses in Colenso. Two laagers of wagons, with which the Burghers would not part, were formed in the depression of the valley North of Plat Kop.

Lucas Meyer, who had only once shown himself on the South bank in the more recent fighting, had placed Vecht Commandant Fourie in command in this part of the field. By him nothing more was expected than a simple frontal attack by the British and consequently he took no measures whatever to protect his left flank, which it was evident could be easily threatened; Cingolo, which lay there, was only occupied by a weak Commando under Louis Botha's brother, Christian, and a picquet of Middelburgers, in strength only about 100 men, was pushed forward on to Hussar Hill.

The connection with the Northern bank of the Tugela was scanty; a circumstance which was certain to disturb the Boers, who were always subject to great anxiety about their line of retreat. The only reliable crossing-place was at a cable-worked ferry about two miles north of the blown-up iron railway bridge at Colenso. Besides this there was sometimes available a bridge, made out of rails and sleepers laid on boulders, and situated a little up-stream from the Falls. Suddenly rising floods frequently made this bridge dangerous of passage for long periods.

The British were well acquainted with the Boer position on the right bank of the Tugela. Buller himself had carried out a personal reconnaissance on the 12th February from Hussar Hill, after Dundonald's Mounted Brigade had driven the Boer picquet off it.

Hussar Hill, of which all the slopes are gentle, lies south-east of Colenso, and its extensive area affords ample space for the deployment for action of a large force of Artillery. On the north it falls away in hillocks towards the broad, mimosa and thorn-clad valley of the Gomba. This stream flows into the Blaauwkranz, of which the deep and broad bed furnishes excellent cover from view when the water is low. North of the Gomba the low-lying hillocks merge, gradually becoming steeper as they rise, into a plateau which is dominated on the west and east by the sharply-defined elevations of Hlangwane and Monte Christo. These are connected by the lower-lying heights of Plat Kop and Green Hill, and thus combine to form a strong line of defence facing south. South-east of Monte Christo and divided from it by a nek, lies Cingolo, which is rocky and difficult of ascent. Behind the line joining Hlangwane and Monte Christo the ground first sinks a little and is invisible from the south, and then, near Bloys' Farm, rises again up to the rocky Bush-rand, thence to descend precipitously to the Tugela on the north. On the plateau the communications are but scanty, and the movement of troops is moreover greatly embarrassed by gorges and by the thick bush which grows in all directions.

In his reconnaissance Buller very clearly recognised the weakness of the left flank of the Boer position, and consequently decided on enveloping it and afterwards rolling up the whole of the Enemy's position from the east, so as to gain possession of the whole of the south bank before proceeding further. With this in view he wanted to bring the Enemy's position under the fire of his heavy Artillery posted on Hussar Hill, that he might prepare the attack so as to be able to work his Infantry round Cingolo and subsequently on to Monte Christo. In the front the Enemy was only to be held, and Burn-Murdoch's mixed Force at Springfield was to ward off any aggressive movements which the Enemy might initiate from the direction of the Upper Tugela. Buller intended to place Hart's Brigade with the 19th Field Battery, No. 4 Mountain Battery, and some heavy guns on Gun Hill, North of Chieveley, for the protection of Chieveley Camp. Bethune's Mounted Infantry was sent towards Weenen on the 10th February to keep a look-out on the right flank.

For some reason which cannot be explained Hussar Hill was evacuated when the reconnaissance was finished; the Boers immediately re-occupied it, and even brought about some casualties among the British as they withdrew.

On the 12th February, too, on the other flank, some shots were exchanged on the Lower Tugela. Louis Botha had here made a reconnaissance of the British Troops at Springfield, through which he learnt that on the Little Tugela they were weak, and that the greater part of their

Force was back again south of Colenso. Hence was deduced the probability of the Enemy making an attack on the positions on the southern bank, and men and guns were accordingly despatched at once to reinforce Lucas Meyer. At the same time there was a disinclination to evacuate the positions on the Upper Tugela entirely and immediately. But the more closely the suspicion that the British would attack east of Colenso approached to certainty, the more frequent became the despatch during the succeeding days of stronger reinforcements to the left flank; these measures were, however, taken with such great deliberation, and at first so tentatively, that the Force at Colenso had not reached the requisite total when the British attack to the east of that place was finally delivered. The result of the ill-defined situation as regards the higher Command there was that there was no one competent and responsible person empowered to issue without delay distinct and reliable orders to meet any situation which might arise.

Early on the 13th Buller received from White a communication which informed him of the Boers' movements as follows:—

> "Yesterday there was considerable stir in the Boer laagers. All the Boers north of Potgieter's Drift have been taken away, some in the direction of Potgieter's Drift, others towards the east."

This made it plain that the Boers were aware of the intentions of the British, and should have urged Buller to expedite matters with a view to taking decisive action on the south bank before the Adversary could collect all his forces there.

But Buller, on account of the excessive heat of the 13th, postponed the attack which had been planned for that day till the 14th. According to the orders issued on the evening of the 13th he intended on the 14th only to "capture Hussar Hill and its eastern spurs north of Moord Kraal, and to occupy the position with Artillery." The Fifth Division (Warren's), protected by the Cavalry Brigade, was to seize Hussar Hill and its eastern spurs as far as Moord Kraal, while the Second Division (Lyttelton's) was to co-operate and take up a position extending to the junction of the Blaauwkranz and the Gomba. While the Divisions were entrenching themselves the whole of the Field Artillery, the Howitzer Battery, the four Naval 12-prs., and both the 5 in. Guns were to be taken into position on Hussar Hill and there also be put in entrenchments.

The advance was begun at dawn on the 14th; Dundonald's Brigade furnished the strong advanced guard. When it approached Hussar Hill it came under the fire of the Boer picquet posted there, which was hurriedly reinforced from Hlangwane. After a short but sharp fire-fight the Brigade, fighting dismounted, and effectively supported by its machine-gun Battery, succeeded in once more seizing Hussar Hill: this was immediately occupied by the Fifth Division which had meanwhile arrived. Dundonald's Brigade moved off into the Blaauwkranz valley on the right flank, and here, not far from the mouth of the Gomba, fell in with the Second Division which had just come up.

The Troops immediately began to strengthen their positions, the Fifth Division on Hussar Hill, the Second extending thence eastwards as far as the Blaauwkranz; the Artillery took up its appointed position in the course of the afternoon. On account of the great heat all further operations on this day were countermanded, and the Troops went into bivouacs in rear of the entrenchments they had constructed.

From their elevated positions the Boers had accurately observed the British movements, which were betrayed far and wide by the great clouds of dust. Hlangwane was occupied by reinforcements sent thither by Lucas Meyer and by those which were following one another down from the Upper Tugela; two Krupp Guns and a Maxim were sent to Green Hill, and a second Maxim was placed in position on Plat Kop. But large Forces still remained halted on the Upper Tugela.

The fighting during the morning had been heard in Ladysmith; on the evening of the 14th White sent the following by heliograph to Buller:—

"55 wagons and about 400 Boers have moved from the Upper Tugela to Onderbrook."

This information once more made it clear that the adversary was ceaselessly sending reinforcements to his left flank, and consequently that the reasons which should have induced Buller to attack as soon as possible were hourly becoming more urgent. He, too, intended that Lyttelton's Division should effect the envelopment of the Enemy's left flank on the 15th February, but finally gave up the idea again on account of the great heat, and except for some few movements of no consequence, the Troops did not leave the bivouacs they had occupied.

Lord Roberts' Troops on the same day, also in burning heat, did a march of some 32-34 miles, and Buller's proceedings show that he was wanting in energy, for he could not, though in an extremely critical situation, bestir himself sufficiently to call on his Troops for a special effort. Except for a rather ineffective cannonade, to which the Boers made but a weak reply, nothing whatever was done on the 15th and 16th on account of "the great heat."

On these hot days special difficulties did certainly arise in connection with the supply of water to the Troops, for it had to be brought by train from the lower-lying districts up to Chieveley, and to be thence transported out to the Troops in receptacles of all sorts loaded on ox-wagons.

The attack, which had been planned for the 15th, was

finally to be delivered on the 17th. While Warren's Division was to remain stationary on Hussar Hill, opposite the Enemy's front, Lyttelton's Division and Dundonald's Mounted Brigade were to move forward to make the enveloping attack on Cingolo Nek and Monte Christo. Barton's Brigade was to join in with this movement on the left, but for the moment was not to cross the Gomba. The whole of the Artillery posted on Hussar Hill was to support the attack.

It had been ascertained during a reconnaissance made by some of Lyttelton's Division on the previous day, that Cingolo was only weakly held by the Enemy. It appears that a patrol of the 13th Hussars had ascended the hill on the evening of the 16th without finding any trace of him.

Lyttelton decided that he would first of all take Cingolo and that he would thence proceed by way of the Nek to the attack of Monte Christo. Hildyard's Brigade was to take Cingolo, and Norcott's Brigade, co-operating with it on the left, was to advance against the Nek.

At 6 a.m. on the 17th the whole of the 50 guns opened fire on Cingolo, Monte Christo, and Green Hill, and under cover of this Lyttelton's Division crossed the Gomba. The Brigades, with the right flank thrown forward, advanced on a front of about three miles, Hildyard's Brigade on the right flank being in advance with Norcott's Brigade echelloned on its left rear, while south of the Gomba was Barton's Brigade. Each Brigade was within itself in a very deep formation. Deployments were made immediately bivouacs were left, at a distance of some 3,000 yards from the Enemy, Hildyard's and Norcott's Brigades each having two Battalions in first line formed in three chains extended in thin skirmishing order with intervals of three to four paces between files.

The unnecessarily early deployment of the Brigade,

which might perhaps have been suitable in quite level ground, was in this instance, as a German eye-witness testifies, ill-adapted to the hilly and bush-grown country in which it was made. Some 800 or 900 yards in front of the Enemy a line of hills stood out and presented a favourable fire-position; to this the Brigades, in close formation and distributed at most into a few small columns, of which the movements could easily have been adapted to the undulations of the ground, could have advanced unobserved, under the protection of a thin line of scouts; arrived there, they might have been deployed under cover into a dense firing-line, which by immediately developing its utmost force might have overwhelmed the Enemy.

In the awkward formation of long, widely-extended lines the progress was extremely slow, and it was not till 9 a.m. that the Brigades reached the line of hills, mentioned above, about 1,000 yards north of the stream; there they came under fire from the southern slopes of Cingolo. The weak Boer detachment which was on the line of hills, under the Command of Christian Botha, had moved to a position on the southern slope of Cingolo, where the field of fire was more favourable, as soon as it was seen that the British were attacking; a strong patrol was left on the summit. Christian Botha's men were soon supported by parties of Boers who, creeping forward through the bush from their positions on Green Hill, opened fire on Norcott's Brigade. At ranges varying from 800 to 900 yards there developed in this quarter an indecisive frontal fire-fight. No progress was made, so General Lyttelton sent orders to the Mounted Brigade to make an outflanking movement against the Boers on the slopes of Cingolo and to force them from their positions. But the Brigade was nowhere to be found; all connection with it had been lost.

General Hildyard consequently called on one of the

Battalions left in rear by his Brigade, viz., the Queen's, to carry out this outflanking movement. The Battalion, after moving eastwards, was to scale the south-eastern side of Cingolo and advancing thence was to drive the Boers in action there off the hill. Owing to thick bush growth and the steepness of the slope, the ascent was very slow, and it was not till 2 p.m. that the Queen's reached the top. Their surprise was great when they quite unexpectedly came on Dundonald's long sought Brigade up there. Dundonald had been ordered by Buller to follow on with his Brigade in the right rear of the Infantry, to watch the development of the action and to seize favourable opportunities for joining in it. But such an almost passive *rôle* was by no means congenial to one so keen for a fight as the Commander of the Mounted Brigade, and he determined to push forward with it, alone and unaided, against the flank and rear of the Boers.

His first objective was the capture of Cingolo. In spite of the extremely severe ascent, during the whole of which the horses had to be led, the Brigade succeeded in reaching the top as early as between 11 a.m. and noon. The Boer patrol posted there was soon driven off and the hill was forthwith occupied. Why Dundonald contented himself with this and why he did not immediately advance against the Boers in action on the southern slope is not clear. It was left for the Queen's to do it.

The Boers, threatened in rear, hurriedly retired over the Nek in the direction of Monte Christo. Lyttelton's Division, which was making the frontal attack and which had meanwhile been strengthened by Barton's Brigade which had advanced across the Gomba, immediately made its way on to the south-western edge of Cingolo, and soon afterwards a Battery was brought across the Gomba and taken up into position there too.

Lyttelton's Troops were now extended in a curve fronting to the north-west, and were thus favourably formed for the enveloping attack on the Enemy's position on Monte Christo. The fight had been successfully begun, the situation was full of promise, when suddenly, just as everything was progressing favourably, Buller ordered that the action should be broken off on account of the great heat, and that the delivery of the decisive attack should be postponed till the next day. Barton's Brigade withdrew to its old bivouac on the southern bank of the Gomba, while the other Troops occupied bivouacs in the positions they had reached during the action.

Later in the afternoon a second Battery was brought forward across the Gomba and taken into position near the first. Otherwise nothing whatever was done towards the preparation of the attack on Monte Christo. Not a single effort was made during the evening or the long night to get some guns up on to the commanding position of Cingolo whence the whole of the Boer position could have been enfiladed. An excuse for this omission was subsequently sought in the excessive steepness of the slopes. The Boers, however, had without so very much trouble taken their heavy guns up on to Hlanwange which is much steeper. It would also have been quite possible during the night to bring more Field Batteries to the north of the Gomba, which would have been a particularly useful measure as, owing to the range being more than 4,000 yards, it was impossible for Batteries posted on Hussar Hill to produce satisfactory fire-effect on the Monte Christo position.

The Boers had clearly recognised the danger which threatened their left flank and employed every moment left to them in sending reinforcements to Monte Christo, continuing to do so even during the night of the 17th-18th. Lucas Meyer, however, considered that the ground presented such difficulties that a serious British attack in this quarter was not to be expected, but rather that the principal frontal blow would be once more delivered from the direction of the Gomba. The majority of the Boers, however, did not share his views. When the British appeared on Cingolo they lost faith in the impregnability of their positions and, as a consequence, the fear of being cut off from a sufficiently early retirement across the Tugela was added to their misgivings about their left wing. During the night of the 17th-18th, therefore, a number of them thought it better to clear out promptly under cover of darkness, and what with the complete absence of discipline and the insufficient respect in which they held their leaders, there was no possibility of preventing them acting on their own impulses. Consequently on the 18th the positions, and specially those on the left wing, were but feebly held, which will partly explain the insignificant resistance which was offered in this quarter.

The following orders for the continuation of the attack on Monte Christo, fixed for the 18th, were published early in the morning of that day:—

" 1. The Second Division will advance this morning over Cingolo Nek and attack Monte Christo which appears to be strongly held.

"The Second Brigade will move off at 5.30 a.m. and will take up a position whence the Enemy on Monte Christo and its south-eastern slopes can be brought under fire or, should any Force of the Enemy be found nearer on Cingolo Nek, whence it can be made to deploy. The attack of the Second Brigade will then be delivered as soon as the Brigadier considers it has been sufficiently prepared.

" 3. The Fourth Brigade will advance on the left of the Second Brigade with its left flank directed on the kraal where the 3rd Battalion King's Royal Rifles is now lying. It will prepare the attack on Monte Christo and its southern slopes with rifle fire. Two

Battalions will remain in third line at the disposal of the Commander of the Second Division.

" 4. The Cavalry will advance by the northern spur of Cingolo towards Monte Christo, will protect the right flank of the advance and will co-operate in the attack on Monte Christo.

" 5. The Field Battery will open fire as soon as the Enemy's position is disclosed on the approach of our Infantry. The heavy Guns south of the Gomba will assist in the preparation of the attack.

" Simultaneously with this attack one Brigade of the Fifth Division will threaten the enemy on Green Hill."

At daybreak the British Batteries south of the Gomba opened a violent cannonade on the Boer position on Monte Christo and Green Hill. On account of the very long range, however, the effect on Monte Christo, particularly that of the Field Batteries, was exceedingly small; only the two Field Batteries which had been taken up on to the Western slope of Cingolo were able in some measure to make themselves felt.

At the hour named in the orders the Second Brigade (Hildyard's) advanced towards Monte Christo. The two Battalions in first line, the Queen's and the West Yorks, opened fire from the north-western slope of Cingolo and from the Nek on the Boers who remained in occupation of the southern spur of Monte Christo, at a range of about 1,000 yards. Both the other Battalions of the Brigade were kept back under cover on the south-western slope of Cingolo. On the right Dundonald's Mounted Brigade had advanced towards the eastern spur of Monte Christo, keeping touch with Hildyard's Brigade.

The two Battalions which were engaged in the fire-fight could not make any progress, their own fire at such long ranges being comparatively ineffective. About 6.30 a.m. the Artillery began to join in the fight, for the ground which had yet to be traversed by the attacking Troops being invisible from the position of the Guns south of the Gomba, it was assumed that Hildyard's Brigade was by this time advancing over the Nek. The fire of the Boers, whose eyesight and experience in shooting at long ranges were all in their favour, was by far the superior.

In front of the British firing line there lay several hundred yards of perfectly level ground on the Nek completely swept by the enemy's fire, while a favourable fire position behind little swellings and boulders could be seen at his end of it. To advance to this position across the level through the unsubdued fire of the Enemy would apparently be to court certain disaster, especially if the Boers on Green Hill, who were not occupied in their front, should also turn their fire on to the Nek. At last, after repeated demands that they should do so, the Artillery again opened fire at about 8 a.m. on the Boers holding Monte Christo.

About the same time Norcott's Brigade, in a deep formation in three lines, with the Rifle Brigade in the first, deployed on the undulating and bushy slopes of the Nek for the frontal attack of the heights between Monte Christo and Green Hill, while Barton's Fusilier Brigade joining up on the left, with the Royal Scots and Royal Irish in first line, advanced to attack Green Hill. When about 700 or 800 yards from them, both Brigades opened fire on the Boers posted on Green Hill. In this way the Boer fire was drawn off Hildyard's Brigade, which was thus to some extent relieved, and soon after 10 a.m. was enabled to make decided progress in its attack. Rushing at top speed across the level ground in their front the Queen's and West Yorks succeeded in traversing it and capturing the fire position mentioned above without incurring serious casualties. In this they were also favoured by the very effective fire of the Devons who, lying as it were in terraces on the upper slopes of Cingolo where they had taken up a position, were able to continue to fire over the heads of the Queen's and West Yorks. These two Battalions, from the favourable fire position they had seized, were now able to engage the Boers so effectively that soon afterwards it was possible to bring forward the Devons and East Surreys across the level ground into the cover which was to be found immediately in rear of the firing line. Not long afterwards the Boers on the southern spurs of Monte Christo, fearing that they would be surrounded by the Mounted Brigade which was advancing on Hildyard's right, withdrew to the summit of the hill.

Hildyard's Brigade immediately followed on, and reaching a dead bit of ground on the southern slope of Monte Christo into which the Enemy's fire could not penetrate, continued the advance, climbing up the steep and rocky hillside. Soon after 12 noon the Brigade reached the summit, whereupon the Boers slipped back as fast as they could to behind the western edge of the hill. Hildyard's Battalions charged after them, but had scarcely made good 100 yards when they were suddenly smitten by the annihilating fire of the Boer Guns posted on Green Hill. Two Krupp Guns, a Maxim Nordenfeldt, and all the rifles to be found there had been turned in hot haste on to the Battalions in their victorious career, with such effect that the Brigade, reeling under the sudden blow, fell back again from the hill to the cover of the eastern slope, and the Boers once more took possession. It seemed as if the passing success of the British would degenerate into failure.

But when General Lyttelton, from his point of observation on a hill south of the Nek, recognised that Hildyard's Brigade was falling back, he ordered Norcott's and Barton's Brigades to drive their attack vigorously home; the result was that the Boer Infantry and Artillery fire on Green Hill was once more diverted from Monte Christo on to the adversary in the immediate front. Meanwhile

R

the strenuous efforts of General Hildyard had resulted in the rallying of the Battalions on the eastern slope and in their being re-formed and once more led to the front. In this their second charge they were not subjected to Artillery fire and were thus enabled to make good the hill; the few Boers still remaining there fled towards the passage of the river. Hildyard's Brigade now lost no time in opening fire from the western slope of Monte Christo on the flank and rear of the Boers on Green Hill and thus all further resistance was broken down. About 2 p.m. the Boers, abandoning their large laager with abundant supplies of food, ammunition and water, were streaming back north-west in headlong flight towards the crossing-places. Norcott's and Barton's Brigades followed them up, while Hildyard's Brigade, pressing on from Monte Christo, hurried their retirement. A Field Battery advanced with the Infantry, and in spite of the steepness of the slope succeeded in getting up to the summit of Monte Christo, whence it sent some more rounds plunging effectively into the Boers as they were disappearing into the valley.

It seemed as though the Boers could no longer escape the certain annihilation with which the pursuit of the British Infantry threatened them. But suddenly an order was received from Buller that the Troops were to halt in the positions they had taken and were to press forward no further. Whether it was attributable to the great heat, or whether to the fear of another retirement which should hazard the retention of what had been so far gained, this fateful order saved the Boers from certain destruction and reduced to half its value this the first success of the British arms. Pursuit, which would have carried the British across the Tugela at the same time as the Boers, would have made it impossible for the latter to take up a new position and, it may fairly be assumed, would have effected the Relief of Ladysmith without any of the further sanguinary fighting which was now involved. It has been said that false information announcing the approach of strong reinforcements towards the Enemy caused Buller to issue this unfortunate order.

But the garnering of the full harvest of success was prevented far less by this mistake, which was, moreover, such as may easily arise in war-time, than by the orders for the attack originally issued by Buller, which could in no way bring about a decisive engagement. If the flank attack was to have an effective result it should have been delivered on the Boers completely tied down to the defence of their front by the operations of Warren's Division; it would thus have come on them as a surprise, and they could hardly have got clear of it with such insignificant losses. Instead of this Warren's Division was held in absolute inactivity opposite the Enemy's front, and the flank attack was expected to decide matters without its co-operation. As a result the Boers who were distributed along the front were left free to turn their strength against the threatened envelopment and rob it of effectiveness. It was all the more unreasonable to think that the Boers would be surprised when the flank attack was launched as early as the 17th and when, in consequence, their attention had been drawn in good time to the danger which threatened them. Had the direction of their affairs been only a little more energetic it would have been an easy matter for the Boers to have opposed a new and a strong front to Hildyard's Brigade. General Lyttelton did to some extent remedy the error which had been made in the distribution of the *rôles* of the attacking Forces, when he threw Norcott's and Barton's Brigades on to the front of the Boers at the critical moment when the flank attack threatened to collapse. The success of the day is therefore to be attributed primarily to his judicious action.

The Boers, unmolested by the British, continued their withdrawal across the Tugela in the course of the afternoon; only the Bethel Commando, strengthened during the night by the Heidelberg Commando, occupied the heights south of the crossing-places.

The British occupied bivouacs that evening on the field, viz., Hildyard's Brigade on Monte Christo, Norcott's Brigade on the Nek between that hill and Green Hill, and Barton's Brigade on the western slope of Green Hill. Two Naval 12-prs. and the Artillery of the Second Division were taken up into position on Monte Christo. Both the 5-in. Guns were brought across to the northern bank of the Gomba during the night, while Warren's Division, less Barton's Brigade, remained on Hussar Hill and did not advance to the heights of Hlangwane till the next morning.

Early on the 19th Barton's Brigade occupied Hlangwane and began exchanging shots at long range with the few Boers who remained on the southern bank and who, having evacuated the hill during the night, which they spent a little further north, had come back too late in the morning to resume occupation. Lyttelton wanted to throw them back across the river forthwith, but Buller would not agree to this, as he considered they would be forced to evacuate their untenable position without fighting. But in spite of the Artillery fire which was directed on them and of the advance of Hildyard's Brigade from Monte Christo towards the Tugela, the Boers held on to it during the whole of the day and only retired across the river during the night 19th-20th; at the same time the Commandos immediately north of Colenso moved back across the Onderbrook stream, and only a weak Force was left south of the stream. Thereupon Hart's Brigade was brought forward from Chieveley to Colenso, so that on the 20th the British were in undisputed possession of the whole of the southern bank. The remainder of the 19th was spent in a cannonade of the northern bank by the British Artillery. Burn-Murdoch's detachment at Springfield was brought to Chieveley, and the Troops which composed it were sent back to the formations in which they had previously been.

The engagements of these last few days had cost the British 9 Officers and 197 Men, while the Boers put their losses at 12 Killed and 46 Wounded.

CHAPTER VIII.

THE FIGHTING ON THE NORTH OF THE TUGELA.

The Boers employed the precious breathing-time which the British allowed them in zealously preparing for occupation a fresh entrenched position on the northern bank of the Tugela across the main road to Ladysmith, firmly determined here to oppose the further progress of the Enemy. The right flank of their position lay somewhat withdrawn on the road from Colenso to Arnot's Hill, South of Groobler's Kloof, and was thence prolonged, following the course of the Onderbrook stream and by Wynne's, Hart's and Railway Hills, as far as Pieter's Hill.

On the south of all these Hills there lie rounded knolls, which in some places narrow the field of fire towards the Tugela Valley, and on these small advanced posts were placed. For the rest the whole of the deeply-indented country is roadless and presents great difficulties for the movement of Troops. Groobler's Kloof, visible from a long way off, dominates all the countryside and is rocky and most difficult of ascent, while Hart's, Railway and Pieter's Hills are, though lower, also rather steep and very boulder-strewn. The Onderbrook and Langverwacht Spruits, running in deep cut channels, are streams which were at the time referred to very swollen in consequence of the recent heavy rainfall and from time to time they could only be crossed by bridges.

Aasvogel Kop, which was not held by the Boers, rises steep and dominating on the east of Pieter's Hill, from which it is only separated by the deep cut gorge in which flows Pieter's Spruit. This gorge furnished a favourable avenue of approach for the envelopment of the left flank of the Boers. In this quarter the Command was in the hands of Lucas Meyer, whose activity and alertness were of no high order, while Botha directed the operations of all the Commandos south of the Langverwacht.

The evacuation of the position at Colenso and the retirement during the night of the 19th-20th had brought General Joubert in person to the scene of operations. But instead of promptly throwing himself as the Chief Commander into the task of putting matters on a good footing, he spent half-an-hour on Groobler's Kloof watching the picture which was unfolding itself down in the valley below him. He then thought that there was nothing more to be done in this quarter and rode back again to his Hoofd Laager.

On the right flank at Onderbrook and Wynne's Hills were the Zoutpansberg, Swaziland, and Middleburg Commandos, to which parts of the Bethel, Standerton, Carolina, and Ermelo Commandos had joined themselves. Hart's and Railway Hills were held by the Boksburg, Krügersdorp, and Johannesburg Commandos, while on Pieter's Hill were the men of Lydenburg, Heidelberg, and Piet Retief. The left flank at Pieter's Spruit was but weak, and Lucas Meyer had initiated no sort of measures to ward off the constantly increasing menace of an envelopment.

The musketry trenches of the Boers were for the most part laid out about half-way up the heights, and all advanced posts were only weakly entrenched. The Boer guns were scattered along the whole of the position; on the Colenso-Arnot's Hill road were a Maxim-Nordenfeldt and a 7·5 centimetre Krupp Gun; on the summit of Groobler's Kloof were two 7·5 centimetre Creusot Guns and a 12 centimetre Howitzer; on the heights between the Langverwacht Spruit and the railway two Maxim-Nordenfeldts, one Creusot, one 7·5 centimetre Krupp Gun, and a 12 centimetre Howitzer. The guns were in protected positions and entirely screened by bushes from the view of the Enemy.

The fighting strength of the Boers had been reduced by the withdrawal of numbers of Free Staters who had made off to the Western theatre of operations, to protect their own country, now threat ned by the advance under Lord Roberts; but it still amounted to some 4,000 or 5,000 Men. How many of these actually took part in the fighting cannot be stated with any certainty. During the two days' pause which had succeeded the disaster on the southern bank the Commandos had recovered themselves, and all looked forward with renewed confidence to the fighting in which they were now to take part.

At the British Headquarters no fresh decision had yet been arrived at. While everything pointed to the desirability of promptly following up the success gained on the southern bank so as to allow the Boers no time in which to recover themselves and to strengthen themselves in fresh entrenchments, the British Troops remained more or less inactive during two days, and on the evening of the 20th were still in the positions which, thanks to the exercise of some perspicacity and activity by those who had led them in the fighting, they had occupied on the evening of the 18th.

On the 19th Buller with his Staff had made a reconnaissance of the Enemy's positions on the northern bank from Monte Christo. His advisers constantly urged him to cross the river without delay in the section north of Cingolo and Monte Christo in order to turn in this quarter against the naturally weaker left wing of the Boers, to drive it in and so to lay hold of the Ladysmith Road This advance could always be most effectively supported by the Artillery posted on the heights on the southern bank. Buller also saw the advantages of this, but he considered the country east of Pieter's Spruit impenetrable and deficient in what he considered essential, viz., a good transport-road, the construction of which would require too much time. An advance along the railway and the main road to Ladysmith would meet with no such difficulties. But a thorough reconnaissance of the country north of Cingolo and Monte Christo, or of that on the opposite bank of the Tugela, had never been made. Buller could only base his contention on the inadequate report of a young Engineer Officer. As a matter of fact, however, in this instance also it was not of so much importance where the advance should be made, as that such prompt and vigorous action should be taken to deprive the Boers of all leisure. But that is just what did not occur; want of decision and delay in execution were on this occasion more detrimental than a faulty choice of measures.

At length, after wavering for two days, during which the most precious time for action had run to waste, the General Commanding decided on an advance along the main Colenso-Ladysmith road, although it led straight on to the front of the Enemy's fresh and very strong position and although every movement on the level plain north of Colenso between Onderbrook Spruit and the Tugela could be seen and appreciated from the semi-circle of heights which enclose the valley of the Tugela. Any attack developing here would come under the concentrated fire of Artillery posted in very dominating positions, while on the other hand no effective Artillery support could be furnished to the Infantry.

The reconnaissance of the northern bank during the two

days' pause had been altogether insufficient. On the afternoon of the 20th a party of Thorneycroft's Mounted Infantry had swum the Tugela near Colenso and had found the country immediately north of the town quite clear of the Enemy. But in advancing towards Onderbrook Spruit it had come under fire, whereupon it retired again to the south bank without having ascertained whether the heights beyond Onderbrook Spruit were strongly held by the Enemy or where the flanks of his position lay.

If these points could not have been settled by pushing forward mounted patrols or by sending some round the flanks, dismounted action should have been tried for the purpose. In any case the mounted party displayed a want of thoroughness in carrying out its mission when it turned about and came back to the southern bank as soon as a few shots were fired at it. The results of the unsatisfactory reconnaissance were soon to be felt.

At the British Headquarters the opinion was held that the Boers only held the heights between the railway and Onderbrook Spruit, and that their right flank rested on the hill, subsequently named Wynne's, which was to the north of the stream and the construction of entrenchments on which had been observed from Hlangwane.

Buller's intention after the Tugela should have been crossed near Colenso, was to advance along the valley of the river in a northerly direction so as to push the Enemy away westwards from the river and thus force him to loosen his hold on the road to Ladysmith. That is to say, the Troops advancing to the attack were to squeeze themselves in between the river and the Enemy's front.

Early on the 21st Dundonald's Mounted Brigade was on Cingolo, Lyttelton's Division on Monte Christo, Warren's Division, which had meanwhile been brought forward, was on Lyttelton's left at Hlangwane, while in advance of the ridge of that hill the whole of the Artillery was in position under the protection of Infantry pushed out to its front. As the road and railway bridges at Colenso had been demolished, Buller instructed the Engineers to construct a pontoon-bridge between Hlangwane and Fort Wylie, about 2,000 yards north of Colenso; this work was carried out in the course of the forenoon, and in spite of the Tugela being in flood and very rapid at this point, it was all completed in three hours.

Towards noon Warren's Division was ordered to cross the Tugela and to advance in a northerly direction along the river. At the very moment when Coke's Brigade was moving off at the head of the Division, Buller received a report that strong parties of the Boers were posted on the Onderbrook stream south of Groobler's Kloof. He decided to begin by driving off these parties which were on the flank of his projected advance and entrusted the operation to Coke's Brigade.

About 2 p.m. Coke crossed the Tugela and deployed the three Battalions of his Brigade behind one another in the valley, fronting west; in the first line were the Somersetshire Light Infantry, then the Dorsets and Middlesex, each Battalion being also formed in several lines. Before any Infantry reconnaissance had been made, and before it was known where the Enemy really was, the Somersetshire Light Infantry advanced in a westerly direction in long, widely extended lines to capture the hills along the railway.

From the heights the Boers were able to observe accurately every movement of the British, and their guns had already fired on the point of passage and on Coke's Brigade as it moved forward, without, however, doing much damage, the range being excessive. The Boers south of Onderbrook now occupied the heights which stretched in a semicircle in front of the stream from the Colenso-Arnot Hill road to the railway. In their front lay a perfectly level plain which extended as far as the hills west of the railway, and which furnished a good field of fire up to about 1,200 yards.

Their plan was to allow the Enemy to cross the plain and to enter the curve on which they were posted, and then to crush him with concentrated fire at close ranges. Owing to the absence of any thorough reconnaissance the Somersetshire Light Infantry came on to meet this plan half-way. When they had got over the kopjes west of the railway and had come on to the plain, they were greeted by the first shots from the Boers, although they were still 1,100 yards or so from them. It looked as if the absence of fire-discipline would once more upset the well-laid plan. The British Infantry, however, did the Boers the service of walking into the trap laid by them. Accustomed as they were to bring matters to an issue by a resolute advance to cross bayonets with the Enemy, the Somersetshire Light Infantry continued to move on across the plain until, at a distance of about 600 yards from the Boers, they were suddenly overwhelmed with such violent fire on their right flank and rear that everybody threw himself down on the ground and there lay demoralised and incapable of replying to the Enemy's fire. Coke thereupon sent forward some companies of the Dorsets who were following, that they might drive the Boers away from the flank of the Somersetshire Light Infantry. They succeeded in driving the Boers off two neighbouring kopjes, but this brought about no appreciable diminution of the flanking fire.

Meanwhile it was about 4 p.m. and the 28th and 78th Field Batteries, of Warren's Division, which had crossed the river immediately behind Coke's Brigade, were taken up on to the hills west of the railway; but in spite of the Artillery support thus afforded to the Somersetshire Light Infantry lying out there in the open, the galling rifle fire of the Boers did not cease. To get clear of its insupportable situation the Battalion rushed forward about 200 yards to a little dip in the ground which would give them at least some small amount of cover. Here the men threw themselves down again, crouching close to the ground, to wait till darkness should fall. No attempt was made to relieve the sorely-tried Somersetshire men, at least from the flanking fire, by moving the Dorsets and Middlesex who were in reserve on the railway further to the north, so that their advance along the Onderbrook should take in flank the Boers posted there. When it was dark those portions of Coke's Brigade which were in action were brought back again to behind the heights on the railway, where they rallied on Wynne's Brigade which had also come across the river during the afternoon.

This engagement cost the British 108 Killed and Wounded, while the Boers had no casualties of any kind.

Buller employed the night 21st-22nd and the early morning of the 22nd in bringing across to the left bank of the Tugela first: the whole of the Infantry, except Barton's Brigade, which remained on Hlangwane, and half Norcott's Brigade and one Battalion of Hart's Brigade which formed the Garrison of Colenso: and then the 73rd, 7th, and 63rd Field Batteries and the 61st Howitzer Field Battery, as well as four 12-pr. Naval Guns. Thus on the morning of the 22nd no fewer than 15 Battalions and 40 Guns were closely crowded together in the narrow space between the pontoon bridge and Fort Wylie.

Although the previous day's fighting had clearly shown that the right flank of the Boers was not to be found on Wynne's Hill, but south of Groobler's Kloof, Buller held firmly on to the execution of his original plan of advancing along the railway. He was the more decided about this when Warren offered to capture with his Troops Wynne's Hill, which stood out conspicuously dominating the plain, and thus to pierce the Boer position. Buller agreed and allotted for the attack, which Warren was to conduct, Wynne's and Hildyard's Brigades and the two Battalions of Norcott's Brigade which had crossed the river, viz., the Scottish Rifles and King's Royal Rifles. By this arrangement the Divisions were completely mixed up one with another.

All the Artillery available on the left bank was taken into position on the kopjes north of Fort Wylie and Colenso, and thence opened fire, which never produced much effect, on the Boer Guns which were posted in positions far above them. There is no doubt that it would have been more to the point to leave all the Artillery on the southern bank, where a far better position could have been found for it on the heights between the Falls and the Boer's Bridge, from which it could have produced much more effect on the whole of the northern bank and especially on the Boer Artillery.

After a cannonade lasting several hours, in which the whole country between Onderbrook and Langverwacht Spruit, as well as on Groobler's Kloof, was swept with shrapnel, the Infantry advanced to the attack about 2 p.m. Wynne's Brigade, the battalions in deep columns, advanced along the valley in the direction of Wynne's Hill, Hildyard's Brigade followed, while both Battalions of Norcott's Brigade were posted on the left rear for the protection of the left flank. As it moved forward Wynne's Brigade deployed for the attack of Wynne's Hill which is a broad feature; on the right the South Lancashires advanced towards Green Hill, in the centre the King's Own towards Wynne's Hill (East), on the left the Reserve Rifles towards Wynne's Hill (West).

The Boers had occupied Wynne's Hill and the heights on its south-west on the left bank of the Onderbrook as soon as they observed the advance of the three British Brigades towards Wynne's Hill.

Wynne's Hill is a broad level-topped ridge divided into two equal portions by a nek at its centre. The plateau, in parts smooth and in parts cut up and rough, is from 300 to 400 yards broad from north to south. The Boers occupied the southern edge at first, while their entrenchments lay on the northern edge.

When Wynne's Brigade began to pass the Onderbrook it came under heavy fire on its front and left flank. Among the first to fall was Major-General Wynne, Commanding the Brigade, who was severely wounded and in whose place Colonel Crofton took up the command. In spite of the very heavy fire the Brigade continued to advance till it reached the slopes of Wynne's Hill, where it found some cover in the deeply seamed ground.

Taking advantage of this the Battalions succeeded in making good the southern edge of Wynne's Hill and in driving the Boers back to the northern edge. The South Lancashires were now on Green Hill, the King's Own on the southern edge of Wynne's Hill (East), while the Reserve Rifles, keeping in connection, stretched as far as Wynne's Hill (West); the last-named were particularly harassed by the flanking fire of the Boers posted on the spurs of Groobler's Kloof. Both Battalions of Norcott's Brigade in the left rear, from the heights on the right bank of the Onderbrook, covered the left flank of the Brigade engaged on the further bank, from the Boers posted on the spurs of Groobler's Kloof, while Hildyard's Brigade was also on the south bank of the Onderbrook, under cover in the valley, not far from where that stream flows into the Tugela.

Meanwhile it was nearly 6 p.m. and the situation of the Brigade on Wynne's Hill began to take an unfavourable turn; already almost all the supports had been placed in the firing-line and the casualties were increasing; the left flank in particular was suffering much all the time from the flanking fire. Ammunition was giving out and the fire was weakening, while on the other hand it seemed as though the violence of the Boer fire was increasing. Colonel Crofton therefore sent to Norcott's and Hildyard's Brigades to ask for their support. But before this could be accorded a mishap occurred which might have had the most disastrous consequences.

A number of Boers, making good use of the increasing darkness,[*] crept forward close up to the centre and left flank of the British and suddenly opened an overwhelming fire on them. Some companies of the King's Own began to waver. At first a few and then many of the men broke away to behind the edge of the hill. The bad example was contagious, and before the leaders could check it, the whole of the British centre rushed back in wild flight to the protection of the Onderbrook valley. The situation was most serious. If the Boers pressed on now the Reserve Rifle Companies which had remained steady on the left flank would be cut off. But the Boers were far too dull to promptly and energetically derive full advantage from such favourable situations in an engagement. Before they had made up their minds to do so the British had provided against the danger. The King's Royal Rifles, which were the first to arrive in response to Crofton's appeal, did not delay in crossing the Onderbrook to come to his aid, and in spite of the darkness, which meanwhile had quite closed in, set about re-occupying the abandoned edge of the hill. The leading Company had scarcely arrived there when a violent close-range fire was opened on it; whereupon the Riflemen, fixing their swords, charged with wild cheers into the darkness of the night.

Before the Riflemen could get at them even, the Boers rushed back to the northern edge. Pressing on after them

---

[*] The sun had set at 6.30 p.m.

the Company came under very hot fire on its flanks and rear, apparently from some groups of Boers who had remained lying on the ground, possibly also from some of their own Troops at the southern edge. Everybody threw himself on the ground, but the Company had already suffered severely; the remnants driven together under the concentrated fire, rallied in a broken-down cattle kraal which was about 100 yards in front of the Boers. Meanwhile the other Companies of the same Rifle Battalion had occupied the southern edge of the hill completely ignorant, owing to the darkness, of the fate of the Company which had charged ahead.

By this time Hildyard's Brigade had come up too. Its leading Battalion, the East Surrey, was sent to the support of the threatened centre and left flank, while the Devons hurried off to the right flank on Green Hill. When the East Surreys reached the southern edge it was pitch dark and wild confusion reigned, the troops of two Divisions and of three Brigades being tangled up together and nobody knowing who was in command; some wanted to go forward, some to go back, and everybody was shouting and swearing and rushing about; above all the din there rose the paralysing cries of the wounded begging for water and help. The scene was one of perilous disorder, and if only a few resolute Boers had charged down on the troops they would have sufficed to bring about a catastrophe. But even the Boers had begun to suffer under the influence of the night which destroyed their cohesion, and they could not profit by the favourable turn which affairs were beginning to take, because the darkness prevented them from realising the full extent of their success. In their excitement the Boers fired on everything that moved, with the result that in many instances the various groups which were lying scattered about all over the place fired on one another. On their side, too, all plan or purpose was wanting, and confusion reigned supreme.

Colonel Harris, of the East Surreys, very justly recognised that further reinforcements in the centre could only increase the blind disorganisation of the night, and he therefore sent half his Battalion to the left flank while he went with the remaining four companies to the right flank at Wynne's Hill. It was so dark that even on this short march thither two companies lost touch, and they only picked up connection with their Battalion again some hours later.

On Wynne's Hill East there prevailed a similar state of affairs. Colonel Harris, while moving along the slope, came on a crouching mob, without purpose or leader, which he could not get to move backwards or forwards. He decided to re-occupy the abandoned position on the southern slope and there, with bayonets fixed, to stand fast till dawn. As there was no certainty in the darkness whether the front was clear of friendly troops or not, nobody ventured to fire.

Meanwhile the Devons who had been entrusted with the support of the right wing on Green Hill, had got along through the darkness in Indian file holding on to one another's clothes, and after frequent halts had arrived at their destination; but as the South Lancashires, who had not been so hard-pressed, were still holding on all right, the Devons were kept back in reserve, and it was not till about dawn that a call had to be made on them.

A Sergeant of the Company of Rifles which had charged ahead and which, as has been mentioned, was now "lying low" in the cattle kraal, had crawled back as far as to where the East Surreys lay, to bring a report of what had occurred. Thereupon two companies of the East Surreys crawled forward in the darkness to get the Riflemen out of their awkward plight; and this much they managed without attracting the attention of the Boers. It was not till dawn, just as the British companies were moving off on their way back to the southern edge, that a few shots were fired at them from the northern edge, which immediately alarmed the whole Boer line and caused the general resumption of their fire. This firing, which suddenly broke out with great violence, threw the South Lancashires on the right flank into such a state of alarm that they, too, rushed pell-mell down the hill in full flight; their leaders had completely lost control over the terrified mass, and all efforts to bring it to a standstill or to explain that the firing boded no danger to it, were in vain. The fugitives were not brought to a halt till they reached the Tugela. As the positions which had been thus abandoned were occupied without delay by the Devons who were in reserve, this retirement produced no serious consequences.

The half Battalion of the East Surreys came up to the left flank exactly at the right moment to render effective aid to the Reserve Rifles who were being hard pressed there. Hildyard complied with the request for further support by sending the Queen's there too, and so a retirement was averted, and the troops on the left flank continued to hold their own in spite of the repeated violent onslaughts which the Boers made during the night in this quarter.

In the early morning the situation of the British on the right and left flanks was not so perilous as it was in the centre, where the confusion still prevailing gave rise to anxiety lest there should be any more giving way.

The formation in extended lines of the three Brigades which were engaged, was particularly ill-adapted to night fighting, and did not favour the formation of well-defined areas of command or the maintenance of order. The various Brigades and Battalions had got into inextricable confusion along the whole line.

But the fighting organisation of the Boers, too, had been thrown out of gear during the night-fighting, and their losses, to which in the darkness they themselves had contributed the larger share, had robbed them of all wish to take further offensive action: it was evident that all they longed for was to be left as much as possible undisturbed by the Enemy. No decisive results of any kind had been secured on either side during this night engagement, but both adversaries had suffered excessively in spirit owing to the disintegrating influence of the darkness, and it was vain to look during the succeeding days for great deeds of war from these exhausted men.

The fight at Wynne's Hill exhibits all the dangerous symptoms attending night enterprises, and a judicious leader, before he decides on undertaking them, must always bear in mind that the occasions are very rare when the best results can be obtained by night from carefully-planned direction of troops in action. Blind chance frequently governs these enterprises, and it would be a great mistake to attach any importance to contrary opinions based on the favourable course of night operations in peace manœuvres, on which neither real danger or the excitement of men's imaginations exert any influence. In war the results gained will generally bear no sort of comparison with the risks run; of the truth of which the British, too, must have had proof in many a night enterprise during this Campaign. It is easy to show that the darkness should be turned to account in bringing troops close up to an adversary posted in a strong position; but great issues can only be fought out by daylight, and it is all the more important nowadays to keep the troops as fit and fresh as possible to take part in then deciding them: for really serious fighting differs from manœuvres in extending over more than a few hours and in taxing the energies of the troops engaged to an extent to which they cannot possibly be accustomed. No leader can look forward with full confidence to the labours of a long day's fighting if he has to employ for the purpose troops whose energies have been already half-spent in night marches and night operations.

On the 23rd, before daybreak, the Troops were in possession of the following Army Order which had been published in the evening of the 22nd:—

"Headquarters, Colenso,
22nd February, 1900.

"1. The Army will advance to-morrow on the west of the Colenso-Ladysmith Railway at an hour which will be communicated to General and other Officers in Command.

"2. The two Battalions of the Fourth Brigade (Norcott's), which are now on Green Hill, will move off at 2 a.m. and join the remainder of the Brigade on the Onderbrook Spruit.

"3. General Hart will move off from Colenso at 4.30 a.m. with 3 Battalions of the Fifth Brigade, and will place himself under the orders of General Warren on the Langverwacht Spruit.

"4. The remainder of the Second Division will move to its left, keeping connection with the Fifth Division in the advance of the latter along the railway. Each Division will make arrangements about the employment of its own Field Artillery and will, where possible, place one Battery in rear of the leading Battalion of the leading Brigade, the other two Batteries marching between the Brigades.

"5. The Sixth Brigade (Barton's) will leave one Battalion in rear on the northern edge of Hlangwane to command the Tugela and to ensure the safety of the right flank during the advance. The Mountain Battery and the four Naval 12-pr. Guns will take up a position under the orders of the Senior Officer for the same purposes.

"6. The 4·7-inch Naval Guns and the heavy 5-inch Guns* will, before daybreak, take up a position on the Colenso Heights; their ox-teams will be kept close by them. A Battalion of the Sixth Brigade will furnish an escort for these Guns.

"7. The 19th Field Battery and the 61st (Howitzer) Field Battery will advance from the Colenso Heights as soon as instructed to do so. The 19th Field Battery† will cross the pontoon bridge at 4 a.m. and move up to near the Howitzer Battery.

"8. The Sixth Brigade (Barton's) will furnish the rear-guard.

"9. The Tenth Brigade, under command of General Coke, will occupy Colenso and cover the rear of the Army.

"10. The two Mounted Brigades will cross the pontoon bridge at 6 a.m. and 7 a.m. respectively, the First Brigade leading.‡

"11. The Balloon Section will march with the Howitzer Battery.

"12. The General Commanding will be on the railway at Onderbrook Spruit at 5 a.m."

At daybreak Coke's Brigade occupied the heights south of the Onderbrook on both sides of the Colenso-Arnot Hill Road in the front of the Enemy still remaining there. Hart's Brigade advanced from the kopjes north of Colenso by the Ladysmith Road towards the Onderbrook, while Barton's Brigade (having left one Battalion on the southern bank) and the two Mounted Brigades began to cross the river by the pontoon bridge. The whole of the Artillery on both banks of the river opened fire at daybreak, from where

---

* Previously on Hussar Hill.

† Previously still on the right bank.

‡ The First Cavalry Brigade under Burn-Murdoch had joined the Second Mounted Brigade at Bloys' Farm on the 22nd. Both Brigades came under the command of Colonel Lord Dundonald.

they had been in action the previous day, on the Boer positions on Wynne's, Hart's, and Railway Hills.

The troops which had lost cohesion and become mixed up together in the previous day's action were disentangled and re-organised, and Hildyard's Brigade, as well as the two Battalions of Norcott's Brigade, were withdrawn from the fight; only the Devons remained in their positions on the right flank. Hildyard assembled his Battalions south of the Onderbrook, between that stream and the Ladysmith road; Norcott's Brigade was held in readiness in rear of Hildyard's Brigade as soon as the two Battalions which had remained on the right bank had been brought across the river. The Eleventh Brigade, of which Colonel Kitchener took over the Command *vice* General Wynne, remained in its positions on Wynne's Hill.

The Army Order of the evening of the 22nd had been issued under the mistaken idea that the possession of the heights between the Langverwacht and Onderbrook Spruits had been incontestably secured. But when early on the 23rd General Buller was informed about the hard-pressed situation of the Eleventh Brigade on Wynne's Hill, he recognised the impracticability of the Order. Accordingly, while holding to the original plan so far as to push the rest of his troops into the narrow space between the Tugela and the position of the Eleventh Brigade on Wynne's Hill, he decided to advance towards and attack the Boers on Hart's Hill so as to bring about some relief in the situation of the Brigade on Wynne's Hill and, if possible, to pierce the Enemy's position. For this operation he detailed Hart's Brigade, to which were attached the two remaining fresh Battalions of Norcott's Brigade, viz., the Rifle Brigade and the Durham Light Infantry, thus bringing it up to a total of five and a half Battalions.

The entrenchments of the Boers on Hart's Hill could

be seen from afar, and the whole of the Artillery on the northern bank was directed to bring them under fire. How unfavourable was the position of the Artillery in the lower-lying ground in the Tugela valley, and how premature had been its transfer thither from the commanding heights of Hlangwane, now became evident. In order to produce more effect the 7th Field Battery was consequently taken back to the right bank and came into action on the heights south of the old Boer bridge; but for all that the cannonade from some sixty pieces, which lasted several hours, had but a very small measure of success.

Meanwhile, Hart's Brigade had begun to advance from the Onderbrook along the Ladysmith Road, the Inniskilling Fusiliers leading and the other five Battalions, the Connaught Rangers, the Dublin Fusiliers, the half-Battalion Imperial Light Infantry,* the Durham Light Infantry, and the Rifle Brigade following in the order named. When the leading battalion approached the Langverwacht Spruit it came under the long-range rifle fire of the Enemy. To avoid this the Inniskillings took cover in the bed of the Tugela and moved on in single file, in consequence of which the march of the battalions in rear was considerably delayed. When the leading battalion reached the Langverwacht about 1 p.m., the spruit was found to be swollen and deep, and only negotiable by the railway bridge hard by. The head of the column had hardly got on to the bridge when a hot fire was opened on it from all sides; from the Langverwacht Valley and from the hills to the north of it, where a Maxim was in position, the bullets rained in thick. A good deal of time was spent in blocking up the lattice of the girders on the left side of the bridge with sandbags, and behind the

---

* The other Half-Battalion had been left behind at Chieveley as garrison.

HART'S HILL.

shelter thus furnished the men, crouching down and running as fast as they could, tried one by one to get across the bridge which was about 20 yards long. This all took time, during which many casualties occurred, but about 5 p.m. the Inniskilling Fusiliers, the Connaught Rangers, the Imperial Light Infantry, and the Royal Dublin Fusiliers had all been assembled in the cover of Hart's Hollow behind one of the lower ridges which lie at the foot of Hart's Hill.

The Boers who had been there had been driven off by the fire of the 7th Field Battery, and of the battalions which had been left by Barton's Brigade on the southern bank in a position on the heights south of the old Boer bridge. Hart's Brigade therefore occupied the hills which form Hart's Hollow, the Connaught Rangers being on the right, the Inniskilling Fusiliers in the centre, the Imperial Light Infantry on the left, while the Dublin Fusiliers remained in reserve in the valley of the river. The two battalions of Norcott's Brigade were still engaged in crossing the Langverwacht.

The Boers had retired to Hart's Hill, their main position running along the crest of the hill, about 100 yards in front of which a shelter-trench had been rapidly constructed and but weakly occupied; thus the field of fire of the main position was limited. This hankering of the Boers after advanced positions was to prove the salvation of Hart's Brigade which was now lying in Hart's Hollow some 800 yards or so distant from the nearest of the Enemy's trenches. Hart's Hollow is separated from Hart's Hill by an open valley through which run the railway and the main Ladysmith Road; neither the slopes nor the valley furnished much cover, and they lay under the effective fire of the Enemy. Hart's Hollow, in spite of its great distance from the Enemy, had therefore to be taken up as the position from which the Brigade should endeavour to subdue his fire. Any hurried advance from it into the fire of the Enemy before it should be subdued might be disastrous.

But there was no idea of preparing the advance with fire of any kind. It was soon after 5 p.m., and the troops had scarcely taken up their allotted positions, when General Hart gave the order that the battalions, without waiting for the arrival of Norcott's Brigade, were to advance and carry Hart's Hill by assault. For the protection of the right flank from the Boers posted on Railway Hill, the Connaught Rangers were instructed to send forward a half-battalion against them.

The assault was gallantly delivered by the British in rushes which, long to begin with, became gradually shorter and shorter; the half-battalion Connaught Rangers on the right, the Inniskilling Fusiliers in the centre, and the half-battalion Imperial Light Infantry on the left pressed forward towards the Enemy almost without a check and without discharging a rifle, each battalion being formed in several long, thin, skirmishing lines. At this critical moment the Batteries posted below in the Tugela Valley, which had been holding the Boers back in their entrenchments, ceased fire, as it was impossible from the lower level to watch the progress of Hart's Brigade, and as it was feared that if the fire was kept up then some ill-directed shell might work havoc in its ranks.

So when Hart's Battalions of assault had left the shelter of their cover, an annihilating fire broke out against them from all sides, on the right from Railway Hill, in the front from Hart's Hill, and on the left from the kopjes north of Langverwacht. The Boer Artillery, too, was turned on to the British Infantry. Some of the Boer marksmen, being themselves exposed to no fire whatever, stood up to their full height in the trenches so as to be the better able to fire at the Enemy. A German Officer who was watching from the top of Hart's Hill the gallant delivery of the assault by the British Infantry wrote in his journal: "One can really only admire these Troops who hope in such a way as this to remedy the tactical errors of their leaders." The frontal fire was not so hot as that on the two flanks, for the trenches in advance of the main Boer position were only weakly held. Consequently, notwithstanding that there had been no fire-preparation, the Inniskilling Fusiliers and the half-battalion Connaught Rangers managed, in spite of heavy losses, to make headway; principally because their right flank was not harassed at this juncture by the Boer fire from Railway Hill, which had been diverted on to the half-battalion Connaught Rangers now in the act of deploying to deliver its attack on the front of that position. The Imperial Light Infantry, however, could make no headway; they were compelled to turn against the Boers who were taking them in flank, and this was specially necessary as the Boers on the northern edge of Green Hill, who were but insignificantly engaged in their front by the action of Kitchener's Brigade, were turning some of their fire on to the left flank of Hart's Brigade. Just at this very juncture, when it was essential to make every effort to occupy fully the attention of the Boers on Wynne's Hill, the Eleventh Brigade (Kitchener's) was being relieved by the Second Brigade (Hildyard's), and two battalions of the Sixth Brigade (Barton's), viz., the Royal and the Welch Fusiliers.

When the troops delivering the assault on Hart's Hill had got within about 200 yards of the Enemy's advanced position, the few Boers holding it fled back to the main position, and the Inniskilling Fusiliers and the Half-Battalion Connaught Rangers took possession of the abandoned trenches. And now such an impetuous fire broke out in the front that everybody ducked down under cover, not a man venturing to enter on a fire-fight. As soon as Hart noticed this from his position at the Hollow which bears his name, he sent forward half a battalion of the Dublin Fusiliers as a reinforcement, and it came into the line about 6.30 p.m. just as twilight was coming on.

Before it was quite dark Hart succeeded in screwing up the Inniskilling Fusiliers and Connaught Rangers to make another rush at the Enemy. This was the moment for which the Boers had been waiting; they received their adversaries with an exterminating fire at close range, and the troops gallantly dashing forward had not advanced more than 100 yards from their cover when their vigour for the assault suddenly broke down. In the furious blaze they threw themselves down and, crouching close to the ground, waited till complete darkness covered them and then withdrew to their shelter. Colonel Brooke, who was the senior Commanding Officer on the spot, led the battle-blasted remnants of the Brigade back in the darkness and assembled them in the hollow behind the railway where a trench was hastily thrown up for their protection and where the units were re-formed. The half-battalion Connaught Rangers, which had advanced towards Railway Hill, rejoined the remaining companies of the battalion here too. For the protection of the flanks a company of the Connaught Rangers was pushed out on the right, while on the left a company of the Imperial Light Infantry, which had also retired, was placed along the railway as far as to where it enters the valley. Although nothing could be seen, the firing on both sides was kept up unceasingly throughout the night. Towards midnight an order was received from Hart that the position along the railway line was to be firmly held during the night whatever might happen, and in this it was stated that reinforcements of one and a-half battalions would arrive at daybreak.

It was hardly dawn when the fight began afresh; under cover of the darkness individual Boers had crept forward close up to the railway and suddenly opened fire which, while it came as a surprise to the British, did not inflict on them much actual damage. But all of a sudden the Inniskilling Fusiliers were caught on their left flank by a tremendous storm of bullets. For some reason, which has not been explained, the company of the Imperial Light Infantry which had been entrusted with the task of protecting this flank failed to execute it, with the result that the Boers had been able to crawl forward unmolested in this quarter. The ranks of the troops, whose powers of resistance had been affected by the severity of the previous day's fighting, were broken by some ill-directed shrapnel fire from the British Batteries posted on the southern bank, and leaving their Killed and Wounded they had to be withdrawn as quickly as possible behind the protection and cover to be found at Hart's Hollow, where they were re-formed on the two and a half battalions which had been left behind there. General Hart, who apparently attached great importance to the position on the railway, was very indignant about its having been evacuated, and soon afterwards ordered the Durham Light Infantry to take it again, which they did in the course of the forenoon of the 24th without suffering any great loss.

Had the Boers only possessed a little more of the spirit of the offensive, it would have been easy for them to wipe out the troops in Hart's Hollow, but nothing happened the whole day long, and a German Officer, burning to express his feelings of irritation at this, recorded the following about the 24th: " General Botha came to the tent and I proceeded to draw his attention to the advisability at this juncture of assuming the offensive on the left flank. He will not have it, as he thinks it would cost too many lives. I reply that the War will cost many more lives yet if the principle of passive defence is persisted in any longer, and if no advantage is taken of the chance of successful offensive action. . . . It makes me sick to death to think how well everything might yet turn out in spite of the great mistakes which the Boers have already made. It is really heart-breaking that the Boers did not pursue when the British assault collapsed. Things cannot go on in this sort of way and turn out successfully in the end. . . ." As another German who was in the fighting judges, General Botha, as a matter of fact, was "a man with a good military eye, but quite opposed to stern and desperate decisions."

The fighting at Wynne's and Hart's Hills had cost the British more than 1,200 men one way and another; the Inniskilling Fusiliers alone had lost about 230 Killed and Wounded in their assault. The losses of the Boers on the other hand had been quite trifling. The attack by Hart's Brigade shows how much the British Infantry, even at that period was still under the evil influence of shock-tactics. It is unnecessary to reiterate that an assault thus delivered without any Infantry fire-preparation against expert marksmen armed with magazine rifles, is doomed from start to finish.

But in spite of the failures of the last two days Buller stuck obstinately to his original plan of capturing Hart's Hill. He ordered that a fresh attack should be made on the 24th, and appointed General Warren to direct it. Besides the Troops standing already in Hart's Hollow, two Battalions of Hildyard's Brigade, the East Surrey, and the West Yorks, as well as half a Battalion of Scottish Rifles from Norcott's Brigade, were placed under Warren's Command for this purpose. By some misadventure, however, this order of Buller's did not reach Warren till 4 p.m., and he accordingly decided to postpone the attack till the 25th. Buller, in answer to an enquiry by heliograph, approved of this, whereupon Warren proceeded to go back to the kopjes north of Colenso and left the Command of the seven Battalions in Hart's Hollow to General Hart.

The last-named apparently thought that he was relieved of all further responsibility by the transfer to Warren of the subsequent delivery of the attack, and he made no arrangements whatever, either for security during the night or in connection with the preparations necessary for the proposed operation. Closely crowded together, the troops formed a bivouac in Hart's Hollow, each Battalion just where it stood. No measures for security were taken beyond those furnished by the presence of the Durham Light Infantry who were lying in the trench on the railway. Some Boers profited by this carelessness, and as soon as it was dark crept unobserved down from Railway Hill and up from the valley of the Langverwacht till they were close to the Battalions resting behind Hart's Hollow, which they suddenly—about 9 p.m.—overwhelmed with a tremendous fire at almost point-blank ranges. The effect was instantaneous. In one part of Hart's troops there ensued a state of confusion akin to panic; some of the men roused in alarm from heavy sleep started off rushing about here and there, and very little was wanting to extend the nervous disorder and to produce a helter-skelter flight, especially as there was no exercise of control. General Hart could not be found; nobody knew where he had betaken himself. Making up his mind what to do on the spur of the moment, General Norcott's Brigade-Major, who had been left on Wynne's Hill and who happened to be in Hart's Hollow at the critical moment, assumed Command and sent off the East Surreys and the Rifle Brigade to drive off the Boers who menaced the flanks; and in a short time this was managed all right without much trouble. But till nearly midnight the exchange of shots went on; then there was absolute quiet, and it became possible to restore order and organisation among the troops which had been thrown into confusion by the alarm.

When Buller heard about the state of his troops he decided to give up the attack which he had arranged for the 25th and to ask the Boers for a truce of 24 hours for the purpose of burying his Dead and collecting his Wounded on that day, which was a Sunday. His request was as a matter of fact refused, but the Commandos in the front line, without the knowledge of General Lucas Meyer, gave assurances that until 7 p.m. there would be a cessation of fire. The British soldiers were allowed to come unharmed from out of their shelter-places and to collect their Killed and Wounded without molestation and, such even is the good nature of the Boers, much kindly assistance was afforded to those engaged in the mournful task.

In the diary of one who was taking his part in the fighting the following is to be found: " From the entrenchments of the Middelburgers an extraordinary sight can be observed. Boers and British are moving about freely hither and thither quite peaceably, collecting their Wounded and burying their Dead. A state of tacitly-recognised armistice prevails. . . . With so little energy are operations conducted that I feel to-day, as I have often felt before now during this South African Campaign, as if I were engaged in some manœuvres and not in a War in which the actual existence of a Nation is at stake. The Boers are beginning to be sick of the War, and one can scarcely be surprised at that when the operations are simply those of fights for positions. . . . It is certain that matters have so far gone too well for the Boers; they have learned nothing in the war and are far too proud in their own conceit to accept any instruction. . . ."

Nothing could have been more welcome at the British Headquarters than this " tacitly-recognised armistice," which afforded the opportunity of making the preparations and arranging the distribution of troops which were needed in view of a fresh attack. Early on the 25th the British were distributed as follows into Brigades extemporized, as will be seen, by a general re-assortment of Units, viz.:—

In Hart's Hollow—Hart's Brigade, viz., two Battalions of Hildyard's Brigade and two and a half Battalions of Norcott's Brigade.

On Wynne's Hill—The remaining Battalions of Hildyard's Brigade and of Norcott's Brigade, as well as two Battalions of Barton's Brigade; on the left of these and

South of the Onderbrook—Coke's Brigade.

On the Colenso Kopjes were one Battalion of Barton's Brigade, Kitchener's Brigade and both Mounted Brigades, as well as the greater part of the Artillery.

On the Southern bank, on the Northern slopes of Hlangwane, were one Battalion of Barton's Brigade, the Scots Fusiliers to wit, four 12-pr. Naval Guns, the Chestnut Troop Royal Horse Artillery, the 7th Field Battery, and No. 4 Mountain Battery.

Buller now came to the conclusion that a continuation of the attack on Hart's Hill such as he had ordered, would hardly bring about the success desired by him, and so, adopting the plan which his Staff had originally proposed to him, he decided to try an attack on Pieter's Hill forthwith. He was fortified in this decision by the receipt of a report that about 500 yards below the Falls there had been found a crossing-place to which a road, practicable for troops and vehicles, led down from Hlangwane. On the same day, the 25th, Buller himself went down to this section of the Tugela and made a personal reconnaissance of it, on the strength of which his orders were verbally communicated in the evening to the assembled General and other Officers commanding. A right and a left wing of attack were to be formed. While the left under the orders of Lyttelton was to carry on a delaying action between the Langverwacht Spruit and the Colenso Kopjes, the right under Warren was to deliver the decisive attack on Pieter's, Railway and Hart's Hills, combined with an envelopment of the Enemy's left flank. For this purpose all the Battalions not present in the foremost line and all the Artillery were to be brought back again to the right bank, while the Battalions already in the space between the Langverwacht and the Colenso Kopjes were to remain where they were.

Out of the Troops detailed for the right wing, three Columns were to be formed for the attack of the three points selected for capture: the first, under General Barton, was to deliver the attack on Pieter's Hill; the second, under Colonel Kitchener, was told off for the attack of Railway Hill, while the Column destined to engage the Boers on Hart's Hill was placed under Colonel Norcott. With the exception of the Dublin Fusiliers, Hart's Brigade, which was left at Hart's Hollow, was placed at the disposal of the General Commanding in Chief, while the Borders formed the Garrison of Colenso. The attack itself was to be delivered early on the 27th, after a fresh pontoon bridge should have been thrown across the Tugela below the Falls, and, as was the case in the attack on Monte Christo, it was to begin with a flank attack, Barton first of all moving towards the Boers' left flank at Pieter's Hill, and Kitchener's and Norcott's Columns in échelon connecting up with Barton's and making the frontal attack. No Column was to begin its attack before receiving Buller's express order to do so. While every attack had hitherto been made on a narrow front unsuitable, as a rule, for the development of sufficient force, the front of the attack on this occasion was at last to furnish ample space for the simultaneous development of all the force employed.

In accordance with the instructions which were issued, the Troops were to be distributed as follows:—

A.—RIGHT WING OF ATTACK.
GENERAL WARREN.

Barton's Column—
  Irish Fusiliers of the Sixth Brigade (Barton's).
  Scots Fusiliers of the Sixth Brigade (Barton's).
  Dublin Fusiliers of the Fifth Brigade (Hart's).

Kitchener's Column—
  South Lancashire of the Eleventh Brigade (Kitchener's).
  York and Lancaster of the Eleventh Brigade (Kitchener's).
  King's Own (Royal Lancaster) of the Eleventh Brigade (Kitchener's).
  West Yorks of the Second Brigade (Hildyard's).

Norcott's Column—
  East Surrey of the Second Brigade (Hildyard's).
  ½ Scottish Rifles of the Fourth Brigade (Norcott's).
  Rifle Brigade of the Fourth Brigade (Norcott's).
  Durham Light Infantry of the Fourth Brigade (Norcott's).
    As well as the whole of the Artillery (except the 73rd Field Battery), and the two Mounted Brigades.

B.—LEFT WING OF ATTACK.
GENERAL LYTTELTON.

Queen's of the Second Brigade (Hildyard's).
Devons of the Second Brigade (Hildyard's).
King's Royal Rifles of the Fourth Brigade (Norcott's).
½ Scottish Rifles of the Fourth Brigade (Norcott's).
Royal Fusiliers of the Sixth Brigade (Barton's).
Welch Fusiliers of the Sixth Brigade (Barton's).
Somersetshire Light Infantry of the Tenth Brigade (Coke's).
Middlesex of the Tenth Brigade (Coke's).
Dorsets of the Tenth Brigade (Coke's).
Reserve Rifles of the Eleventh Brigade (Kitchener's).
73rd Field Battery.

C.—AT THE DISPOSAL OF THE GENERAL COMMANDING IN CHIEF.
Inniskilling Fusiliers of the Fifth Brigade (Hart's).
Connaught Rangers of the Fifth Brigade (Hart's).
½ Imperial Light Infantry of the Fifth Brigade (Hart's).
And at Colenso, Borders of the Fifth Brigade (Hart's).

The original Divisional and Brigade formations were thus, as a result of the extent to which the troops had been split up in the previous day's fighting, completely broken up and mixed together.

The 26th was spent in making the necessary preliminary movements of the Troops. First of all, in the early morning all the Artillery, except the 73rd Field Battery which remained on the Colenso Kopjes, was brought back again over the pontoon bridge on to the right bank and taken into position on the northern slopes of Hlangwane; after this came the Infantry, which went into bivouacs on Hlangwane, and also the two Mounted Brigades which were placed behind the right flank on Cingolo Nek: the transport brought up the rear. When this passage of the river was finished the pontoon bridge was dismantled and the material was taken down close to the fresh point of passage, about 500 yards below the Falls, and there put in readiness for the construction of the bridge which was to ensue on the following day.

From the heights the Boers had been able to note the movements of their Enemy and might certainly by now expect that their left flank would soon be attacked. But no serious measures were undertaken to avert the danger which threatened them. The Commandos remained inactive in their previously-occupied position the whole of the 26th. All that occurred was that the Second Vryheid Commando, which had been left on the extreme right at the mouth of the Little Tugela, was brought thence to Railway Hill.

The constant fighting of the last few days had not failed to make its impression on the powers of resistance of the Boers, and their keenness for the fight was diminishing from day to day. The number of those who were sick of fighting was visibly increasing. A German writes thus in his diary on the 26th: "Dr. H. (a Swedish doctor) is importuned by

Boers asking for leave, they are sick from lying constantly in the trenches, and do not want to fight any more. As there is no disciplinary code, they cannot be kept. Wagons are seen continually making off, which is a proof that the owners will soon follow, for the Boer never separates himself from his wagon for long." Moreover, the withdrawal of the Free Staters, which had begun on the 18th, had made many of the Transvaalers think it would be well to watch coming events from further off, and so, as the days passed, the firing-line grew thinner and thinner. Hunger, too, contributed towards depressing the Boers' spirits, and caused many of them to quit the foremost lines. For while there was no deficiency of food round the wagons, nobody had once given a thought to sending any up to the men engaged in the front.

The 27th February, Majuba Day, broke dull and cloudy.

In the grey dawn the Engineers began to throw the fresh pontoon bridge over the Tugela at the appointed place, where the river was about 100 yards wide. Its completion was delayed till about 10.30 a.m. The work had not been disturbed by the Enemy's fire, for from early dawn the Boers had been kept under cover by a powerful cannonade from more than 70 guns firing from advantageous positions at favourable ranges. Although, according to the reports of the Boers who were under it, the cannonade was more violent than any which they had previously experienced in this War, its effect was only poor. Major Freiherr von Reitzenstein, well concealed behind a rock near the Boer Artillery, found time to write at his ease during the cannonade, the following trenchant remarks in his diary:

" . . . 12.20 p.m.—Heavy lyddite fire on the Maxim on the left of our position, which is standing in deep shadow under a tree, but otherwise in the open : the barrel and the shield are covered with grey canvas : the gun has been under fire for five days. It must be very annoying to the

British, for they are always firing at it without ever hitting it. It is really wonderful that up to the present not a single gun has been put out of action. The silencing of Artillery is, however, a difficult job. For, after all, how can it be seen that Artillery is silenced? If the detachments are well entrenched, a couple of guns can be retained, even under far superior Artillery fire, until the decisive Infantry fight, provided of course, that the Artillery Commander has got the requisite nerve. The Boers' nerves are good, and therefore they are good artillerymen. . ."

Barton's Column was the first to cross the Tugela about 11 a.m. Both the Mounted Brigades had taken up a position on the southern bank east of the site of the bridge, that they might cover the passage; they overwhelmed the hills on the northern bank with hot rifle fire which, combined with the Artillery cannonade, kept the Boers in their shelters at a distance from the Infantry as it crossed.

At the very moment when Barton's Troops were about to cross the bridge, Lord Roberts' telegram announcing Cronje's surrender at Paardeberg came to hand. The troops greeted the joyful news with loud cheering: it inspired them with greater ardour for the fight.

When they had crossed the river, Barton's Fusilier Battalions in the following order: Scots, Irish, Dublin, moved to the right in file along the narrow ground bordering the river. When the head of the Column approached the southeastern corner of Pieter's Hill it wheeled left-about to get hold of the low line of hills which skirts its base. On emerging from cover the skirmishing line was met by a brisk fire from the southern edge of Pieter's Hill, which, at least at first, was only weakly held by the Boers. The line of hills was reached without many casualties; the Scots Fusiliers on the right and the Irish Fusiliers on the left lay down to engage in the fire-fight, while the Dublin Fusiliers were held back in reserve behind the centre. The fire-

LANGVERWACHT SPRUIT.   PIETER'S HILL.   RAILWAY BRIDGE.

PIETER'S HILL FROM THE SOUTH-WEST.

To face p. 278.

fight now became hotter for the Boers, whose front had not been engaged, received re-inforcements from the right. As Kitchener's Column was only at this period beginning to cross the river, the Boers on Railway Hill directed their fire on the left flank of the Irish Fusiliers which was in the low ground separating the railway from Pieter's Hill.

General Barton determined to capture Pieter's Hill by an impetuous assault before the Enemy on it should be able to receive further reinforcements. While the Scots Fusiliers, who were favoured by the hilly ground, advanced without suffering much loss, the Irish Fusiliers, whose left flank as they advanced was under heavy fire, soon had to swing off against the Boers on Railway Hill, and so left a wide gap between the two Battalions, which was filled up by the Dublin Fusiliers. They and the Scots Fusiliers succeeded in laying hold of the southern edge of the top of Pieter's Hill, which meanwhile had been evacuated by the Boers after a weak resistance. Now it was seen that the more difficult task of attacking the Boers entrenched on the northern edge, across the 500 yards of level ground which forms the plateau of the hill, had still to be accomplished. The fire-fight developed such intensity that the Dublin and Scots Fusiliers had, as time went on, to place all their supports and reserves in the firing-line. As reinforcements reached the Boers they prolonged their firing-line to the left so that the unsupported right flank of the Scots Fusiliers was also brought under flanking fire. The situation of the Battalions was serious; for several hours they had borne the brunt of the fighting without any support, and their powers of resistance were nearly giving out, especially as the Enemy's Guns now joined in the action, and, in spite of the superior force of the British Artillery, directed their fire on Barton's Infantry. Kitchener's Column, on the advance of which was based the hope of early relief from the pressure which was constantly becoming more severe, had not even yet appeared on the scene. Thus it came about that in this very part of the field, where the decisive stroke was to be delivered, no sort of progress could be made.

At last—it was already 4 p.m.—the anxiously-awaited advance of Kitchener's Column made itself felt on Pieter's Hill. The South Lancashires and the York and Lancasters, which formed part of the Column, had crossed the pontoon bridge in rear of Barton's Column, and they waited on the northern bank for the arrival of the two other Battalions of the Column, the West Yorks and King's Own, which had been in Hart's Hollow. Then, like Barton's Battalions, they moved to the right in file along the narrow ground in the river-bed in the order: West Yorks, South Lancashire, King's Own, York and Lancaster. As soon as the head of the Column reached the ravine-shaped and deep-cut valley of Krüger's Spruit it halted in the bed of the river and waited for Buller's order to attack.

When Buller recognized the difficulties of the situation in which Barton's Troops found themselves, he sent Kitchener the order to attack Railway Hill and the Battalions were extended for this under cover. The West Yorks and the King's Own in first line were to advance with their outer flanks on Krüger's and Hart's Spruits, while the South Lancashires and the York and Lancasters were to follow in support. The West Yorks also received special instructions to attempt to surprise the left flank of the Boers on Railway Hill by an attack following on its advance up the deep-cut valley of Krüger's Spruit.

At first all went well with the advance in the broken and hilly ground, and there were but few and unimportant casualties. But when the Battalions got on to the open ground on the further side of the railway they came under heavy fire and were forced to halt and reply to it. In this case, too, a large gap had been created during the advance between the inner flanks of the leading Battalions, and the South Lancashires now came forward to fill it. The West Yorks found very good cover in the valley of Krüger's Spruit, and, in accordance with their instructions, tried to get unobserved on to the flank of the Boers whose attention and powers were completely absorbed in the fighting in their front which was growing in violence every minute; no measures had been taken for keeping a look-out on their flanks during the action.

The efforts of the British troops engaged in the frontal attack, to push it home by crawling and rushing forward in turn, had met with but little success. Nor had they succeeded in reducing the Enemy's fire; on the contrary it was constantly becoming stronger and casualties were becoming more frequent; finally, the last Battalion, the York and Lancasters, till now held back in reserve, had to be thrown into the fight in this part of the field too.

Meanwhile the hour was 5.30 p.m., and it almost seemed as if this attack would be as barren of results as the others. Colonel Kitchener asked for support from Norcott's Brigade which had arrived and had formed up in Hart's Hollow while the action had been going on. It had opened a fire-fight with the Boers on Hart's Hill and was impatiently awaiting Buller's order to attack. In reply to Kitchener's request Norcott sent a half-battalion each from the East Surreys and Scottish Rifles.

But they had not yet reached the scene of action at Railway Hill when an unlooked-for event occurred there which suddenly changed the whole situation in favour of the British. The West Yorks had succeeded in climbing up the valley of Krüger's Spruit unnoticed by the Boers, whose left flank on Railway Hill they suddenly approached before any warning whatever could be given. This gave the Burghers such a fright that most of them immediately abandoned all further attempt at resistance without even making an effort to drive the Enemy back again, which under the circumstances, however, would have been an easy matter. But at this moment such a leader as was required was not forthcoming here at the focus of events. As has been mentioned, General Botha had remained on the right flank out of consideration for Lucas Meyer who, however, was paying no sort of attention to what was going on. When the battle was raging its wildest he was sitting in his tent in the rear smoking his pipe quite peaceably. Still he did try to get some reinforcements, but it was too late, and without them his authority would have been insufficient to induce the Burghers to stand fast. They gave way first of all on Railway Hill, then those on Hart's Hill followed the example, and soon afterwards those north of the Langverwacht fell back too. Only a few gallant-hearted men tarried in the positions.

When Kitchener's Battalions which were in the front line noticed the cessation of the fire from the top of Railway Hill they fixed bayonets and charged. By Warren's order Norcott's Battalions joined in this charge on the left and dashed up Hart's Hill. When the Troops reached the tops of the Hills not a Boer was to be seen; they had avoided contact with the assault in hasty flight towards the Onderbrook Hill. The hills between Krüger's and Langverwacht Hills were found to be in possession of the British, and so the Boer centre was pierced.

But the Boers on Pieter's Hill and south of the Langverwacht still held on to their positions as strongly as ever. From early morning a fire-fight had been going on south of the Langverwacht, in which neither adversary had so far succeeded in getting the upper hand. When General Botha heard of the mishap in the centre he considered the whole position untenable, especially as no reserves whatever were available to re-capture the positions which had been abandoned. He therefore determined to retire on to the line Onderbrook Hill-Bulwana Hill, and first of all to withdraw the Burghers from his menaced right flank. The positions on the left flank at Pieter's Hill were maintained till darkness fell and so the line of retreat to Ladysmith remained open. The retirement of the Boers was not interfered with and was carried out in perfect order, for the British did not make the slightest effort to pursue. They contented themselves for the rest of the day in taking up the positions which had been abandoned by the Boers and in there re-organising their Units.

The attack had taken quite a different course from that which had been intended, for the plan was to envelope the Enemy's left wing so as to roll the position up from East to West. But the same mistake was made as at Monte Christo; instead of beginning by establishing the largest possible force to attack the Enemy's front, the flank attack was that which opened the proceedings. This, however, as events proved, did not fulfil its purpose: the troops taking part in it did not follow the valley of Pieter's Spruit which furnished a favourable approach to the Enemy's flank, and so struck straight against the front of his left wing, which the Boers, not being tied down all along the line, could continually reinforce with the result that in due course it threatened in turn to envelope the British right wing. But in spite of this the success might have been made complete had the action of the troops which pierced the centre been more effective, and had the Cavalry been employed more judiciously. If Kitchener's and Norcott's Columns after taking Railway and Hart's Hills had immediately wheeled to the right and left against the rear of the Boers who were still holding on to Pieter's and Wynne's Hills, and if the Mounted Brigades had been more judiciously employed, the Boers, particularly those on their right wing, could never have got away unmolested.

During the whole day the Mounted Brigades had remained almost idle on the southern bank. When their Commander, Dundonald, wanted to take them over the pontoon bridge in the evening which closed the fight, that they might take up the pursuit of the Boers, Buller held him back because he thought it was already too late, and that there was small prospect of obtaining any advantage in an advance by night in the rough and difficult country between the Tugela and the Klip River. If, however, these Brigades had, early on the morning of the 27th, crossed the river unobserved anywhere lower down, they would have been on the rear of the Boers in ample time to harass their retreat and to convert their mishap into a severe defeat. How much this was in the minds of the Boers themselves is quite clear from an observation recorded by Major Freiherr von Reitzenstein on the evening of this day: . . . . "If the British Cavalry and Horse Artillery had been in their proper places to-day they could have gained a great success. A couple of shrapnel would have produced a panic, and the result would have been a great Boer defeat. Instead of this, everything went off smoothly, and one only sees faces as contented as if a battle had been won. The homeward movement appears to be welcome to most of them. They have not yet clearly grasped that the Relief of Ladysmith is bound to ensue to-morrow."

After General Botha had made all the arrangements for the withdrawal of the right wing, a Council of War was summoned with all speed, and the question of further resistance on the line Onderbrook Hill-Bulwana Hill was then discussed. Although Botha was in favour of it, the general opinion of the other leaders, that the Burghers' powers of resistance were by now so reduced that any fresh stand south of Ladysmith would have little prospect of success, gained the day. It was therefore decided to continue the retirement towards Ladysmith in two groups, over the northern slopes of the Onderbrook Hill and along the main road, under the protection of small rear-guards, that very night.

About 8 p.m. firing ceased along the whole line. The British Troops went into bivouacs on the positions they had taken.

The Boers continued their retirement throughout the night, General Botha being charged with ensuring its safety from molestation. Early on the 28th he got into position again on Bulwana, north of the Klip, with several Commandos and some guns, while the main body continued to withdraw on to Ladysmith in the hope that they would there be backed up by the Troops investing that place. But General Joubert had ordered the raising of the Siege as early as midday 27th when he received the first news of the loss of the positions on the Tugela, and during the night 27th-28th he had actually marched off northwards with most of his Commandos. When the Boers withdrawing from the Tugela heard of this, such a state of alarm set in among them that their hitherto well-conducted retirement suddenly degenerated into a wild helter-skelter flight. Fearing that the Garrison of Ladysmith would be able to cut off the retreat, everybody hurried off northwards as quickly as possible, and even the wagons were abandoned. As a matter of fact, however, the capacity for action and the will-power of the Garrison were so reduced that no attempt was made to cut off the Boer retreat until too late. Unmolested by their adversaries, the Transvaal Boers continued their retreat along the Dundee and Newcàstle Road on the 28th, while the Free Staters on the same day drew off westwards towards the Drakensberg and hurried to the defence of their Capital, Bloemfontein, which was threatened by Lord Roberts' advance. There was ample time to entrain the heavy siege guns at

Modderspruit railway station; the last train did not leave there till the 1st March, and the railway bridge was blown up when it had crossed.

Early on the 28th Buller allowed the two Mounted Brigades to move forward in pursuit. If they had pressed on energetically they would still have found opportunities to make good the omissions of the previous day, for it was only during the 28th that the ranks of the Boers dissolved in flight. But when the Brigades found themselves confronted by Botha's rear-guard on Bulwana, they came to a dead halt and did not even attempt, by working round to the right or left, to cross the Klip River and strike on to the flanks of the retreating Boers. In the afternoon they carefully followed up Botha's rearguard when it retired, and in the evening they reached Ladysmith. The rest of the British Army spent the forenoon in clearing up the Battlefield, and in the evening moved on as far as Nelthorpe.

On the following day, 1st March, Buller started from Nelthorpe to make his triumphal entry into Ladysmith, where he was joyously welcomed by those now liberated after four months of investment. The Natal Army went into camp on the hills west of the town.

After a struggle extending over almost three months the goal had been reached and Ladysmith had been relieved, true though it is that the Boers had never been decisively beaten. The success which had been finally gained bore no proportion to the stakes hazarded and lost. The four attempts at the Relief had cost the Natal Army altogether more than 5,000 men.*

In his anxiety to avoid heavy losses Buller had, on almost every occasion, broken off an action as soon as it began to be costly in lives, and so these actions and the

---

* See Appendix III.

smaller fights which had occurred during the two months' operations, though not a single one of them was attended with really heavy casualties had, taken all together, certainly caused far more sacrifices than would have been caused by one single big battle fought out energetically to its bitter end, regardless of consequences; such a battle would naturally have cost many lives, but it would have promptly produced decisive results. There is no doubt that the moral value of the Troops was reduced by these half-decided contests and frequently vain sacrifices. In war some sacrifices must be made and the anxiety of Commanders to curtail their Casualty List will only increase the number.

After White's release the Natal Army began to enjoy some time of repose which was as much needed by the Relief Force as by the terribly exhausted Garrison of Ladysmith, for the recovery of their fitness for action. White's troops joined Buller's Army as the Fourth Division which was placed under Lyttelton's Command. White himself proceeded to Cape Town.

In order to make things as comfortable as possible for the troops by giving them better accommodation, Buller spread his Army over a widely-extended area bordered on the north by the line Elandslaagte-Walkers Hoek, and on the south by the Tugela.

Buller himself thought that after giving the Natal Army three weeks rest he would employ the bulk of it under his own orders in moving over the Drakensberg in the direction of Harrismith and effecting a junction with the Principal Army, while a part should undertake the clearance of Northern Natal. Lord Roberts on the other hand thought that it would be impossible for the Natal Army to push its way through the solid barrier of the Drakensberg, and therefore wished to have its further advance postponed until his own progress with the Principal Army should bring about the opening of the passes without fighting. Consequently the pause in the operations of the Natal Army was prolonged till the beginning of May, for not till about then did the Principal Army under Lord Roberts start from Bloemfontein on its march to Pretoria.

Meanwhile the Headquarters of the Army ordered the formation of a fresh Division—the Tenth—under General Hunter, out of the unallotted Infantry Brigades.

The Boers, in strength about 6,000 men, took up positions in the Biggarsberg, at first under Command of Louis Botha and later of Christian Botha. They only disturbed the repose of the British on one occasion, when they made a surprise-attack on Clery's Division in its Camp near Elandslaagte, from which, however, no results were gained. Events in the Free State caused the Boers to send away many men thither about the middle of April, with the result that there was perfect calm in the Natal Theatre of Operations until the beginning of May.

SURVEY OF THE EVENTS DURING THE SUMMER OF 1900.*

---

* The battles of this period furnish in their details but little instruction of tactical value. The narrative is therefore limited to a general description of the operations.

PART I.

THE OPERATIONS IN THE SOUTH-EAST OF THE FREE STATE.

CHAPTER IX.

Preparing for Further Advance.

A continuance of offensive operations immediately after Lord Roberts had entered Bloemfontein on 13th March, 1900,* was no doubt most desirable on military as well as on political grounds; but it was quite impracticable in view of the prevailing insecurity of the situation in rear of the Army, especially in the southern part of the Free State, of the condition to which the Troops† had been reduced in their rapid advance through hostile country and of the great difficulties which existed in connection with supply. The outbreak of an epidemic of typhoid fever in Bloemfontein made the British situation the more serious.

Reports of the incapacity of the British Army to show much activity in the Field for the present, soon spread about among the Boers, whose drooping spirits were in consequence revived afresh. The internal dissolution

---

* p. 40.   † p. 43.

which had seized on their ranks* gave place to a more confident frame of mind, and about the end of March several thousand men belonging to Commandos which had been on furlough, began to assemble between Brandfort and Thaba Nchu under Christian de Wet and Delarey. From this quarter it was an easy matter for them to operate against the flanks and rear of the British and to destroy the only available railway, viz., that from Springfield to Bloemfontein. The energetic Christian de Wet therefore decided, by means of such enterprises, to turn the temporarily precarious situation of the British to the profit of the Boers. On the 31st March he succeeded in surprising and defeating with much loss General Broadwood's† Column which had been pushed out to Thaba Nchu and Sannah's Post for the protection of the waterworks in that neighbourhood. The capture of the Waterworks by the Boers cut off the supply of good water from the British Troops, who consequently suffered all the more from the typhoid epidemic.

Only three days after this stroke of luck the same de Wet surprised and captured a British Battalion (Irish Rifles) and a detachment of Mounted Infantry near Reddersburg. Soon after that, however, an attempt to prepare a like fate near Wepener for a detachment of Colonial Troops under Colonel Dalgety,‡ failed to meet with similar success; after several attacks had been repulsed, de Wet had to content himself with investing with one part of his force the British detachment at Wepener and taking up with the remainder a strong position near Dewetsdorp for the protection of the investment against an advance which threatened it from the west.

---

* pp. 40, 41.
† One Cavalry Brigade, a detachment Mounted Infantry, and two Batteries R.H.A.
‡ About 1,600 men, who had been pushed forward to Wepener from the Colonial Division then at Aliwal North under General Brabant.

At the British Headquarters it was perfectly well recognised that the resumption of operations towards Pretoria could not be thought of until the rear of the Army had been rendered secure, and large masses of troops were therefore assembled to clear the eastern and south-eastern portion of the Free State and to protect the railway from the danger which threatened it. The Eighth Division, which had just arrived from England, under General Rundle, and Hart's Brigade which had been detached from the Tenth Division just brought round from Natal, were to be employed for this purpose.

Rundle's Division joined, at Edenburg, General Gatacre's Troops which had advanced thus far from Bethulie *viâ* Springfontein, and which, having been brought up, by the addition of several Militia Battalions, to the strength of a Division, were now under the command of General Chermside, who had taken the place of General Gatacre, recalled. General Hart's Brigade joined the remainder of the Colonial Division under General Brabant at Aliwal North. The newly-formed Eleventh Division,* two Brigades of Cavalry and a Brigade of Mounted Infantry were at the same time sent from Bloemfontein to Dewetsdorp under the command of General French, to make a concerted movement with the Third and Eighth Divisions against the Boers under de Wet (whose strength was daily increasing and whose numbers were already estimated at from 8,000 to 10,000 men), and to relieve Colonel Dalgety at Wepener.

At the same time, too, General Ian Hamilton was sent with the Nineteenth Brigade of the Ninth Division and a

---

* This was formed out of the Guards' Brigade and the Eighteenth (Stephenson's) Brigade, which was detached from the Sixth Division. The Sixth Division was then completed by General Clements' Troops, which had advanced from Norval's Pont through the western part of the Orange Free State, and which had reached Bloemfontein about the beginning of April.

strong force of Mounted Infantry towards Thaba Nchu to disperse the Boers there and to re-occupy the waterworks near Sannah's Post.

The Third and Eighth Divisions, which formed a part of the Relief Columns, proceeded to attack de Wet's very extended position at Dewetsdorp on the 20th and 21st April without waiting for French to join in the operations; their attack was unsuccessful, and the Boers delivering a counterstroke on their right flank, they were in a somewhat serious plight, from which they were only released on the 23rd by General French's Column which hurried up from Bloemfontein. Hart's and Brabant's Columns advancing *via* Rouxville had encountered a Boer force pushed out to meet them at Bushman's Kop on the 21st; they certainly were successful in driving the Boers out of this position, but the gallant resistance which they encountered checked their further advance towards Wepener.

De Wet, however, after having invested Dalgety's Force for sixteen days, had to give way before the overwhelming superiority of the British on the 25th April, and retired northwards with all his Commandos in the direction of Ladybrand and Thaba Nchu. Between these two places, in the mountainous country which was favourable to the Boers' fighting methods, he took up a new and a strong position. Of the British Forces which had been assembled near Wepener, the Eleventh Division was kept back at Bloemfontein and the Third Division at Edenburg for the protection of the railway, while the Eighth Division and two Brigades of Cavalry co-operated with the Colonial Troops under General Brabant in following the Enemy northwards in order to join with General Hamilton's Troops (which had remained west of Thaba Nchu after re-occupying the waterworks) in driving the Boers north of the line Ladybrand-Thaba Nchu. In pursuance of this plan a series of actions was fought during the last few days of April in the neighbourhood of Thaba Nchu and Hout Nek, which resulted in the Boers being forced to evacuate their strong positions and to retire into the country north of Thaba Nchu. Hart's Brigade was railed round to Kimberley, and there rejoined its own Division, which, in co-operation with Methuen's Division, was to disperse the Boers still investing Mafeking, and to effect the Relief of that place.

In the beginning of May the south-eastern part of the Orange Free State was also in the undisputed possession of the British, and by this time the Army, having been reinforced* and abundantly remounted, as well as having received from the Base plenty of Commissariat and other Supplies, was once more fit to take the Field, and attention could be turned towards making an offensive movement on Pretoria. By their bold action in pushing forward under de Wet into the south-eastern portion of the Orange Free State, the Boers had placed themselves in a situation more desperately critical than any which the British could possibly have sought to contrive for them, and had this opportunity been more resolutely turned to advantage, it would have been quite possible to cut off the retreat to the North of the by no means small and still increasing Boer Forces and to deal them a blow which should annihilate them. If the concentric advance of the various Columns of relief arriving from the South and from the North had only been directed with better appreciation of the requirements of the situation towards ensuring more concerted action, it must have resulted either in de Wet's being surrounded or in his being forced to cross into Basutoland, where the

---

* The following reinforcements had arrived from England, viz.: the Eighth Division (of which mention has already been made), a Brigade of Cavalry with two Batteries R.H.A. Thus French's Cavalry Division from this time onward was composed of four Brigades; moreover the Mounted Infantry had also been considerably increased in strength.

Natives were hostile to the Boers. The fate of the 1,600 Colonial Troops invested at Wepener, even if matters came to their worst, and if they had to lay down their arms, was of no importance whatever in comparison with the attainment of such a success. If de Wet had been wiped out, the revival of the Enemy's resistance would have been smothered from the very first, and the two Republics would have lain practically defenceless before the British. But as it was, the various Columns, hurriedly despatched one after another to relieve the small number of Troops shut up in Wepener, were employed as they came to hand in making this single effort, and that moreover with no sort of co-ordinated direction to ensure their working in concert. The result was that de Wet succeeded in getting away to the North unmolested. There is no doubt that the British Commander here let slip a favourable opportunity for bringing the War to a rapid conclusion. Later on, in the course of the War, the frequent attempts by the British to round up the Boers, although more skilfully planned, could hardly ever be brought to a successful issue, for the Boers never fought again in forces of any great size; they never came on the scene except in quite small, dispersed parties, and consequently they generally succeeded in slipping unobserved through the British lines by night.

PART II.

THE MARCH ON PRETORIA.

CHAPTER X.

The Advance of Lord Roberts and Sir R. Buller.

At the beginning of May the opposing Forces were disposed as follows:—

The British were distributed in three groups over an area of which the breadth, fronting the Boers, was about 375 miles; Buller was on the right flank in Natal with about 35,000 men and 100 guns near Ladysmith, Lord Roberts was in the centre in the Orange Free State with about 65,000 men and 210 guns in and around Bloemfontein; Lord Methuen and General Hunter were on the left flank in the western portion of Cape Colony, with about 20,000 men and 68 guns in the area—Kimberley, Boshof, Warrenton. Mafeking had not yet been relieved. The total strength of the British Forces amounted at this time, in round numbers, to 200,000 men, including 55,000 in Garrisons and on the Lines of Communication, and 23,000 sick in the Hospitals.

The Boers also were formed in three groups: between Warrenton and Hoopstad about 6,000 Boers under Hoofd Commandant Wessels were in front of Lord Methuen; in the centre there were about 8,000 men under Delarey and Christian de Wet near Brandfort and Thaba Nchu, and also some 7,000 Boers still in process of assembly near Kroonstad. The chief command of these Forces was in the hands of Louis Botha, who had been appointed Commandant-General of all the Boers still in the Field, in the place of General Joubert deceased.

In Natal about 6,000 Boers under Christian Botha closed the Biggarsberg, while some 2,000 men under Fourie guarded the Drakensberg.

Early in May the advance northward was begun by all the three groups of British troops. The next objective of the Operations was to be the occupation of Pretoria, the capital of the Transvaal.

The Troops in the centre, under the personal command of Lord Roberts, were the first to advance. They started on the 3rd May from the neighbourhood of Thaba Nchu and Bloemfontein in two columns, which roughly followed the general direction of the Pretoria Railway. The right Column, commanded by General Ian Hamilton, consisted of three Brigades of Infantry, one Brigade each of Cavalry and Mounted Infantry, and the Artillery allotted to these Formations, making a total of 18,000 men and 48 guns; the left Column, under Lord Roberts, consisted of two Divisions of Infantry, a Brigade of Mounted Infantry, and the Artillery allotted to them, a total of about 20,000 men and 78 guns. French's Cavalry Division, with a mounted strength of 3,400 and with 18 guns, was not quite ready to march; it did not follow on till the 6th May, when it proceeded to take post on the left flank. For the protection of the Communications in rear of the Army, the Eighth Division was left near Thaba Nchu, the Sixth Division in Bloemfontein, and the Third Division on the Railway Line between Springfontein and Bloemfontein in the neighbourhood of Edenburg.

The Boers near Brandfort and Thaba Nchu retired behind the Sand River after making only a small show of resistance. The British Army, marching *viâ* Winburg and Smaldeel, reached the southern bank of the river on the 9th May, the right Column being then at Boomplats, the centre Column at Merriesfontein, while the Cavalry Division, which had joined the previous day, and which now formed the left Column, was at Vermeulen's Kraal. The Boers were on the northern bank of the river, in position on both sides of the Bloemfontein-Kroonstad Railway.

Lord Roberts advanced to the attack on the 10th May. While the centre column, which deployed a rather weak force of Infantry, but which had with it the whole of the Artillery, fought a holding action in its front, Hamilton's and French's Columns pushed forward on both flanks and tried to envelop the Boer position. As this position was very extended, the Boers were unable to dispose of force in sufficient depth to deal with the enveloping column: consequently they had no alternative but to withdraw and so to extricate themselves from the grip which threatened to encircle them. As a consequence of their own mobility and in the absence of an energetic frontal attack they had no difficulty in quickly disengaging themselves from the action which had been begun.

In this, as in most of the subsequent actions, was exemplified the frequently adopted plan of holding the Enemy in front while an enveloping movement was in progress. The object in view was to cause the Enemy to evacuate his positions merely as a consequence of a threat on his flanks and rear—a procedure which, though it tended to the reduction of the "butcher's bill," could never culminate in the delivery of a knock-down blow.

After destroying the Railway Bridge the Boers withdrew *viâ* Kroonstad across the Vaal, that they might there resist afresh the advance of the British, who, following them up, occupied Kroonstad on the 12th May without opposition. At this point the necessities of Supply imposed a halt of ten days on the Army.

Meanwhile Buller had also resumed the offensive with the right wing " in order to attract to himself the attention of the Boers in the Biggarsberg," and to tie them down as much as possible in Natal. The provision of support to the advance of the centre group towards Pretoria was thus indirectly aimed at.

To cope with Buller, the Free Staters had occupied the passes of the Drakensberg, while the Transvaalers had entrenched themselves strongly from the Ladysmith-Newcastle road as far eastward as Helpmakaar, on the routes which lead over the extremely difficult Biggarsberg range.

Till the 7th May Buller was concentrating the Natal Army* in the country north of Ladysmith. Leaving two Divisions in front of the Biggarsberg, he then marched to the right with one Division and his Mounted Troops on Helpmakaar; advancing from the south-east, he attacked the Boers who were posted there on the 13th May, and after a weakly-contested engagement drove them back towards Dundee. In the course of the 14th and 15th the Boers evacuated all their positions in the Biggarsberg, and drew back into the northernmost portion of Natal. Buller followed them without delay, and concentrated his Army again on the 18th in the neighbourhood of Newcastle. The Cavalry advanced on the 19th towards Laing's Nek and acquired information that the country as far as the Nek was free of the Enemy, but that the pass itself was still held by strong Boer forces. Within ten days, and without any serious fighting, the Boers had been cleared

---

* Three Divisions and a Brigade each of Cavalry and Mounted Infantry.

out of Northern Natal which was thus once more in British occupation.

Buller temporarily delayed his further advance on account of the necessities of Supply, and, moreover, received orders from Lord Roberts to postpone his attack on the heights near the pass until the centre group should have occupied Johannesburg.

In the westernmost theatre of operations, after Kimberley had been relieved, Lord Methuen had been charged with the task of clearing the Boers out of the country between the Vaal and the Modder, and of completely mastering it. Early in April, after encountering a gallant resistance in a fight near Boshof, at the close of which the French Colonel Villebois Mareuil Commanding the Boer Forces engaged lost his life, he succeeded in partly dispersing and partly making prisoners of a strong detachment of the Enemy, of which foreign volunteers formed the large majority.

After the arrival of the Tenth Division (Hunter's), Lord Methuen remained near Boshof with two Brigades, while Hunter with two Brigades was near Warrenton. On the 5th May, after a severe engagement with a strong party of Boers at Warrenton, Hunter forced the passage of the Vaal there and reached Fourteen Streams. By Lord Roberts' order, a Flying Column of about 1,100 Mounted Infantrymen with four guns was despatched from Fourteen Streams under Colonel Mahon for the hasty Relief of Mafeking. While this Column, working along the west of the Railway, endeavoured to reach Mafeking without coming into contact with the Enemy, General Hunter went on after the Boers whom he had put to flight, and, having reached Christiania, he too directed his march towards Mafeking along the Railway. Small parties of Boers tried once or twice to stand in Mahon's way near Vryburg and on the Maritsani, but he managed to brush them aside without much loss of time, and, by co-operating with

Plumer's Force, succeeded in relieving Mafeking on the 18th May, when it had withstood the Siege for seven months. This event split up and had a very dispiriting effect on the Boers engaged in this part of the Theatre of War, and Commandant Du Toit only succeeded in rallying from 2,000 to 3,000 near Klerksdorp; the bulk of them made for their homes.

General Hunter, advancing with his Column *viâ* Vryburg and Doorn Bult, and meeting with no resistance, reached Lichtenberg on the 1st June. Meanwhile, on the 14th May, Lord Methuen had begun his forward movement from Boshof, *viâ* Hoopstad, on Bothasville, that he might co-operate with Lord Roberts' Army in its march into the Transvaal. But this intention had to be given up subsequently, as the protection of the communications in rear of the Main Column during its advance on Pretoria necessitated the employment of Methuen's Division near Kroonstad.

During its ten-day halt at the last-named place the Main Army had thoroughly repaired the Bloemfontein-Kroonstad railway, which had been seriously damaged by the Boers, and which was essential for the bringing forward of all requirements. The advance on Pretoria was accordingly begun again on the 22nd May, on the 23rd the Rhenoster was crossed without opposition, and on the 24th the Troops had reached the neighbourhood of Vredefort Road Station.

Intelligence having come to hand that President Steyn and the members of the Orange Free State Government were to be found at Lindley, General Hamilton had been sent there as early as the 15th May with orders to make a surprise attack and capture the President and the members of his Government. The enterprise, however, failed, Steyn escaping to Heilbronn and thence taking flight to the Transvaal. Hamilton marched his troops in pursuit as far as Heilbronn, and did not recover connection with the Main Column till the 24th. Only the Ninth Division and the Highland Brigade were left at Heilbronn for the protection of the Railway in that district.

On the 24th May, the Queen's Birthday, Lord Roberts issued a proclamation to the inhabitants of the Orange Free State, in which he announced with all formality the annexation of the country by Great Britain, and that this, the youngest of the British Possessions, would henceforth bear the name of "The Orange River Colony."

During the subsequent movement towards the Vaal, Hamilton's Column, which had been brought across the railway from the right to the left bank on the 25th, crossed the river at Lindeque's Drift on the 26th, and advanced towards the Riet, while the Main Column under Roberts did not finish its passage of the river at Viljoen's Drift till the 27th. French's Cavalry Division had crossed the river at Parys as early as the 24th.

The Boers under Botha had planned an obstinate resistance on the northern bank east of the railway, but they abandoned their positions without fighting when they saw that their right flank was threatened by French's Cavalry Division and by Hamilton's Division, the transfer of which to the west of the railway had been concealed from them. Their Forces now separated, the Transvaalers under Louis Botha retiring on Johannesburg, while the Free Staters under de Wet were desirous of remaining in their own country, that they might carry on minor operations in the rear of the British.

As de Wet expressed it, "It was clear that owing to Cronje's surrender and the desertion of many Burghers, the 45,000 men with whom we had begun the war had been reduced by a third of the number, and that we could no longer think of employing Artillery against the British. We had to pit our Force, thus reduced, against an Army of

240,000 men with from 300 to 400 guns. . . . We had, therefore, to examine where it was possible for us to score an advantage, and failing such a possibility, to make a bolt of it." De Wet, with his Free Staters, moved into the Heilbronn and Lindley districts, where he saw a chance of operating against the rear of the British.

Having crossed the Vaal, Lord Roberts continued his forward movement on Johannesburg. The Boers in strong positions on the west and east of the town, at Doornkop and Germiston, awaited the attack of the British.

On the 29th Lord Roberts, with the Main Column, attacked the Enemy east of Johannesburg, while Hamilton moved against the Boer position at Doornkop. The Cavalry Division had moved out in a north-westerly direction, in order to get round the right flank of the Boers. No decisive issue was arrived at in the front on this day, and it was not till the night of the 30th—31st, when the Boers saw that their rear and flanks were threatened by the Cavalry Division, which had meantime arrived at Florida, that they abandoned their positions and retired on Pretoria. Lord Roberts immediately invested Johannesburg, and early on the 31st the town was surrendered. On the 1st and 2nd June the Army rested in the vicinity of Johannesburg.

Meanwhile, very disquieting news came to hand from the Orange River Colony: the Free State Boers who had remained in the Field there were scattered about in numerous small Commandos in the quadrilateral of Heilbronn—Lindley—Bethlehem—Senekal, whence they initiated a series of small operations in the rear of the British, and especially against their single Line of Supply, the Bloemfontein-Kroonstad railway. On the 29th May, Piet de Wet, a brother of Christian de Wet, succeeded in surrounding and in four days compelling the surrender of the Irish Yeomanry who were on the march from Ventersburg, *viâ*

Lindley, to Heilbronn, to reinforce the Ninth Division posted there. The efforts of the First and Eighth Divisions, which hurried up to the rescue from the vicinity of Kroonstad and Senekal were in vain : the former arrived too late, while the Eighth Division, which was represented only by a weak detachment, was driven back again. On the 2nd June the First Division drove the Boers out of Lindley and occupied that town.

Immediately after this, Christian de Wet inflicted another blow on the British Lines of Communication. On the 3rd June a large British Supply Park, under escort of two Companies of Highlanders on the march from Rhenoster Station to Heilbronn, was surrounded and captured by a part of de Wet's Commando : the men surrendered.

Under the influence of the disturbing news from the Orange River Colony, an opinion began to spread at the Headquarters of the Army that the forward movement should be postponed for the moment, and that all the Force should be employed to crush the Boers in the rear, so that the railway to Pretoria might be made thoroughly secure once and for all. The British were at that period about 1,000 miles away from their Base of Operations, and they were deep in the heart of a hostile country in a district which was poorly cultivated and deficient in routes for communication, and where nothing but a few head of cattle and some grass could be found by way of subsistence. They were consequently obliged to rely for all their supplies of every kind on the railway, the security of which was therefore a matter of life or death to them. But this precarious state of affairs did not distract Lord Roberts, who determinedly stuck with all his energy to the objective which he had originally selected for his operations, the capture of Pretoria.

If the advance had been postponed, the Transvaalers, who formed the strongest assembled Force remaining in the Field, but who had already begun to show signs of disorganisation, would have had time to rally afresh for further resistance and to construct works of defence.

Consequently, the Army resumed the advance on Pretoria on the 3rd June. The Capital was reached on the 5th June, after some Boers lying in wait strongly entrenched at Six Mile Spruit to make another effort at resistance had been forced, after a short fight, to withdraw, under the now conventional menace of their flanks. There then ensued the unconditional and unopposed surrender of Pretoria, into which Lord Roberts made his triumphal entry on the afternoon of the 5th June.

The Boers, quite taken aback by the rapid advance of the British, had begun their retreat eastwards in such haste that they had been perforce obliged to abandon their wives and families, as well as the greater part of the British Prisoners of War who were in the town, altogether 158 officers, 3,029 men. Only about 1,000 prisoners could be railed off to Middelburg; all the rest regained their freedom.

In four weeks, inclusive of a ten-days' halt at Kroonstad, Lord Roberts' Troops had covered nearly 320 miles, under great difficulties as regards supplies, in a country which was deficient in water, in roads and in cultivation, and where the communications with the rear were in a most insecure condition. This was a performance which furnishes a striking and eloquent proof of the energy of the Chief Command and of the devotion and endurance of the Troops, and which must ever remain remarkable in the History of War.

The Boers occupied and strongly entrenched a widely-extended position near Diamond Hill, about 15 miles east of Pretoria, and Lord Roberts having determined to drive them away at once from such dangerous proximity to Pretoria, moved out to the attack on the 11th June in

x

three Columns. The right and left Columns, under Hamilton and French, were to envelop the Boer position on the south and the north, while the Eleventh Division, under Pole-Carew, forming the centre Column, was to hold the Enemy in the front. But the Boers recognised this frequently-employed manœuvre in ample time, and making a fresh front against the outflanking Columns, endeavoured in their turn to outflank the British. The fight went on for two days with varying success, but never came to anything serious at close quarters, except on the right flank, in front of Hamilton's Column, where the Boers made a determined onslaught against a Battery of Horse Artillery, but where the loss of the guns was obviated at the last moment by a dashing and vigorous charge by the 12th Lancers. The Composite Regiment of Household Cavalry also charged home successfully on the Bethlehem Commando. But still the British had not succeeded, even on the second day, in driving the Boers out of their positions, far less in inflicting a decisive defeat on them, and it was not till the night of 12th-13th June that the receipt of a false report of the movement of a strong Force of British against his rear, induced Botha to give the order for a retirement to Middelburg. The British made a feeble attempt at pursuit, but marched back to Pretoria again on the 14th June.

Fresh, and still disquieting, news about the state of affairs in the Free State had also come to hand there. De Wet had succeeded in holding up various railway trains conveying supplies, and even in capturing another whole Battalion on the 7th June.

Before a resumption of operations against Botha in the Middelburg-Koomati Poort direction could be thought of, it was urgently necessary to ensure the security of the rear of the Army. For unexpected trouble had broken out, not only in the Orange Free State, but also in the western portion of the Transvaal, in the Lichtenburg and Rustenburg District, where the Burghers who had returned to their farms were streaming back in large numbers to the Commandos forming under General Delarey, and were threatening the weak British Garrisons. The enormous extent of the Theatre of War and the irregular warfare which had broken out and which was increasing in violence in the rear of the Army, presented far graver difficulties to be overcome by those directing the British operations than the defeat of the organised Boer Forces still in the Field.

PART III.

THE OPERATIONS NORTH-WEST AND SOUTH-WEST OF PRETORIA.

---o---

CHAPTER XI.

DE WET'S MOVEMENTS.

Lord Roberts decided to begin by restoring the superiority of the British Forces in the north-west of the Transvaal, and then to turn against de Wet with all the force at his disposal. The first of these purposes was effected without much trouble. The Boers retired northwards from the whole area without offering serious resistance to Baden-Powell's, Plumer's and Mahon's Columns, which advanced against them from Mafeking towards Rustenburg. Hunter, who had turned towards the south-east from Lichtenburg, found the neighbourhood of Potchefstroom clear of the Enemy. Wessels' Commandos which had retired in that direction had apparently dispersed. It was therefore believed at the British Headquarters that the occupation of Rustenburg by 1500 men under Baden-Powell and the maintenance of connection between them and Mafeking by means of intermediate posts at Eland's River and at Zeerust, would suffice to fulfil all requirements. Of the other Troops which had previously been employed in the west, Hart's Brigade occupied Heidelberg on the Ladysmith-Johannesburg railway, and the remainder were taken to form the Columns which were to operate against de Wet.

On the 19th June, de Wet had attacked Methuen's* Force, which was east of Kroonstad, guarding the Bloemfontein-Pretoria railway, but had met with no success. On the 22nd June he drove off the garrison of Honingspruit Station, captured a train, and after some heavy fighting with the reinforcements sent from Kroonstad, retired into the Elandsberg.

At the end of June the undernoted Columns were assembled for operations against this dashing Boer leader:—

At Frankfort, the remainder of the Tenth Division, two Cavalry Brigades, and 3,000 Mounted Infantry under Hunter.

At Heilbronn the Third (MacDonald's) Brigade of the Ninth Division.

At Paardekraal, Methuen's Force.†

At Lindley, the Twentieth (Paget's) Brigade of the First Division.

At Senekal, the Twelfth (Clements') Brigade of the Sixth Division.

In the south Rundle held the line Ficksburg-Trommel-Winburg with the available portion of his own, the Eighth, Division and Brabant's Colonial Division. The intention was to surround the whole of the Boer Commandos in the north-east of the Free State by a concentric advance of all the Columns in the direction of Bethlehem. But they were widely separated from one another, and the efforts to bring them into co-operation at the right moment failed. While the rest of the Columns were still in process of assembling, Paget and Clements moved forward at the end of June towards Bethlehem, and arrived there on the 7th July. Although Rundle had also begun his northward movement,

---

* At this period the distribution of Units into regular formations was almost completely broken up by the despatch of Troops to form garrisons, and by the provision of detachments for all sorts of purposes. The groups were enlarged as needed by the allotment to them of any Troops available.

† Only took part in the beginning of the operations.

Paget felt himself too weak to make a decisive attack on de Wet, who had withdrawn towards the South before the British Columns as they approached him, and who was able to lead the whole Boer Force, 8,000 strong, with an immense train of wagons and herds of cattle, back into the Roode Berg without having been seriously molested. This range, which was approachable by only a few neks, offered them a safe place of retreat for the moment, but was certain to prove a fatal trap to the Boers as soon as the Britsh Columns should have barred the exits.

Although the road towards Harrismith was open for several days, de Wet was unable to get his Commandos away in good time owing to the impossibility of arranging for any concerted action among them. It was not till the middle of the month that the decision was formed to fight a way out in three Columns, each taking a different direction, through the barrier of the British Columns, which meanwhile had drawn nearer, and which were now roughly on the line Ficksburg-South of Bethlehem-Harrismith. This decision, however, was only acted on by the Column with which de Wet himself and President Steyn were present and by some Commandos under Olivier. The latter turned westwards, while de Wet, with about 2,000 men, five guns, and many waggons, broke through the right wing of the British. The Free Staters who remained behind, numbering about 4,000, of whom Prinsloo took the command, laid down their arms on the 29th July, although, in de Wet's opinion, there was even then a chance of escaping by way of Witzie's Hoek. The Commandos which had escaped westwards, amounting to about 2,000 men with six or seven guns, still carried on the guerilla warfare, and during the next few weeks scored many successes by threatening the railway south of Kroonstad; but after the capture of Olivier in a fight near Winburg, on the 25th August, all energy died out of them.

Meanwhile de Wet, pursued in a north-westerly direction by the Second and Third Cavalry Brigades, had reached the neighbourhod of Lindley on the 19th July, after a small rear-guard action. On the 22nd July he crossed the railway at Serfontein, capturing at the same time a railway train loaded with valuable stores, and from the 23rd halted in the hills south of the Vaal about Vredefort and Reitzburg. There he entrenched himself so well that Broadwood did not venture to attack him with his Cavalrymen.

Lord Kitchener now took up the direction of the subsequent operations against de Wet. Large reinforcements had been collected, and on the 5th August the following were all in position to round up the redoubtable Boer leader:—two Cavalry Brigades, Brabant's Colonial Division, two Infantry Columns under Hart and Knox south of the Vaal, Methuen's Force (which had been employed in the interval in the Western Transvaal) and Smith-Dorrien's Column on the Krügersdorp-Potchefstroom railway.

De Wet, meanwhile, being favoured by the mountainous character of the district, crossed the Vaal at Schœmann's Drift on the 5th August, and by a feint lured away all the British south of the Vaal towards Lindeque's Drift, while he himself moved off northwards with all speed. On the 9th he reached Welverdiend, after some unimportant fighting with Methuen's advanced Troops: there he came on Smith-Dorrien, and drew away westwards on Ventersdorp, whence, after more fighting with Methuen, who, meanwhile, had swung round towards the north, he turned away to Rustenburg. Ian Hamilton* was to block the Witwatersrand and the Magaliesberg against the Boers, in order that de Wet's capture should be somehow contrived. De Wet, however, marched round Hamilton's Column during the night of the 16th-17th August, near Rustenburg, vainly

---

* See p. 317.

summoned Baden-Powell, who was posted there, to surrender, and then made eastward to the Pretoria-Nylstroom railway. Although Paget and Baden-Powell were watching the railway as far as Warm Bath, de Wet put President Steyn and an escort across it into the Bushveld on the 14th August; making his way through the Bushveld, President Steyn proceeded to Machadodorp, which was at that time the seat of the Transvaal Government.

De Wet himself turned about; threading his way clear of roads and paths, right through the British Columns he crossed the Magaliesberg the second time and at the end of August was back home again in the Free State. His aim was to put fresh life into the partisan warfare in the eastern portion of the Orange Free State, to keep on disorganising the Capetown-Pretoria railway, and after that to invade Cape Colony too. In his march from the Roodeberg to the Railway north of Pretoria, during which he was accompanied by his transport train, he had covered about 375 miles in 19 days, exclusive of his halt at Reitzburg, and had twice fought his way through hostile forces which were far superior to him in numbers, and which had the aid of the railway and of the telegraph at their disposal—a remarkable performance from every point of view.

The powers of resistance left in the Boers in the Western Transvaal had been considerably under-estimated by the British, and especially by Baden-Powell. Hunter and Mahon had hardly gone back into the north-east of the Free State at the end of June,* when Baden-Powell was shut up in Rustenburg by Commandant Lemmer, while a British detachment sent to restore communication with Pretoria was utterly defeated on the 11th June by Delarey at Nitral's Nek.† Baden-Powell was relieved for the time

---

* See page 309.
† In this action a whole Squadron of the Scots Greys, 90 men of the Lincolnshire Regiment, and two Guns were captured by Delarey.

being by a detachment of Carrington's Force* sent by way of Zeerust about the middle of July, but as soon as ever it went back again he was once more invested by Lemmer. Thereupon, Methuen's Force, which had originally been told off for the operations in the north-eastern portion of the Free State was brought up *viâ* Krugersdorp, and after heavy fighting at Olifant's Nek on the 21st, forced Delarey to retire eastwards, but had to leave this neighbourhood itself on the 25th July, to take part, on the Krugersdorp-Potchefstroom railway, in the most recently-arranged operations for rounding up de Wet. Consequently, Delarey was able, at the end of July, to shut up Baden-Powell for the third time in Rustenburg and a similar fate befell Lieut.-Colonel Hore's Column at Eland's River, as it was marching from Mafeking, at the beginning of August. Ian Hamilton from Pretoria, and Carrington from Mafeking were started off to relieve these two detachments. Hamilton reached Rustenburg, after a fight at Nitral's Nek, on the 5th August, and Baden-Powell was taken out of Rustenburg on the 7th August, that place being difficult to defend and not easy to supply. His Force was transferred to Commando Nek, which is situated on the border of the Magaliesberg to the east of Rustenburg. Hamilton turned his attention to de Wet.†

Carrington, coming on a strong party of Boers during his advance, turned back without having accomplished anything, so it was not till the 16th August that Hore was relieved by some of the Troops employed under Kitchener against de Wet. By the middle of August the situation was so far cleared up that after de Wet had left the district west of Pretoria, Lord Roberts was able to proceed with his long-planned operations towards Koomati Poort.

---

* Carrington's Force consisted of 5,000 Irregular Troops, who had been landed at Beira and marched through Rhodesia. It was at this time halted on the western border of the Transvaal about Mafeking.

† See page 311.

PART IV.

EVENTS IN THE EASTERN TRANSVAAL. THE MARCH TO KOOMATI POORT.

—o—

CHAPTER XII.

SIR R. BULLER'S OPERATIONS.

In the Natal Theatre of the War Buller had resumed operations on the 6th June, after having vainly negotiated with Christian Botha for a surrender. On the 8th June the Fifth Division (Hildyard's) which was reinforced, took Botha's Pass, and passing along the western edge of the Drakensberg, defeated Christian Botha on the 11th June, after a hot fight at Alleman's Nek, in consequence of which Laing's Nek was also evacuated by the Boers. On the 13th June, Hildyard occupied Volksrust, while Clery followed along to Laing's Nek. Buller halted for a time in the south-eastern corner of the Transvaal, and found employment to hand in bringing forward supplies, restoring the Natal Railway which had been damaged in various ways, and in settling the districts he was occupying. In the middle of June Lord Roberts directed that some parts of the Natal Army should be pushed forward along the Laing's Nek-Johannesburg railway, so as to ensure for himself a second line of supply, supplementary to the Bloemfontein-Pretoria railway which was under continuous menace. Buller accordingly starting on the 20th June with a Division and a half and a Mounted Brigade from Sandspruit, which is north-west of Volksrust, reached Paardekop on the 21st and Standerton on the 22nd. The Boers drew back without resistance, but they had previously broken up the line in various ways, and specially by blowing up the bridges over the Vaal, had destroyed the supplies which had been collected, and had made at least a part of the rolling-stock useless. On the 30th June a small Column under General Clery continued the march to Heidelberg, so as to join hands with Hart's Brigade* and complete the occupation of the Natal-Johannesburg railway. Clery's Force, which was continuously skirmishing with the Enemy, reached Greylingstad on the 3rd July and Vlakfontein on the 4th, whence it established connection with Hart by means of Mounted Troops.

The railway line in this section too had been considerably damaged by the Boers, and it was not till the 26th July that traffic could be fully resumed. But even then the Commandos, which had only withdrawn a short distance towards the North, did not cease their interruption of the railway traffic. The whole of Buller's Army was therefore employed for the moment in guarding the railway, and Clery had to march once more through the district north of the Greylingstad-Standerton section in order to keep the Boers in check.

Under instructions from Army Headquarters, Buller assembled the Fourth Division under Lyttelton and two Mounted Brigades, with a large force of Artillery, at Paardekop early in August, in order to support the advance of the Main Army on Machadodorp by a forward movement from the south. He began his own advance on the 7th August, and the same day came on Christian Botha's Commandos drawn up in an entrenched position at Amers-

---

* Page 308.

foort. After an insignificant show of resistance, however, these withdrew. On the 10th the march was continued to Ermelo, which the Mounted Troops reached on the 11th, the Infantry on the 12th. During these days also the Boers drew off northwards without entering on any serious fighting. On the 14th the advanced parties of the Natal Army occupied Carolina, and got in touch with General French's Advanced Patrols, he having, meanwhile, been pushed to the front from Pretoria, *viâ* Middelburg. On the 15th Buller himself crossed the Koomati at Twyfelaar, and consequently was now directly in front of the principal Boer Force, which had concentrated at Machadodorp under Louis Botha. Christian Botha, who was Buller's opponent up to this stage, had meanwhile swung out eastwards and then turned back towards the south again, that he might harass the British Lines of Communication in the south-eastern Transvaal and in Northern Natal. For the moment, Buller refrained from coming to a decisive fight with Louis Botha, for, in accordance with Lord Roberts' instructions, he was to wait for the arrival of Troops which were marching from Pretoria *viâ* Middelburg.

Early in July the Boers, refreshed in spirits by the repose which the British, who were completely occupied by the events in progress in the west and south-east, had perforce granted them, resumed a menacing attitude east of Pretoria. Roberts, therefore, being anxious for the safety of the section of the railway between Johannesburg and Pretoria, despatched two Columns under French and Hutton towards the south-east from Pretoria, and on the 10th July these Columns drove the Boers back across Bronkhorst Spruit, whereupon French returned to Pretoria. As early as the 13th July, however, Hutton found himself in the toils of an attack made on him by 2,000 Boers east of Irene Station; the result of this attack was actually *nil*.

After Hamilton had made a short expedition towards

Hamann's Kraal in the north, Lord Roberts, in the last ten days of July, began his eastward movement in three Columns: in the centre, moving along the Delagoa railway line, was Pole-Carew's Eleventh Division; on the right flank was French with the Cavalry Division, with Hutton some 30 miles to his south moving *viâ* Witpoort and Rietolei; on the left flank was Mahon, who had started from Kameel Drift with a force of Mounted Infantry; still further out on the left was Hamilton, who reached Rustfontein on the 22nd July, *viâ* Doornkraal, and who by threatening the retreat of the Boers caused them to retire without resistance before the advance of the Eleventh Division. On the 24th Hamilton and Pole-Carew reached Bronkhorst Spruit, and the same day French and Hutton, by working round the left flank of the Enemy, who stood in their way about six miles south of Balmoral, forced them to withdraw towards Middelburg. On the 25th July Hamilton reached Balmoral and Pole-Carew Wilge River, while French and Hutton crossed the Olifant's River and on the following day occupied Middelburg, which had till then been the seat of the Transvaal Government. The Boers now retired hurriedly, but without incurring any great losses, on Machadodorp. Although the eastward movement of the British had considerably increased the area of the territory occupied by them, and had rendered the situation in Pretoria more secure, it had not conduced to any material weakening of the fighting strength of the Boers. Events in the west, and the pursuit of de Wet, which was now beginning, necessitated Ian Hamilton's return to Pretoria. General French's Troops, distributed on a big curve east of Middelburg, assured the safety of that town, while Pole-Carew guarded the Pretoria-Middelburg railway.

It was not till the end of August, when de Wet had quitted the Transvaal and Buller had drawn nearer, that

Lord Roberts judged that the eastward movement could be resumed. On the 23rd, therefore, Pole Carew's Division was assembled at Wonderfontein and the despatch of reinforcements from Pretoria began. Buller came closer to the Cavalry Division south of the railway. During this movement he came in for some heavy fighting, in the course of which two Companies of the Liverpools were surrounded and captured by the Boers at Geluk Farm. On the 24th Pole Carew occupied Belfast after slight resistance, and on the 25th Lord Roberts arrived there and took over command. The Boers under Botha, numbering, it is said, only about 4,000, held a very extended position, of which the right flank rested on the Steenkampberg, and the left on the Koomati River.

Roberts decided to envelop the right flank of the Boers with the Cavalry Division, which was accordingly brought towards the North in rear of Pole-Carew's Division on the 26th, but on account of the excessively difficult nature of the ground the attempt at envelopment proved unsuccessful. On the same day Buller confined himself to throwing back the advanced parties of the Boers under heavy Artillery fire. On the 27th, however, after bombarding it for hours with about 60 guns, he succeeded in taking by storm the small kopje of Bergendal, which dominated the centre of the Boer position, and which was held by only 74 of the Johannesburg Police. After this misfortune, which was in itself of no importance, the Boers' powers of resistance broke down completely. They retired incontinently on Machadodorp, whence some went northwards to Lydenburg under Botha, and some retired eastward along the railway under Viljoen. Here again, then, the Boers were driven back, but in no sort of way defeated, and they still retained plenty of useful force for the prosecution of the guerilla warfare which soon afterwards broke out in this district too.

On the 28th Buller occupied Machadodorp with his advanced Troops at Helvetia, and the following day he moved the bulk of his Army to the last-named place. Pole-Carew and French reached Elandsfontein. On the 30th French was once more brought, as was the Guards' Brigade, on to the railway at Waterval Onder. At this place about 1,800 British Prisoners of War, who till French arrived had been kept at Nooitgedacht, regained their freedom and joined him.

During the last few days of August considerable reinforcements arrived at Belfast, and Buller began to move on Lydenburg, reaching Elandspruit on the 1st September. The Boers took up a strong position to oppose him at Badfontein, and he was averse to attacking their front. Consequently a second Column under Hamilton was moved off from Belfast, *via* Dullstroom, that it might threaten the Enemy's flanks and rear. Under this pressure the Boers retired through Lydenburg on the 6th, and took up a new position which entirely commanded the town. On the 8th Buller successfully attacked it, and on the 9th he reached Mauchberg.

The Boers now retired, some going northwards over the Sabie River and some southwards along the Nelspruit. In the latter half of September Buller followed them as far as Krüger's Post, and marched through the whole district east and north-east of Lydenburg. But when it seemed that the Boer Commandos about there were turning westwards towards Pietersburg, his Troops were gradually brought back out of the unhealthy region round Lydenburg into the neighbourhood of Middelburg.

On the extreme right flank French reached Hlomohomo, on the Koomati River, on the 10th September, moved on the 11th towards Barberton, being lightly engaged by the Enemy *en route*, and on the 13th occupied the last-named town, where he liberated a number of British Prisoners of War and captured a great quantity of railway material and of food supplies.

On the Delagoa railway the Eleventh Division had concentrated at Nooitgedacht on the 11th, and Hamilton on this day drew nearer to the line again. On the 15th Pole-Carew, followed by Hamilton, began to advance towards the Portuguese border. On the 19th the Guards' Brigade, which was leading, arrived at Kaapmuiden Station, Hamilton and Stephenson remaining at Godwan Station and Nelspruit. On the 24th the Guards' Brigade at last reached Koomati Poort, to which point Hamilton also came forward on the 26th. On this day it became possible to work traffic on the railway between Delagoa Bay and Pretoria. In their latest advance the British had secured abundant stores of all kinds and much railway material, for the Boers had only managed to effect a partial destruction of the quantity which existed.

The 3,000 Boers who, according to British accounts, were on the Delagoa Railway made no sort of resistance, although a range of heights running north and south furnished advantageous positions for defence. 700 of the combatant Boers, among whom were a great number of foreigners, crossed the Portuguese frontier and were disarmed. Others struck out for the mountains south of the railway in readiness to begin minor operations here too as soon as the attention of the British should be occupied elsewhere.

President Krüger had quitted the Transvaal on the 11th September, to proceed to Europe, while Steyn returned to the Free State. Krüger left a representative behind him in the person of Schalk Burger, but from this time onwards there was neither a permanent Transvaal Government nor any organised military Force. This, however, by no means involved the cessation of opposition to the British annexation of the Transvaal, which had been proclaimed: it merely took a form which presented no less serious difficulties to the British. It was only at this juncture that the operations assumed everywhere the characteristics of guerilla warfare, in which a whole people were engaged, and partisan fighting began to be carried on with increasing bitterness along the communications in rear of the British, exactly as de Wet had initiated it some months previously.

In this class of warfare also the tried leaders furnished the soul of the resistance—Louis Botha in the north and east of the Pretoria-Pietersburg railway; his brother, Christian, in the extreme south-east of the Transvaal and in Northern Natal; Delarey in the north-west; and de Wet and Steyn in the east of the Free State. They even succeeded about the end of 1900, when Cape Colony was invaded, in endangering—at least for a time—the prospects of the British by their conduct of such operations.

Another year and a half were yet to pass before the British suppressed this opposition. It was only the complete exhaustion of the Boers, the melting away of their forces, their want of clothing, ammunition and food, the limitation placed on their freedom of movement by the system of blockhouse lines, and the destruction of their homes, which, after they had made a heroic fight of it, induced the Commandos still remaining in the Field to accept the British terms of Peace.

TACTICAL RETROSPECT OF THE COURSE OF THE SOUTH AFRICAN WAR.

CHAPTER XIII.

TACTICAL RETROSPECT.

In common with other wars, that in South Africa teaches that methods of warfare adapt themselves to the experiences which are gained during the progress of the Campaign, and that they are subject to many modifications.

Two adversaries met in this Campaign, each of whom possessed an armament which comprised all the most recent technical inventions and developments. Small calibre rifles with almost smokeless powder, and Artillery firing high explosive and shrapnel shells were here employed for the first time on a large scale. Heavy, long-range guns, with low trajectories, as well as those constructed for high-angle fire, were also for the first time brought into the sphere of field operations. Bearing in mind, then, the effect of modern weapons, the great bed-rock question for decision in the first bloody encounters in this War was whether masses of Troops could still stand up against lines of riflemen, or, in other words, whether the bayonet was still a match for the bullet.

The very earliest engagements in the Campaign, in which the British suffered heavy defeats, and which resulted in the utter collapse of the procedure in action which they had formulated as the result of their studies in peace-time, illustrated most clearly the contrast between the tactical views held by the two opponents. The Boers almost always fought on the defensive. As their adversaries possessed a superior Artillery they utterly refused to engage in a decisive duel with it. Their own guns were concealed as long as they could be fired on by those of the British, and were not exposed to view until the Enemy's Infantry advanced to the attack; they were, moreover, distributed throughout the area of the engagement in isolated groups, which were widely separated one from another and which were so placed as to be difficult to distinguish, and as to favour as much as possible a concentration of fire. Consequently, not only was the picking up of the targets and the observation of effect rendered difficult to the hostile Artillery (which, as a rule, was employed as a single unit of command, and of which the fire came generally from one direction), but they also often caused it to disperse, and therefore to weaken the effect of, its own fire. Thus the Enemy was often prevented from profiting by the advantages due to his possession of a superiority in Artillery, and the Boer Artillery itself was able, notwithstanding its inferiority, to maintain itself in position till the very last.

It was, however, to his rifle that the Boer trusted for the decisive effect. From his youth up he had been accustomed to using it, and, moreover, he knew all there was to know about the natural features of his own country: he knew, consequently, how to get the best work out of his weapon in a fight at extreme ranges, how to add to his own power by an ingenious use of the natural features of the ground, and how, by skilfully strengthening sections of the ground, to call a powerful ally to his assistance in increasing the effect of his weapon.

The Boers dispensed with all direction of fire: each individual directed the fire-power of his weapon entirely on his own initiative, usually against that target which he could best distinguish, which he judged to be the most important, and which, taking into consideration its distance from him and its size, promised the most favourable results from his fire. Seeing how great an effect, as it was, was produced by such uncontrolled fire, the question may be asked what force would it have attained under the conditions obtaining under a firm and clearly-defined direction of the combat and of the fire-action.

For these was substituted healthy common-sense, and this quality, unprejudiced by any sort of methodical training, but in its own unsophisticated originality, frequently suggested the happiest innovations and expedients; but, brooking no control, it could never subordinate itself to the intention or will of a superior. Here and there the activity of an individual made good the deficiency of peace-instruction, but the inability to brook any control made the execution of the plans and wishes of a superior impossible.

The Boer methods of fighting were therefore quite unmethodical. Interdependent lines of fire were only formed if the ground furnished favourable cover for them; as a result, there was an absence of contiguity between the groups of marksmen, which were separated from one another by more or less wide gaps of unoccupied ground— a condition of affairs which the long-ranging power of the weapon employed, robbed of danger.

Nothing was known by the Boers about a distribution of Troops for the combat: the whole of their strength was, from the very commencement of the action, thrown into the first line. Although in their great mobility the mounted Boers possessed the power of quickly reinforcing a firing-line, and could thus in some degree compensate for the want of depth in their formations, the ever-present fear of being outflanked led them away, on the other hand, into giving an altogether excessive extension to their front. It is true that this often facilitated the concentration of their own fire on an Enemy who began his advance on a narrow front, and who generally delivered a purely frontal attack, but it also made it quite impossible for the Boers to effect any increase of fire-power during the fight, and, more than that, deprived them of all chance of assuming the offensive when the attack should be repulsed. However good a model this method of fighting may furnish for an action in which the sole object is to hold a section of ground or to gain time, *e.g.*, Advanced or Rearguard Actions, and the conventional dismounted action of Cavalry, it is defective in that it does not provide for the enjoyment of the advantages of a hardly-attained superiority of fire, in the vigorous delivery, with fresh fire-power, of an assault on the enemy.

The purely defensive fighting methods of the Boers, designed solely to repulse attacks, and based on the clinging to ground, originated in the sense of their own weakness of which they were forced to be more and more conscious when they recognised their want of military training, organisation, and leadership, and, more than all, their complete lack of discipline. That their leaders, even in the hey-day of their success, never aspired to so much as even contemplate the annihilation of their adversary, is in itself, an avowal of their military incompetence. The outcome was that they limited themselves to negative efforts, which can never result in positive gains. To hold on as long as they could to the position they had selected was the sole object of their fighting, which consequently exhibited none of the elementary characteristics of a serious life or death struggle.

The British leaders, on the other hand, as represented by General Buller early in the Campaign, sought victory in impetuous, decisive action: they were governed by the sound idea of destroying their Enemy in a resolute attack. But the real struggle for the issue of the combat lay far less in a tough and keen contest for superiority in the combined fire of gun and rifle, than in a determined advance to close quarters, there to deal the death-blow with a formed mass of troops. This is expressed in most drastic terms in Buller's Order of the Day, dated 12th January, 1900: ". . . . the men must get to close quarters with the Enemy—that is the way to victory and to safety! Any retirement is fatal. The only thing the Enemy cannot withstand is a hand-to-hand fight with us."

The prelude to every fight was a bombardment by the superior force of British Artillery which lasted for hours and even days. It was imagined that in this alone lay the ultimate decision of the first phase of the combat, the fire-fight, and that no support need be furnished by the Infantry as long as it lasted. No doubt the experiences of the Franco-German War had contributed to the adoption of such a method of employing Artillery. The cruel losses suffered by the German Infantry in the early battles of the War, and particularly at St. Privat, had been primarily caused by a want of co-operation on the part of the Artillery. But while during that period the Infantry attempted to push home the attack in the absence of Artillery support, the Artillery was now, by an exchange of tasks, supposed to be able to decide the fire-fight in the absence of any combined action on the part of the Infantry. There was a complete want of harmonious effort by the two Arms combined to attain the maximum of fire-effect. On more than one occasion, as long as the Artillery was engaged in its own fire-fight, the Infantry did not come on to the field at all, or remained so far away from the Enemy as to be perfectly innocuous. Just as had been sometimes recommended to us, the Artillery and the Infantry engagements formed two distinct operations as regards time, and the Artillery even went so far as often to begin one or two days before the real attack. The result of this was that the Enemy kept his Infantry under cover and protection during this Artillery bombardment, and did not so much as show his guns to the superior force of the British Artillery. As a thorough investigation of the points to be fired on seldom preceded the opening of fire, and as the silence of the Enemy's guns precluded all knowledge of their whereabouts, the British guns proceeded to sweep an enormous extent of ground with their shell—generally fired at random. Consequently the Artillery bombardment was, as a rule, quite ineffective. The advance of the Infantry which next ensued was, it is true, supported for a certain period by Artillery fire, but when the Infantry got within close range, and just when the Enemy's rifle-fire began to produce the maximum of effect on it, at the very moment, that is, when the support of the guns was most essential to it, they ceased fire, owing to anxiety lest any shell should by accident fall in its ranks. How deceived the British Commanders were about the effect of their own Artillery bombardments, and how completely they failed to understand the need for co-operation and harmony between the Infantry and the Artillery action, is clearly shown in General Warren's report about the first engagement on the Upper Tugela, in which he declared that the best course would be "to keep the Boers, as they lay in their trenches, under an overpowering fire of Artillery, until they should be disheartened, and till their position should be almost ripe for assault, and that then the Infantry should be sent forward to rush them."

The supposed fire-preparation of the attack existed, as a matter of fact, only in the imagination of the British leaders, and the Infantry actually advanced to the attack of an absolutely unshaken adversary. Leaders and Troops showed that in their peace-training they had been inadequately instructed how to conduct a decisive fire-engagement with an Enemy armed with modern long-range rifles. In the opinion of their own Commander-in-Chief the

British Infantry lacked the qualities necessary for this. After the War, Lord Roberts criticised their performances in the following words:—

" The self-reliance of the British soldier had not been sufficiently developed, with the result that he did not know how to act for himself; this was particularly the case at the beginning of the War. In his want of appreciation of ground and of knowledge how to use it, he was the exact opposite of the Boer: also in his poorly-trained talent for observation. His marksmanship cannot be pronounced good. His calmness in action and the way he husbanded his ammunition were points in his favour, but he failed, owing to his slowness in firing, to profit by fleeting opportunities, and also to get good results under difficult or strange conditions. At close ranges, where, as a rule, there is a protracted fire-fight between two adversaries more or less protected, the aiming was unsatisfactory; long ranges were seldom correctly estimated. . . . The splendidly-developed faculty of every single Boer for constructing artificial cover was completely deficient in our Infantry of the Line. . . . The men thought less about the use of cover in the attack than they did in the defence. . . . In many respects remarkable progress was made during the course of the Campaign, which shows that it was not intelligence, but suitable training, which had been deficient. Far too much importance had been attached to the preservation of order and regularity, and far too little to the development of individuality. It had not been universally recognised that quickness and handiness in the fire-fight are of no less importance than good order and preciseness in close formations."

The Infantry specially failed in the power to take an effective part in a fire-fight with an enemy under cover at very extreme ranges, which is essential in these days of far-ranging weapons: it neither possessed the requisite qualities of marksmanship nor had it received the essential training of the eyesight. At distances beyond 500 yards the men could only with difficulty distinguish their enemy; much less could they obtain good results from their fire.

The leaders—superior and subordinate—had, moreover, no mental grasp of the requirements of a modern battle.

In the endeavour to keep the Troops tightly in hand as long as possible, and, regardless of the far-reaching effect of the hostile rifle-fire, to bring them steadily forward to the closest possible quarters without firing a shot, all deployments were in the earlier actions made too late and into too dense a line, and the result was that the Troops, quite insufficiently protected as they were by any attempt at scouting during the combat, were only too often exposed to the disintegrating effects of fire opened on them unawares.

The distribution of the Infantry for action showed, in its outward form, a firm reliance on the principles expounded in the Instructions of all the other European Armies, and fulfilled the requirements of modern battle direction. But as it was incorrectly applied, it remained an empty form. There was a marked absence of recognition of the principle that the force held back in deep formations should be employed towards the gradual attainment of superiority in fire-effect, and that it ought to be incorporated, section by section, in the foremost firing line. The view of the British leaders was that the issue of the fight would have to be decided first and foremost by shock-action, and on this account the weight of the deep formations was generally held back to throw into the balance at the last. But when the time came, instead of at any rate then throwing the whole weight of this force into the fight, so as to give the intended impetus to the final blow, some part of the Troops held in reserve—on many occasions more than half the total numbers engaged—were still held back to cover a possible retirement, or to meet some other subsidiary requirement of sorts, and thus consequently took no part in the decisive action, in which it is impossible to be too strong.

From this it resulted that only on the rarest occasions was a volume of fire even approximately equal, much less superior, to his brought to bear on the Enemy, but worse still, that assaults were almost always delivered prematurely, half-heartedly, and at half-pressure. It was only natural that under the storm of hostile fire which burst upon them they should go under at once, especially as they were generally not launched simultaneously along the whole front of attack, but quite independently one of another. The bloody defeats of that "Black Week" in December, 1900, had conclusively demonstrated the superiority of small-calibre rifle-fire over the shock of troops in masses. That old maxim of Suvarow's, "The bullet is a fool, only the bayonet is wise," the open and secret believers in which were to be found not only in the British but in every other Army, had lost all its point if applied to encounters with an adversary who knew how to get full value out of the capabilities of improved fire-arms.

General von Moltke had clearly expressed his own acknowledgment of this forty years previously, in his "Tactical Essays,"* in the writing of which he had received many instructive suggestions from his study of the Italian Campaign of 1859. In his opinion, the "Bayonet Charge" in a period of improved fire-arms is to be understood rather in the figurative sense. He writes: "If the frequent records of bayonet encounters contained in the French reports of the Italian Campaign of 1859 were stripped of their theatrical adornment, the simple prosaic truth would be arrived at, and by far the greater number of them would

---

* Observations on the influence of improved fire-arms on Tactics during the period 1861–65.

be found to amount to this—that the Enemy, shaken by more or less heavy losses, had escaped actual collision by retiring."*

"The bayonet assault is the way to finally press the life out of the Enemy: no soldier would wish to be deprived of its employment. The confidence of the man in his *arme blanche* cannot be sufficiently aroused or encouraged; but, firstly, the progress of the action, and, secondly, fire-effect, must make the opportunity for using such weapons. Besides this, leaders must bear in mind that the most brilliant courage avails nought against obstacles which cannot be overthrown, and they should recognise that the bayonet charge is not the first but the final action in every encounter."

"The Infantry fight is decided by fire-effect": this leading principle of the German Regulations for the employment of Infantry, founded on the experiences of the War of 1870-71, had been embodied in almost the same outward form in the English instructions, but it had not been inwardly digested by the British leaders. Governed by vicious ideas, and accustomed during their peace-training to the force of a conviction that success would primarily result from a rigid adherence to outward forms, they failed, as a consequence, to grasp the true and deep-seated origin of their failure, and held the superiority of the Enemy's armament and the inadequacy of the forms of combat employed, responsible for their misfortunes. They, therefore, sought refuge principally in new forms.

This was emphatically demonstrated in the battles which preceded the Relief of Ladysmith and the Capture

---

* General von Moltke expresses the same idea in the narrative of the Battle of Solferino, contained in the Account of the Italian Campaign by the General Staff, as follows:—"General Niel certainly ascribes his victory to the bayonet. That depends on how often the attack culminated in actual personal collision. As a rule it is only so distinguished with the premise that the opponent did not wait for the bayonet."

of Bloemfontein. At the same time, a great deal of real progress is to be noted as regards certain points. In the first place, much more intelligence was displayed about the co-operation between Infantry and Artillery: the purposeless, one-sided cannonading, unaccompanied by a deployment of Infantry, was of far less frequent occurrence, and Infantry and Artillery joined in a combined attack. As a result, the Battle of Driefontein was a perfect model of the interdependent action of the two Arms. The Infantry, too, had learned something. Their formations for attack, based on a juster appreciation of fire-effect, were, generally speaking, thinner and on broader fronts. All deployments were made in plenty of time and outside the zone of effective hostile fire, and no denser formations than swarms of skirmishers were to be seen within rifle-shot of the Enemy.

On the other hand, to protect the Troops from being taken unawares by the Enemy's fire, a very loose sort of grouping, in dispersed formations, was adopted quite early in an engagement at very great distances, sometimes more than six miles from the Enemy; thus distributed, the Brigades with their four Battalions—each in a deep column with all its eight Companies following one another very widely extended—advanced in a sort of double column.* In such awkward and inelastic formations the Troops could only carry out movements straight to their front, and were thus prematurely committed to one definite direction. As a result of this, it was impossible to employ the Troops held back in rear otherwise than straight to their front.

The difficulty of bringing forward the Troops in rear under the Enemy's fire sometimes conduced to the mistaken employment in the foremost lines of far too strong a force at the beginning of an action, and consequently to

---

* p. 31.

excessive frontal extensions; in fact, it was not of rare occurrence that all the Troops intended to participate in an action were placed in first line as soon as the action began.

In this way all influence over the subsequent course of the action, and, worse still, all chance of increasing the volume of fire was irretrievably lost. It was, moreover, evident that the knowledge that they could no longer dare to hope for vigorous support during the long action which was to ensue, and the consciousness that they had no backing, would perforce tell disadvantageously on the keeness and endurance of Troops when under the stress of the battle.

The new "Order of Combat," therefore, as a matter of fact, only effected a change in outward forms: with regard to elementary characteristics there was no alteration. The issue of the Infantry fight was still sought less in fire-effect than in shock action, and the Infantry continued to manifest the same fatal desire to capture the Enemy's position as quickly as possible by an unfaltering rush at it, without engaging in a serious fire-fight. In certain instances there were signs of greater discernment and of a more correct method of procedure—for example, at Driefontein. But these formed exceptions. Generally speaking, vicious memories of bygone days, and with them the cut-and-dried forms of barrack-square drill prevailed. An example of a carefully-planned and well-maintained fire-fight, in which the contest for superiority of fire was conducted with definite purpose or in which perseverance and tenacity were displayed, was but very rarely furnished.

In almost every engagement the British Infantry-fire remained, as previously, weaker than that of the Boers, and, as previously, the assault was attempted in the face of the unsubdued fire: the only difference lay in the assault being delivered in long, thin lines instead of in close formation. Consequently almost every British Infantry attack, whether on a level and open plain or in broken and mountainous country, was made in the same constantly-employed formations which had been adopted when their use was quite misunderstood, and which had then often brought about the most disastrous results. An importance was attributed to formations to which they are in no way entitled, and the whole subject was judged more by its outward appearance than by its essential characteristics; thus the mistake made by the Russian leaders in the Russo-Turkish War of 1877-78 was repeated. Then, too, the real cause of failure was overlooked and it was erroneously attributed to the superior armament and to the fighting formations of the Turks. As Kuropatkin says: "From this originated that endeavour to discover and adopt for ourselves new methods of fighting, which resulted so miserably for us." There was a failure to discern, firstly, that in the modern battle that formation is correct and applicable which best meets the demand for the development of the greatest possible fire-effect; and, secondly, that the course of the modern fire-fight can, by reason of its complexity, be so little foretold that it cannot be formulated in any cut-and-dried routine. In South Africa the contest was not merely one between the Bullet and the Bayonet, it was also between the soldier drilled to machine-like movements and the man with a rifle working on his own initiative, and so little under control indeed as to be actually unmanageable: War had been proclaimed between rigid formulas and untrammelled healthy common sense.

When, in spite of the new formations, the British attacks —notwithstanding their being made in an overwhelming numerical superiority—still resulted in failure, the leaders thought that they were face to face with an insoluble problem, and despaired of ever being able to make a successful frontal attack. Misapprehending the true cause of their failure, they came to the conclusion, which had such a baneful influence on the subsequent course of the campaign, that a frontal attack is impossible under the fire of modern rifles. They, therefore, adopted a course which was bound to render it impossible for them ever to gain a decisive success.

Most of the battles in the period which ensued up to the Capture of Pretoria and up to Koomati Poort were indecisive in character, and, owing to the dread in which the Enemy's fire-effect was held, they took over and over again, as if it were inherent to the solution of the problem, the form of a holding frontal attack combined with an envelopment of the Enemy's flank.

The Artillery and Infantry opened, at extreme ranges in the Enemy's front, a fire-fight, which was, as a rule, completely ineffective, while the Cavalry and Mounted Infantry worked round the Enemy's flanks and rear. As he was not tied down to his own front, the Enemy extricated himself from the threatened envelopment and retired a few miles to a strong position, in which he once more opposed his strength to the advance of the British.

The old lesson had been forgotten that, no matter what may be the nature of the country, no enveloping movement can be effective and decisive unless made in combination with an energetic frontal attack, and that a flank attack should always arrive at its destination when the Enemy is thoroughly occupied with what is proceeding in his front. The more energetically he is engaged in his front the more force must the Enemy apply there and the better prospect will the enveloping attack have of meeting with only feeble resistance and of possibly falling on the Enemy unawares, and therefore with the maximum of effect.

In these indecisive affairs Leaders as well as Troops lost all the strength of will needed to conquer in a Battle, no matter what the victory might cost; the fight was begun with wills half-formed and with plans half-laid, and the Troops had to dispense with the backing of which they would have been conscious had their leaders possessed the inflexible will-power which was urgently needed at critical moments to re-animate the exhausted spirits of the men engaged. The dread of the Enemy's front was not due to the small-calibre rifle with smokeless powder, nor to the severity of the losses (which were but trifling in comparison with those in other wars) but to the want of confidence of the Leaders in their own powers, and, as a reflected result of this, to the broken confidence of the Troops in their own Leaders.

Even though the fighting-methods adopted by the British may be looked on as the natural outcome of the inferior quality of a mercenary army, and of the difficulties of filling the gaps in its ranks, justice demands the acknowledgment of the fact that the British soldier, if only he was well and skilfully led, did not fail in the devoted and thorough performance of his duty, and that he understood how to make a forward movement with great dash. Moreover, it would be a great mistake to assume that the sacrifices of war were diminished by the methods adopted by the British Leaders in the conduct of the Campaign. Even granting that occupation of the Capitals was effected without much trouble or bloodshed, these successes were illusory, seeing that the live force of the Enemy was not crushed out of existence. Another eighteen months of fighting was still needed to break down all resistance, and the failure to take advantage of the opportunity, which presented itself early in the War, of inflicting a crushing defeat on the Boers, by reason of the consequent prolongation of hostilities actually cost the British far heavier losses than the bloodiest of decisive battles would have. The number of victims of sickness and exhaustion among the Regular Troops and Volunteers during the last twelve months of the Campaign, was more than four times the number of those lost in action—a proportion but seldom reached in any war in which raging epidemics did not thin the ranks.

Not the crushing of the Enemy, but the occupation of towns and districts became more and more the purpose of British military endeavour. Manœuvring was substituted for fighting. This mode of conducting warfare, in which, to judge from the impression of recent contemporary opinion, it was imagined that a perfectly fresh phenomenon of modern war had been discovered, was nothing more or less than a reversion to the bad old times. More than three generations ago, Clausewitz wrote, in the true spirit of prophecy: "It is thus that all Government and Leaders in War have from time immemorial endeavoured to evade the decision of a battle, either by attempting to attain their object through some other channel or by unexpectedly renouncing it. Historians and theorists have then proceeded to search for some higher art in these campaigns and wars. . . . . But contemporaneous history has done away with this vain conceit, though nobody can guarantee that it will not reappear here or there at longer or shorter intervals of time, and allure the leading men into such perverse actions as originate in weakness, and which are consequently the more attributable to Human Nature."*

War can never change its character: its true essence is found at all times in the destruction of the live force of both sides, and this is true not only of stupendous decisions between great and cultured States, but also, in full measure, with respect to smaller colonial operations.

Even the War in South Africa—notwithstanding the improvements in firearms—discovered no fresh element

---

* Clausewitz "On War," Book IV., Chapter II.

which can alter the essence of fighting. That lies to-day as it did a hundred years ago in fire-effect, which has during the interval gradually increased with improvements in fire-arms until it has now become the dominant force in all fighting.

The endeavour to produce increased fire-effect also led in this Campaign to the employment of heavy Artillery in the open field. The astonishing mobility which was found to be an attainable quality of such Artillery in South Africa, notwithstanding the poverty in quantity and condition of the communications in the Theatre of War, and notwithstanding the great weight of the pieces,* justifies the hope that under the far more satisfactory conditions obtaining with regard to communications in Europe, it may be possible, if they are brought forward with energy, to place such pieces at the really decisive point at precisely the right time: the reflection that the larger the masses of troops become, the slower must be their movements, specially justifies this hope.

The importance of fire-effect is on all-fours with the irresistible force furnished by the intelligently combined action of the two principal fire-producing Arms—the Infantry and the Artillery. Nothing, however, has been altered with regard to their mutual relations in the fight. To-day, as of yore, the Infantry is the Arm which decides the Battle. It is true that no sound conclusions can be drawn from the experiences of the South African War with regard to the capabilities of modern Artillery: the imperfection of the material, the disproportion of the numbers of guns, and the inability of the Leaders to effect the harmonious co-operation of the powers of gun and rifle prevent that: but the course of the fighting shows that Artillery alone cannot

---

* For instance, weight of the 4·7 inch Naval Gun, 4½ tons. In February, 1900, these Guns covered the distance from Jacobsdal to Paardeberg (about 32 miles) in 23 hours, on bad roads.

decide an action—the Infantry must still do this as they did in bygone days. In fact, the latter Arm, owing to the potentialities inherent to its weapon, is now in a position to prepare for itself the path to victory in those cases where the performances of the sister Arm do not fulfil expectations. The perfectly natural endeavour not to launch the Infantry for the decisive attack until the power of the hostile Artillery is reduced, which endeavour is often dignified with the appellation of a fixed principle, will not be always practicable in war, even if the Infantry is associated with a greatly superior force of Artillery. Even in South Africa the British Infantry, notwithstanding the overwhelming superiority of their own Artillery, suffered in their attacks from the Artillery as well as from the Infantry fire of the Enemy. When all Field Artillery is equipped with shields the assailant will have to take this consideration even more into account, for an inferior Artillery will then be in a position to turn all its force against the advancing Infantry, in the full knowledge that any fear of its own annihilation by the Enemy's Artillery is ungrounded.

The nature of the modern fire-fight makes it self-evident that the task of the assailants, who by reason of their being in motion must from time to time interrupt the continuity of their fire, has gradually become more difficult than that of the defenders, who can use their weapons uninterruptedly; further, it is not a phenomenon produced by this War that the assailants' losses were heavier than those of the defenders in instances when no pursuit succeeded the fight. History records that the difficulties of the Infantry attack are of quite as old standing as the doubts whether it could succeed. Nor did Moltke fall into the error of minimising these difficulties in his "Tactical Studies." He said that "in the improvements in fire-arms was involved the increase of strength of the defence against attack," but that the balance of the advantages inherent to the offensive, which manifestly exists in various other respects, make it indisputably superior to the defensive; the attack should endeavour to assimilate the strong points of the defence and to derive the utmost benefit from the manifest and solid advantages which accompany it into the fire-fight, before making the final charge. He therefore considered that "any desire to lay down as a regulation that no body of Troops was to advance across an open plain against an enemy in position, under cover, would be unjustifiable." Every superior officer must, however, satisfy himself quite clearly as to the bearing which the subject has on his own situation. The value of the offensive in war will be established scientifically: it depends entirely on the judicious selection of the moment for adopting it, and does not lie in dashing forward in nervous haste at a juncture when it would manifestly be more advantageous to remain halted.*

Another question which was specially agitating the military world at that period was "What alterations in principle should be made in the Instructions in view of the influence of improved fire-arms on the combat-methods of Troops?" Moltke's reply to this was: "Our authorized instructions fulfil the new requirements: the point of them lies in their application, and that is the business of the Commander. The leading principles of our instructions, too, retain their value notwithstanding the improvements in fire-arms, and, although there may be considerable need for alteration in outward forms. The constant improvements in the accuracy and handiness for action of our rifles and guns, necessitate alterations in our fighting formations. Modern fire-effect allows no movement in the open within the danger-zone to remain unpunished; it makes nothing of distances, and forces massed bodies of Troops to dissolve into smaller groups ; it makes its mark on the

---

* "and to fire" is to be understood from the context.

form of the swarms of skirmishers, and raises that formation, which used to be the principal, to the status of being the only one permissible on a battlefield; it compels the most circumspect attention to ground, and it loosens the external connection and compactness of all movements."

The application of forms and principles is, in War, of far higher value than these subjects themselves. The disorganising influences of modern fire-effect, which make the direction of Troops such a difficult matter, demand from individual marksmen no small measure of clear appreciation of the task before them, of self-reliance, and of well-directed action. Only those men in the ranks who can think and act on their own initiative will be able to extract full value from the employment of their weapon.

But in these days of loosely-knit fire-fights and of incalculable complexities in their own situations, Leaders, too, stand more than ever in need of unlimited development of all their mental powers, that they may direct their energies with success. The rigid fettering with forms and rules, to which a false system of peace-training condemned Leaders, avenged itself bitterly during the South African War. In this experience, so pregnant of warning for the future, is contained the most important lesson of the whole War.

No one can dispute that formations are of great importance in the training of Troops. The endeavour to run that on lines adaptable to the practice of war, and to exercise Troops during peace time in such formations as can be retained under an Enemy's fire is an important feature in the work of serious peace-training. Ill-judged contempt for formations would be avenged as bitterly as would too bigoted a devotion to them. But the first battles in a war always give rise to the same constantly-recurring phenomenon—that, notwithstanding every effort to run it on lines adaptable to the practice of war, even the best peace-training cannot provide for all the requirements of war itself, and that it must result in the adoption of some formations which are found to be valueless when employed for serious purposes.

In a long period of peace it will probably be found that no Troops will have attained the supreme standard of having nothing to unlearn on the battlefield of that which they have learned on the drill-ground. To harbour any illusion on that point would be a fatal form of self-complacency. But those Leaders who, being under no tyrannical sway of the Form, have grappled to their souls a profound knowledge of the Essence and Needs of the modern fight, will know how to suit their action to the requirements of any situation and to create something fresh and useful, even when under the rain of the Enemy's bullets: trained to self-reliance in all they undertake and yet conscious of the restrictions imposed on them, such Leaders will know how best to serve the great common purpose in the combination of forces, by which alone success can be attained.

Fortunate is that Army whose ranks, released from the burden of dead forms, are controlled by natural, untrammelled, quickening common-sense.

APPENDICES.

APPENDIX I.

ORDER OF BATTLE of the NATAL ARMY during the Fighting on the Upper Tugela.

GENERAL COMMANDING-IN-CHIEF: GENERAL SIR REDVERS BULLER.
CHIEF OF THE STAFF: COLONEL WYNNE.

SECOND DIVISION.
LIEUTENANT-GENERAL SIR C. F. CLERY.

Fifth Infantry Brigade.
MAJOR-GENERAL HART.

- Parts of 1st & 2nd Rl. Dublin Fusiliers.
- 1st Connaught Rangers.
- 1st Border Regiment.
- 1st Royal Inniskilling Fusiliers.
- Supply column.
- Field Hospital.
- 16th Bearer Company.

Second Infantry Brigade.
MAJOR-GENERAL HILDYARD.

- 2nd Devonshire.
- 2nd West Surrey (The Queen's).
- 2nd East Surrey.
- 2nd West Yorkshire.
- Supply Column.
- Field Hospital.
- 2nd Bearer Company.

DIVISIONAL TROOPS.
Brigade Division Field Artillery.

- 17th Field Co. R.E.
- 73rd Field Battery.
- 64th Field Battery.
- 7th Field Battery.
- 1 Squadron 13th Hussars.
- Field Hospital.
- Supply column.
- Ammunition column.

APPENDIX I.—*continued.*

FIFTH DIVISION.
LIEUTENANT-GENERAL SIR CHARLES WARREN.

Eleventh Infantry Brigade.
MAJOR-GENERAL WOODGATE.*

□ 1st York and Lancaster. □ 1st South Lancashire. □ 2nd Lancashire Fusiliers. □ 2nd King's Own (Royal Lancaster).

||| Supply Column.
||| Field Hospital.
□ 6th Bearer Company.

Fourth Infantry Brigade.
MAJOR-GENERAL LYTTELTON.

□ 3rd King's Royal Rifle Corps. □ 2nd Scottish Rifles. □ 1st Rifle Brigade. □ 1st Durham Light Infantry.

||| Supply Column.
||| Field Hospital.
□ 14th Bearer Company.

DIVISIONAL TROOPS.

Brigade Division Field Artillery.

⊣⊢ 63rd Field Battery. ⊣⊢ 28th Field Battery. ⊣⊢ 19th Field Battery. ⊠ 1 Squadron 13th Hussars.

|| Field Hospital. || Supply column. || Ammunition column.

□ 37th Field Co. R.E.

* Later Major-General Wynne.

348   APPENDIX I.

APPENDIX I.—*continued.*

MOUNTED BRIGADE (COLONEL LORD DUNDONALD).

Mounted Infantry.

- South African Light Horse.
- Thorneycroft's Mntd. Infantry.
- Bethune's Mntd. Infantry.
- 1st Royal Dragoons.
- Imperial Light Horse.
- Natal Carabineers.
- Natal Police.
- R. Dublin Fusiliers (1 section).
- 2nd King's R. Rifle Corps (1 Co.)

Supply column. Field Hospital (section of). 4 Machine Guns.

CORPS TROOPS.

Tenth Infantry Brigade (MAJOR-GENERAL COKE).

- 2nd Middlesex.
- 2nd Dorsetshire.
- 2nd Somersetshire Light Infy.*
- Imperial Light Infy.*

Supply column. Field Hospital. No. 10 Bearer Company.

8 Naval 12-pndrs. 2 4·7 in. Naval Guns. H, Q, and 1 Squadron 13th Hussars. 78th Field Battery. 61st Howitzer Field Battery. No. 4 Mountain Battery.†

Field Telegraph Section. Ammunition column. Balloon Section. Pontoon Train.

Supply Park. Supply Column.

* Only joined the Brigade shortly before 24th January.   † Only arrived at Springfield from Estcourt 23rd January.

APPENDIX I.—continued.

GARRISON OF CHIEVELEY.

Sixth Infantry Brigade (MAJOR-GENERAL BARTON).

2nd Royal Irish Fusiliers. 1st Royal Welch Fusiliers. ½ 2nd Royal Scots Fusiliers. 2nd Royal Fusiliers.

Supply column. Field Hospital. No. 17 Bearer Company.

200 Men from Mounted Brigade.   2 5-in. Guns.

GARRISON OF FRERE.

LIEUTENANT-COLONEL BLAGROVE (13th Hussars).

Composite Reserve Rifle Battalion. ½ 2nd Royal Scots Fusiliers.

2 4·7-in. Naval Guns. 400 Men from Mounted Brigade. 2 Guns of the 66th Field Battery.

TOTAL: 25 Battalions, 6 Squadrons Regular Cavalry, about 1,900 Mounted Infantrymen, 8⅓ Field Batteries, 1 (Howitzer) Field Battery, 1 Mountain Battery, 14 Heavy Guns, 4 Machine Guns, 2 Field Companies R.E.: roughly, 27,000 Men and 76 Guns.

APPENDIX II.

ORDER OF BATTLE of the NATAL ARMY at the beginning of the Last Attempt to relieve Ladysmith.

GENERAL COMMANDING-IN-CHIEF: GENERAL SIR REDVERS BULLER.

CHIEF OF THE STAFF: COLONEL MILES.

SECOND DIVISION.
MAJOR-GENERAL LYTTELTON.

Fourth Infantry Brigade.
COLONEL NORCOTT.

- 3rd King's Royal Rifle Corps.
- 2nd Scottish Rifles.
- 1st Rifle Brigade.
- 1st Durham Light Infantry.

Second Infantry Brigade.
MAJOR-GENERAL HILDYARD.

- 2nd Devonshire
- 2nd West Surrey (The Queen's).
- 2nd East Surrey.
- 2nd West Yorkshire.

DIVISIONAL TROOPS.

- 17th Field Co. R.E.
- Brigade Division Field Artillery.
  - 64th Field Battery.
  - 63rd Field Battery.
  - 7th Field Battery.
- 1 Squadron 13th Hussars.

APPENDIX II.—*continued.*

FIFTH DIVISION.
LIEUTENANT-GENERAL SIR CHARLES WARREN.

Tenth Infantry Brigade.
MAJOR-GENERAL COKE.

2nd Middlesex.   2nd Dorsetshire.   2nd Somersetshire Light Infantry.

Sixth Infantry Brigade.
MAJOR-GENERAL BARTON.

2nd Royal Irish Fusiliers.   1st Royal Welch Fusiliers.   2nd Royal Scots Fusiliers.   2nd Royal Fusiliers.

Eleventh Infantry Brigade (MAJOR-GENERAL WYNNE, later COLONEL KITCHENER).

Reserve Rifle Battalion.   * 1st York and Lancaster.   1st South Lancashire.   2nd King's Own (Royal Lancaster).

DIVISIONAL TROOPS.

Brigade Division Field Artillery.   1 Squadron 1st (Royal) Dragoons

78th Field Battery.   73rd Field Battery.   28th Field Battery.

37th Field Co. R.E.

352   APPENDIX II.

APPENDIX II.—continued.

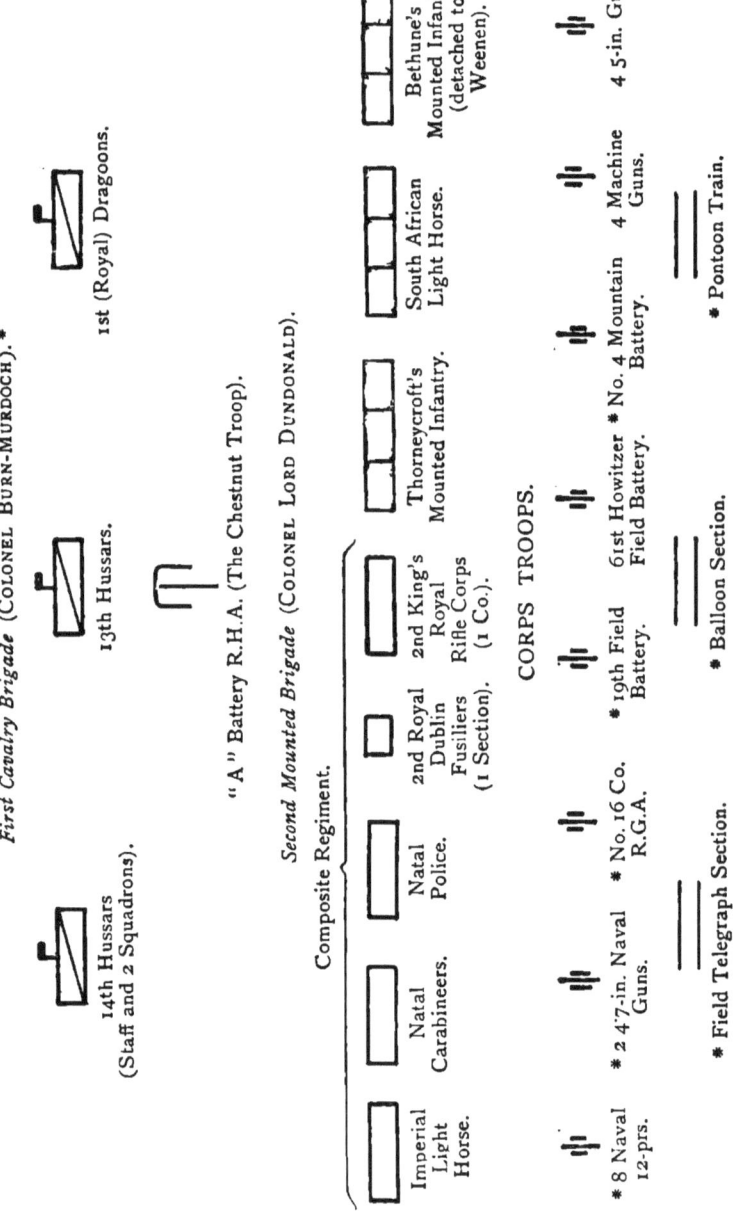

APPENDIX II.—continued.

APPENDIX II.

Fifth Infantry Brigade.

MAJOR-GENERAL HART.* (Until 20th, Second GARRISON OF CHIEVELEY.)

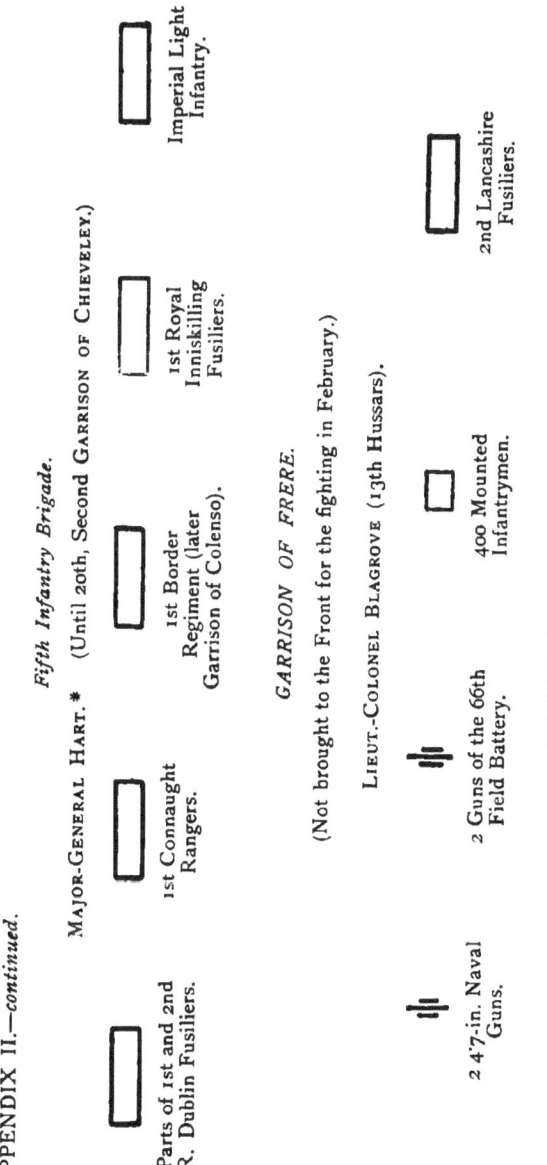

GARRISON OF FRERE.

(Not brought to the Front for the fighting in February.)

LIEUT.-COLONEL BLAGROVE (13th Hussars).

REMARKS:—

1. The distribution of Troops underwent constant variation during the course of the fighting.
2. The Units marked * came on to the scene of operations partly about 17th, partly about 27th February.

APPENDIX III.

SUMMARY OF BRITISH CASUALTY LISTS.

Unit.	Officers. Killed.	Officers. Wounded.	Men. Killed.	Men. Wounded.	Officers. Captured or Missing.	Men. Captured or Missing.	Total. Officers.	Total. Men.	* Percentage of Losses. Officers.	* Percentage of Losses. Men.
Second Attempt at Relief.										
ACTION AT THABA MYAMA, 20TH JANUARY.										
1st and 2nd Dublin Fusiliers* (parts of)	1	1	5	35	—	—	2	40	10	5.5
1st York and Lancaster	—	2	10	71	—	—	2	81	8	10.1
2nd Lancashire Fusiliers	—	7	18	90	—	—	7	108	28	13.5
Total Casualties of Hart's and Woodgate's Brigades and of Dundonald's Mntd. Brigade	—	—	—	—	—	—	2	34	295	—	—
ACTION AT BASTION HILL, 21ST JANUARY.										
2nd Queen's	—	5	4	31	—	2	5	37	20	4.6
2nd West Yorkshire	1	1	4	35	—	4	2	43	8	5.4
2nd East Surrey	—	1	4	18	—	8	1	30	4	3.8
Total Casualties†	—	—	24	223	—	4		251	—	—
ACTION AT SPION KOP, 24TH JANUARY.										
2nd King's Own (Royal Lancaster)	3	4	34	98	1	1	8	133	32	16.6
2nd Lancashire Fusiliers	3	5	39	97	3	34	11	170	61	24.3
2nd Middlesex	3	4	20	58	1	—	8	78	32	9.8
2nd Dorsetshire	—	—	—	1	—	—		1		
2nd Scottish Rifles	3	6	20	64	—	1	9	85	36	10.6
3rd King's Royal Rifles	2	4	19	65	—	1	6	85	24	10.6
Imperial Light Infantry (1,000 men)	?	?	31	72	?	19	?	122	?	12.2
Thorneycroft's Mntd. Infantry (about 180 men)	6	5	20	40	-..	—	11	60	?	33.0
Total Casualties‡	28	34	175	520	6	281	68	976	?	about 5
Total Casualties in Second attempt at Relief	30	53	292	1060	4	303	87	1655	?	about 6

APPENDIX III.—BRITISH CASUALTIES.

Unit.	Officers.		Men.		Offi-cers. Captured or Missing.	Men. Captured or Missing.	Total. Officers.	Total. Men.	* Percentage of Losses. Officers.	* Percentage of Losses. Men.
	Killed.	Wounded.	Killed.	Wounded.						

Third Attempt at the Relief.
ENGAGEMENTS AT VAALKRANZ, 5TH TO 7TH FEBRUARY.

Unit	K.O.	W.O.	K.M.	W.M.	Cap/Miss O.	Cap/Miss M.	Tot O.	Tot M.	% O.	% M.
1st Durham Light Infantry	2	6	12	76	—	—	8	88	32	11·0
1st Rifle Brigade	—	5	5	76	—	—	5	81	20	10·1
11th Brigade (Wynne)	—	—	—	—	—	—	—	23	—	0·7
4th Brigade (Lyttelton)	—	—	—	—	—	—	—	225	—	6
2nd Brigade (Hildyard)	—	—	—	—	—	—	—	40	—	1
Total Casualties in the Third attempt at the Relief	2	18	23	326	—	5	20	354	—	about 1·7

Fourth Attempt at the Relief.
ENGAGEMENTS FROM 15TH TO 18TH FEBRUARY (CINGOLO—MONTE CHRISTO).

Unit	K.O.	W.O.	K.M.	W.M.	Cap/Miss O.	Cap/Miss M.	Tot O.	Tot M.	% O.	% M.
Total Casualties	1	8	13	180	—	4	9	197	—	—

ENGAGEMENTS FROM 19TH TO 27TH FEBRUARY (WYNNE'S, HART'S, PIETERS HILL).

Unit	K.O.	W.O.	K.M.	W.M.	Cap/Miss O.	Cap/Miss M.	Tot O.	Tot M.	% O.	% M.
Total Casualties	22	91	245	1530	1	3	114	1778	—	—
Total Casualties in the Fourth attempt at the Relief	23	99	258	1710	1	7	123	1975	—	7·6

Casualties of individual Units during the last Attempt at the Relief.
ACTION AT HART'S HILL, 24TH FEBRUARY.

Unit	K.O.	W.O.	K.M.	W.M.	Cap/Miss O.	Cap/Miss M.	Tot O.	Tot M.	% O.	% M.
1st Inniskilling Fusiliers	3	8	54	165 above	—	—	11	219	44	31·3
1st Connaught Rangers	—	7	19	100	—	—	7	? 120	28	17·1

Casualties in the Period 14th to 27th February.

Unit	K.O.	W.O.	K.M.	W.M.	Cap/Miss O.	Cap/Miss M.	Tot O.	Tot M.	% O.	% M.
2nd Somersetshire Light Infy.	3	1	11	80	—	—	4	91	16	11·4
2nd Queen's	—	7	7	120	—	—	7	127	28	15·9
1st South Lancashire	1	3	10	81	—	—	4	91	16	11·4
2nd King's Own (Rl. Lancaster)	2	8	28	145	—	—	10	173	50	24·7
2nd Scots' Fusiliers	4	9	26	72	—	—	13	98	52	12·3
2nd Royal Fusiliers	1	4	3	70	—	—	5	73	20	9·1
2nd East Surrey	1	6	27	86	—	—	7	113	28	14·1

APPEXDIX III.—BRITISH CASUALTIES.

SUMMARY.

	Officers.	Men.
Losses in the First Attempt at the Relief (Colenso)	62	892
,, Second ,, ,, (Spion Kop)	87	1655
,, Third ,, ,, (Vaalkranz)	20	354
,, Fourth ,, ,, (Monte Christo—Pieters Hill)	123	1975
Total Casualties during the Relief of Ladysmith	292	4876

= 18 per cent. of original strength.

---

* The strength of the Battalions is taken at 25 Officers and 860 Men, or where actual losses had previously been incurred, correspondingly lower. Only those Battalions in which casualties were specially severe are specified.

† Including Troops which did not actually take part in the action at Bastion Hill.

‡ According to Botha's report the number of killed was considerably greater. It is said that 650 corpses lay on the plâteau of Spion Kop and 150 on the slope facing the British.

INDEX.

EXPLANATION OF ABBREVIATIONS.

B. H.—Bastion Hill.
D. F.—Driefontein.
H. H.—Hart's Hill.
M. C.—Monte Christo.
P. G.—Poplar Grove.
S. K.—Spion Kop.
T. M.—Thaba Myama
V. K.—Vaalkranz.
W. H.—Wynne's Hill.

Abandonment of, Boer laager Green Hill, 242; Siege of Ladysmith, 285; of Wepener, 291; Capitals and territory do not involve loss of fighting force, 317, 318, 338.

Action P. G., 9-22: D. F., 23-38: comments on, 46: Wagon Hill, 73: Acton Homes, 105-107, 109: T. M., 113-131: B. H., 122, 123, 127: V. K., 186-220: M. C., Cingolo, 232-245: Onderbrook, 251-253: W. H., 254-261: H. H., 263-272: P. H., 273-284: Sannah's Post, 291: Dewetsdorp, 293: Hout Nek, 294: Sand River, 298: Helpmakaar, 299: near Boshof, 300: Relief of Mafeking, 301: E. of Johannesburg, 303: Six Mile Spruit, 305: Alleman's Nek, 314: Bronkhorst Spruit, 317: Bergendal, 318.

Acton Homes, Dundonald's Mounted Brigade at, 105; importance to *Boers*, 105; dangers of route to *British*, 107.

Address General Buller's to Natal Army, 85; comment on, 327.

Advanced Guards. *See* Tactics.

Afrikander, De Wet on, 41.

Alexandra Berg, struggle for possession of, D. F., 30.

Ambush, Boer, failure of, 27.

Ammunition, Artillery, Boer, ineffective, 9, 31, 129, 206; effective, 149.

Annexation by British of Orange Free State, 302; of Transvaal, 320.

Armistice, tacitly recognised, H. H., 272

Artificial thirst, 156.

Artillery. *See* Tactics.

Artilleryman, Boer qualities as, 278.

Athletic sports in British camp, 202.

Atmosphere, deceptive clearness of, 11.

Attack. *See* Tactics.

Balloon section, position on march for action, 262.

Bastion Hill captured but abandoned by British, 122; unprepared assault of, 127.

Battle of S. K., 132-185; Diamond Hill, 305.

Bayonet. *See* Tactics.

Biggarsberg, Boers inactive in, 288; turned by General Buller, 299.

Bloemfontein, British cut railway N. of, 39; march on and bloodless capture of, 39; President's hurried departure and Lord Roberts' entry, 40; situation after capture of, 42, 290; outbreak of typhoid fever, 290; Lord Roberts advances northwards from, 297.

Boer: Disordered retreat after P. G., 12; rally at D. F., 26; stout resistance, 30; retreat, 36; temporary dispersal, 40. In Natal after Battle of Colenso: Inactivity in Colenso position, 64; attack Ladysmith south front, 72; reinforce position on Upper Tugela, 77;

Acton Homes, 105-109; T. M., 113-131; S. K., 132-179; V. K., 186-220; M. C.—Cingolo, 232-245; final operations preceding abandonment Siege of Ladysmith, 246-288; rally under de Wet, 290-295; retirement towards Pretoria, 296-307; de Wet's movements, 308-313; in Eastern Transvaal, 314-321; opposition finally suppressed, 321.
Confidence in own invincibility, 64, 202, 272; quickly restored after disaster, 248, 290; in marksmanship, 205.
Exaltation of spirits, 64, 187.
Good-nature, instance of, 272.
Government: Kroonstad, 40; Lindley, 301; Heilbron, 301; Middelburg, 317; Machadodorp, 312; extinction of does not involve cessation of hostilities, 320; flaccidity of regarding desertion, 227.
Individuality well developed, 155, 325, 326.
Routine in position, 64.
Sanitary arrangements faulty, 65.
Botha, Christian, at Cingolo, 228, 235; commands in Biggarsberg, 288; finally refuses negotiate surrender with General Buller, 314; opposes General Buller's northward advance in Transvaal and circles round him, 316; prominent leader in guerilla warfare S.E. Transvaal and N. Natal, 321.
Botha, Louis, assumes command U. Tugela, 113; profits by Boer mobility, 119; energy and *coup d'œil*, 147, 163; vainly urges offensive action after S. K., 188; furlough, 188; relations with Lucas Meyer, 227; S. of Langverwacht, 247; loses confidence, 282; commands rearguard Boer retirement northwards in Natal, 285; Chief Commandant *vice* Joubert, 297; leader in guerilla warfare N. and E. Transvaal, 321.
Brakfontein Heights strongly defended, 91; demonstrative attacks on, 96, 102, 108, 125, 160; influence of position on action V. K., 198; Krupp gun on, 203; demonstrative attack on, 204.

Bridges: Pontoon, 99, 196, 206, 214, 251, 276.
Railway: Bethulie and Norval's Pont destroyed and reconstructed, 41, 42; N. of Bloemfontein cut by British, 39; Moddespruit by Boers, 286; Sand River do., 298.
Road Bethulie intact, 42; Little Tugela do., 84; Langverwacht Spruit Railway, advance by, H. H., 264.
British Government, despatches to and from, 59, 60, 93, 133, 178, 180-185, 188, 192, 194, 211.
Soldier, tributes to merit of, 34, 36, 179, 185, 267, 338.
Buller, General Sir Redvers, after Battle of Colenso, 59-62; withdraws southwards, 63; Lord Roberts relieves in Chief Command S. Africa, 71; during Wagon Hill fight, 73, 74; resumes offensive, 75; looks for annihilation of Enemy, 76; on wood-fighting, 76, 217; moves westwards, 77; address to troops, 85, 328; projects an enveloping attack, 91, 92; dispenses with co-operation Ladysmith garrison, 93, 129, 190; confides principal task to General Warren, 95; dissatisfaction with operations, 100, 133; relations with General Warren, 107, 133, 134; ignorance of intentions regarding S. K., 112; position during Battle S. K., and nomination of Col. Thorneycroft for command on summit, 153; breaks off demonstrative attack Brakfontein Heights, 161; first withdrawal across Tugela, 178; report on S. K., 179; retains confidence of troops, 186; persistence in offensive, 188, 190, 193; variableness of spirits, 188, 190, 193, 194; fresh plan, 194; on situation, 195; Council of War, 196; V. K. position during action, 201; breaks off action, 211; indecision, 213; report on V. K., 215; encouraged by Lord Roberts, 216; Council of War, 217; depressed, 221; urges offensive and Lord Roberts approves, 224, 225; consideration for troops, 231-233, 237, 287; checks pursuit M. C., 242; P. H., 284; decides on advance by Ladysmith road, 249; holds to plan,

253, 261; W. H. and H. H., 263, 270; asks for truce to bury killed, 272; orders attack of P. H., 273; reconnoitres Hlangwane crossing, 273; centralisation of command, 274, 280; enters Ladysmith, 286; proposals for further operations overruled, 287; advances and turns Biggarsberg, 299; clears N. Natal and halts at Newcastle, 300; resumes operations after negotiations with C. Botha, 314; guarding railway, 315; advance to Machadodorp and operations in support of Lord Roberts, 315-319.

Burger, Schalk, on Upper Tugela, 90, 102, 113; at S. K., 147, 164, 175; commands in L. Botha's absence, 203; indecision after V. K., 219.

Cable, use of in crossing river, 97; in moving heavy guns up Zwart Kop, 196.

Cape Colony: Lord Kitchener proceeds to quell threatened insurrection, 23; invaded by Boers, 321.

Capitals of Enemy: occupation of an inconclusive strategical measure, 20, 338.

Capitulation of Bloemfontein, 40; suggested of Ladysmith rejected by General White, 61; of Johannesburg, 303; of Pretoria, 305.

Capture by *British* of ammunition P. G,, 16; of laager on Green Hill, 240; of Prinsloo and 4,000 Boers, 310; of rolling-stock, 39, 42, 320.
By *de Wet*, 291, 306, 311.

Casualties: *Boer*—P. G., 17; D. F., 37; T. M., 131; S. K., 180; V. K. 219; M. C., etc., 245; Onderbrook, 253; W. H. and H. H., 270. *British*—P. G., 17; D. F., 37, 54; summarised, 55; T. M. and B. H., 125, 354; S. K., 180, 354; V. K., 206, 219, 355; M. C., etc., 245, 355; Onderbrook, 253, 355; W. H. and H. H., 270, 355; P. H., 355.

Cavalry, P. G., 9; delay in movement, 19; no pursuit, 36, 284; with advance on Pretoria, 297, 298; Diamond Hill, 306; in Eastern Transvaal, 317-319. *See* Tactics.

Chance favourable to Boers, 142, 164; reliance of Boers on, 203.

Character: force of General Kelly-Kenny, 48; General White, 61; Louis Botha, 119, 147, 163, 175, 177; Lord Roberts, 304.

Cingolo, capture of by Dundonald's Mounted Brigade, 236; of Nek, 242.

Clausewitz on pauses in operations, 45; on evasion of battle, 339.

Clery, General, instructions from General Warren, 110; T. M., 114-129; in Council of War before S. K., 132; V. K., 199; falls ill, 220; Division attacked near Elandslaagte, 288; in Transvaal, 314, 315.

Climatic influences, 63, 87, 202, 231-233, 237.

Coke, Major-General, commanding 10th Brigade, 351; crosses Tugela, 128; S. K. reconnaissance, 133; directs right wing of attack, 134; lame, 135; temporary command 5th Division, 137; operation order, 138; prepares rallying point, 143; sends reinforcements to summit and ascends, 152; ignorance of Lt.-Col. Thorneycroft's appointment to command on summit, 153; meets fugitives, 156; forms a reserve, 158; reports favourably, 166; recognises crisis, 167; called to General Warren's head-quarters, 173, 174; Lord Roberts' report, 183, 184; V. K., Spearman's Farm, 204; covers withdrawal, 218; crosses Tugela and moves against Boers on Onderbrook, 251-253; covers rear of army on heights S. of Onderbrook, 262, 273.

Colenso, situation after Battle of, 59, 75; British withdrawal from, 63, and its moral influence, 64; inactivity of Boers in position, 65; British advance north of, 251.

Colonial troops, 42, 291, 295.
Warfare qualities needed for conduct of, 70; essence of should be annihilation of Enemy's live force, 339.

Colour of clothing should harmonise with local surroundings, 150.

Column, Supply; deficient in Natal Army, 69; improvised, 70; difficulties encountered, 84.
Transport, formation on march, 109.
Command, *British*, in S. Africa, Lord Roberts *vice* General Buller, 71. *Boer*: Louis Botha on U. Tugela, 113; of all forces on Tugela, superseding Lucas Meyer, who not informed, 227.
Confusion of at S. K., 135, 153, 158, 167, 170, 173, 174, 184. *Also under* Tactics.
Comments, P. G., 18; D. F., 45, 46-53; supply columns, 69, 70, 86; passage of Tugela, 92, 93, 95, 98, 102, 104, 106, 107, 111; T. M., 115, 116, 117, 121, 124, 128, 130; S. K., on orders for, 136; on Battle, 132, 169-172; on General Buller's plans, 191, 193, 197, 198; on orders for V. K., 202; on passage of Tugela, V. K., 206, 207; on action, V. K., 210, 211, 213, 214; M. C., Cingolo, 231, 233, 235, 237, 242, 243; operations in final attempt relief of Ladysmith, 248-250, 252-254, 256, 259, 260, 264, 265, 267, 269, 270, 272, 274, 276, 282-284, 286, 287; operations April-November, 294, 295, 298, 302, 304, 305, 312, 318, 321; general retrospect, 324-344.
Communication, line of, dominant *British* regard for, 25, 43, 69, 290, 301, 304, 309, 314-316; defects in *Boer*, 130.
Confidence of his troops in General Buller, 186; of Lord Roberts in his own plans, 192, 222, 304. *See* Boer.
Council of War: *Boer*, before surrender of Bloemfontein, 38; after S. K., 188; V. K., 129; P. H., 284. *British*, General Warren's before T. M., 109; before S. K., 132; General Buller's before V.K., 196; after V. K., 217.
Cover, malign attraction of to Boers, 89, 160, 163.
Cubic capacity of a biscuit tin, 138.

Darkness, withdrawal of compromised troops under cover of, T. M., 123, 127; Onderbrook, 253; H. H., 268; of Boers from S. of Tugela, 238; disintegrating influence of, 257-259, 260, 263.
De Aar, Lord Kitchener proceeds to, 23.
Decision: Independence of essential, 121; Louis Botha's prompt, 147, 163; want of, 249; Brigade-Major's prompt, 271.
Defensive attitude in Natal, divergent views of Lord Roberts, General Buller, and War Office, 75, 191-196, 216, 221-225.
Boer reliance on originates in sense of weakness, 327.
Tactics, comments on, 341.
De la Rey, 21, 26, 312, 313, 321.
Delay in British operations, 3; of cavalry, P. G., 19, 44; in operations on U. Tugela fatal, 92, 104, 107; in transmission messages, S. K., 166; M. C.-Cingolo, due to great heat, 231-233, 237; N. of Colenso, 249; at Bloemfontein, 290.
Demoralisation: *Boer*, after P. G., 12; after D. F. recognised by leaders, 40; on U. Tugela under prolonged strain, 131, 143; S. K., 176; M. C.-Cingolo, 242; W. H., 260; H. H., 277; after Siege of Ladysmith raised, 285.
British, Onderbrook, 252; W. H., 257-260.
Desertion, Boer, 227, 277.
De Wet, Christian, acting Chief Commanding Free Staters, 6; P.G., 12; D. F., 26; before Bloemfontein, 38; knowledge of Afrikander, 40; rashness of operations, 294; remarkable success, 306, 310-312; leader in guerilla warfare, 21, 321; quotations from 12, 26, 41, 302.
Diamond Hill, action at, 305.
Discipline, *Boer*, need of, 21, 41, 160, 163, 187, 205, 227, 238, 277, 327. *British*, firmness of counterbalances temporary loss of moral force, 219.
Paramount need of in training to arms, 41, 205.
Disorganisation, W. H., 263; H. H., 273, 276.
Disregard of Enemy, 47, 202.
Distances increased in modern battles, 52, 342.
Distribution: *Boer*, P. G., 5; D. F., 26; after Battle of Colenso, 64; Wagon Hill, 72; U. Tugela, 77,

INDEX.

90, 103, 108; T. M., 113, 126; S. K., 142, 147; V. K., 203, 212; M. C.-Cingolo, 227, 228, 231, 233; N. of Tugela, 247, 251, 254, 276, 279; beginning of May, 296. *British*, after Cronje's surrender, 3, 4; P. G., 7; D. F., 24, 29; after Battle of Colenso, 63, 71, 346; for operations U. Tugela, 78, 79, 94, 103, 109; T. M., 114; S. K., 134, 139; V. K., 187, 196, 203, 218; M. C.-Cingolo, 232, 234, 238, 241; N. of Tugela, 250, 253, 261, 263, 270, 273, 275; S.E. Free State, 292; beginning of May, 296; operations against de Wet, 309; march to Koomati Poort, 314.

For combat: *Boer*, all in first line, 326; *British*, conventional but incorrectly applied, 331. See Tactics.

Driefontein, action of, 23-38; turning movement planned, 24; Boer strength, 26; Sixth Division at, 28, 52; Boer entrenchments, 30; formation for attack, 30; rifle ammunition deficient, 34; well-developed fire-fight, 35; effective volleys, 36; bayonet attack, 36; resolute frontal attack, 36; absence of Cavalry pursuit, 36; loss of connection, 37; casualties, 37, 54; General French's unusual inactivity, 46; local rank, 47; excessive detail in plans, 47; excellence of General Kelly-Kenny's dispositions, 48; 81st Field Battery, 50; Welch regiment, 51; suitable formations, 51; opportune shock action, 51; "a model of interdependent action of the two arms," 334.

Dundonald, General Lord, commands Mounted Brigade Natal Army, 348, 352; Upper Tugela, 105, 106; Acton Homes, 109; B. H., keen action, 122; offers take machine guns up S. K., 155; by prompt action captures Cingolo, 236; eagerness for action and pursuit, 284.

Eighth Division, joins Lord Roberts' force, 292; in relief column Dewetsdorp, 293; near Thaba Nchu, 297; detachment of moves northward, 304; in N.E. Free State, 309; co-operates in capture Prinsloo in Roode Berg, 310.

Emergency ration, prejudicial absence of, 104.

"Emptiness of battlefield," 67.

Encampments, Boer, concealed on U. Tugela, 89.

Enemy, annihilation of, prime object of warfare, 20, 21, 76, 104, 128, 216, 294, 298, 317, 318, 338, 339; illusions regarding, and disregard for his possible action, 47, 202.

Engines, steam traction, inefficiency in bad ground, 79.

Enlistment, voluntary, baneful influence of, 21, 338.

Enteric fever: *Boer*, 64; *British*, 290.

Entrenchments. See Tactics.

Escort, D. F., for transport excessive, 48; for transport moving to Venter's Spruit, 109.

European Press, falsely informed by Boers, 37.

Exhaustion caused by night marches, 18, 144, and enterprises, 260; of both adversaries on summit S. K., 171, and after Battle of, 186, 187.

Expedients: biscuit-tins, etc., for water, 138, 233; cable in passage of rivers, 97; canvas for masking guns, 278; for head-cover, 114, 228; for shelters, 228; wire cable for hauling heavy guns up Zwart Kop, 196.

Eyesight, British need of training, 120, 331; superiority of Boer, 240.

Fifth Division, General Sir C. Warren commanding, 347, 351; arrival in S. Africa, 71; proceeds to Springfield, 79, 84; passage of Tugela, 91, 94, 95, 98-100; T. M. and S. K. (*which see*); Coke's Brigade rejoins, 187; V. K., 201, 204, 207, 217, 218, 220; M. C.-Cingolo, 232, 234, 239, 240, 243; advance to Ladysmith, 250-253, 261, 263, 274, 275, 278-281; commanded by General Hildyard, takes Botha's Pass, 314.

Fog at S. K., 148.

Forage, scarcity of, 13, 44 (*footnote*).

Foreigners with Boers, advice of spurned, 203; under Villebois-Mareuil, 300; cross Portuguese frontier, 320.

Fourth Division, Commanding General Sir G. White, Garrison of Ladysmith under Sir R. Buller's command, 93; General Lyttelton appointed to, 287; in operations supporting Lord Roberts' eastward movement, 315.

Franco-German War, 1870, references to, 154, 328.

Free Staters, General Warren foresees withdrawal of from Natal, 224; withdraw from Natal, 248, 277, 278; separate from Transvaalers, 302.

French, General, P. G., 12, 13; D. F., commands left column, 24, 27, 28, 32, 37; comments, 46, 47; operates towards Wepener, 292, and Hout Nek, 293; commands Cavalry Division in advance to Pretoria, 297, 298, 302, 303; left column of attack Diamond Hill, 306; in Lord Roberts' operations E. of Pretoria, 316-319.

Furlough, Boers proceed on, 41, 64, 188, 226; return from, 291, 307; origin of practice, 226.

German Corps, Wagon Hill, 72; between T. M. and S. K., 108, 120; S. K., 142, 147.

German officers and others, narratives and remarks, 16, 26, 32, 34, 36, 64, 127,* 130, 148, 151, 176, 198, 213, 269, 270, 272, 277, 284.

German regulations retain value, 52, 333, 342.

Ground. *See* Tactics.

Hart, Major-General, Commanding Fifth Infantry Brigade, 346, 353; to Frere, 63, 71; to Upper Tugela, 78, 82, 83; crosses at Trichardt's Drift, 99; advises night attack of Boer position, 104, 107; to Venter's Spruit Valley, 109; T. M., 110, 114, 117-119, 121, 125, 126; S. K., 135, 150; V. K., 204, 206, 215, 217, 218; final advance to Ladysmith, 230, 244, 253, 261-271, 273 - 275; S.E. Free State, 292-294; Heidelberg, 308, 311, 315.

Hart's Hill and Hollow, 246, 263-274.

Heat of weather, 60, 202, 231, 233.

Hildyard, Major-General, Commanding Second Infantry Brigade, 346, 350; to Chieveley, 63, 71; march to U. Tugela, 78, 82-85; passage of Tugela, 89, 94, 98, 99, 104, 106, 109; T. M., 117, 124, 127; S. K., 132, 135, 171; V. K., 199, 204, 207, 209, 211, 215, 218; M. C.-Cingolo, 232, 234-236, 238-244; N. of Tugela, 250, 253, 256-259, 263, 270, 273, 275, 280, 281, 288; succeeds General Warren, Commanding Fifth Division, 314.

Hlangwane, flanks Boer position at Colenso, 226; Boer works on, 228; outflanked but held on to by Boers, 244; passages over Tugela N. of, 276, 278; as Artillery position, 254, 274, 276, 278.

Horses, exhaustion of, 3, 12, 15, 16, 18, 43; gun teams of ten, 13; receipt of, 294.

Hussar Hill, topography, 229; captured by Mounted Brigade, 232; unsatisfactory Artillery position on, 237.

Impression false of Enemy, orders for advance on Bloemfontein framed under, 47; produced by invisibility of Boers, 67.

Information accurate about Boers, 108; defects in transmission of in action, S. K., 168; false supplied by Boers to Press, 37†; influence of false and faulty on operations, 126, 149, 192, 243, 306; Kaffirs furnish, 65, 77; signalled from Ladysmith, 191, 231, 233.

Insurrection, threatened in Cape Colony, 23.

Johannesburg police, sole Boer disciplined force, D. F., 26; Bergendal, 318; surrender of; 303.

Joubert, Commandant General, makes vigorous attack on Ladysmith, 72; views on the war, 226; regard for Lucas Meyer, 227; lack of interest, 247; raises Siege of Ladysmith, 285; death of and replacement by Louis Botha, 297.

Kaffirs employed carrying ammunition, 5, entrenching, 90, 114, in furnishing information, 65, 77.

Kelly-Kenny, Lieut.-General, Commanding Sixth Division: P. G., 7, 13, 15; D. F., 23-38; comments, 47-52; in Bloemfontein, 297.

King's Royal Rifles, skilful capture of Twin Peaks, 162, 163; resolute action, W. H., 256.

Kitchener, General Lord, proceeds to De Aar, 23; talent for organisation, 70; directs operations against De Wet, 311.

Kroonstad, Boer Government at, 40; British occupation of, 298.

Kruger, President, stimulates Boers, 11, 25, 72; leaves Bloemfontein, 40; appoints Louis Botha to command on Tugela, 113; quits South Africa, 320.

Kuropatkin, General, on overrated importance of formations, 336.

Ladysmith, suggestion of capitulation of rejected by General White, 61; political importance of, 60, 62; attack on (Wagon Hill), 72; Lord Roberts suggests evacuation of after relief, 75; co-operation of garrison not arranged for operations U. Tugela, 93, 129, 135, nor for V. K., 191; General White proposes to break out from, 189; public clamour for relief, 224; information supplied by, 231, 233; Siege of raised, exhaustion of garrison, 285, which forms Fourth Division under General Lyttelton, 287.

Leaders, Boer, recognise demoralisation, 40, 284; in guerilla warfare, 21, 321.

Leaders, superior, control of reinforcements by, 154.

Lethargy, Boer, 64, 97, 226, 260.

Linear tactics, example of, 100.

Lines of communication, British, 23, 43, 68, 291, 304; de Wet's operations against, 291, 294, 303, 309, 311.

Local rank, D. F., influence of system, 47; S. K., confusion of command arising from, 153, 158, 167, 170, 173, 174.

"Long Tom," V. K., more noisy than noxious, 214.

Lucas Meyer, commanding Boers at Colenso, character, consideration for, 227; slowness of action, 231; erroneous impressions, 237; on left flank N. of Tugela, 247; P. H., lethargic, 282.

Lyddite, effects of, 130, 210.

Lyttelton, Major-General, Commanding Fourth Infantry Brigade, 347; Second Infantry Division, 350; Fourth Infantry Division, 287; to Frere, 63, 71; to Springfield, 79, 83; to Spearman's Farm, 84; to Potgieter's Drift, 90, 94; demonstrations, 96-98, 102, 108, 125, 160; Twin Peaks, 161-163; One Tree Hill, 180; V. K., 196, 199-201, 204, 206, 209-215; to Chieveley, 218-220; commanding Second Division, 220; M. C.-Cingolo, 232-245; operations N. of Tugela, 250, 253-267, 269-271, 273-275, 281, 282; commanding Fourth Division, 287, 299, 315.

Mafeking, operations for relief of, 300.

Magazines, formation of Natal Army, 68-70.

Manœuvres or pitched battles? 6, 20, 47, 76, 244, 298, 302, 303, 305, 317, 318, 338-340.

Manœuvres, Natal Army wanting in mobility for, 86, 107.

Manœuvres, peace, false views acquired at, 51, 260; V. K., resemblance of action to, 207.

Manœuvring, space for need of, 250, 274.

Maps, British defective, 92, 145.

March on Bloemfontein, Force divided for, 24, 47; flank to Springfield, 77-86; forced, 40, 233; Lord Roberts' to Pretoria, commendation of, 305; night, exhaustion due to, 18, 144, 260; order of, 25, 261; cause of slow rate of, 86.

Marksmanship, ill-advised confidence of *Boers* in, 205; *Boer* gift, 325; Lord Roberts on *British*, 330.

Mental power, need of, 121, 343.

Methuen, General Lord, operations after Relief of Kimberley, 300; in operations against De Wet, 311.

Militia Army, weak characteristics of, 21, 41, 90, 187, 327.

Militia, British, incorporated in General Chermside's Division, 292.

Mobility: *Boer*, D. F., 46; value in extended positions, etc., 89, 103, 106, 279, 283, 326; appreciated by L. Botha, 119, 142; facilitates evasion of enveloping movements, 298. *British*, deficient in for manœuvre, 86, 107, 198.

Modern battle, fire action essence of, 52, 162, 235, 270, 340; distances increased in, 52, 330; close formations impossible, 52, 334; need of independent decisions in, 121, 344, and of mental development of all ranks in, 331, 343.

Monte Christo—Cingolo, action of: Objective, occupation of Hlangwane, 226; Lucas Meyer, Boer Commandant, incapacity, 227, 238; Boer disposition, 228, 233, 238; topography, 229; weakness of Boer left flank, 230, 238; deliberation in Boer reinforcing movements, 231; information supplied by Ladysmith garrison, 231, 233, 235; need for prompt British action, 231, 233; British dispositions, 232, 234, 238; Dundonald's Mounted Brigade seizes Hussar Hill, 232; Cingolo, 236; Artillery position Hussar Hill, 232; great heat, 231, 233; Second Division advance on Cingolo, 234, 236; on Monte Christo, 239–241; Fifth Division on Hussar Hill, 232; threatens Green Hill, 239; inactivity, 243; General Lyttelton's action, 241; Boers retire unpursued, 242, 244; comments, 243.

Moral effect of Artillery overrated, 116; of enfilade lyddite fire, 130.

Moral influence of withdrawal from Colenso, 64, from Vaalkranz, 219; of indecisive measures in warfare, 337.

Moral qualities of adversaries. *See* Qualities.

Mounted Brigade (Natal Army): Composition, 348, 352; march to Potgieter's Drift, 84, 94, 98, 100, 103; Acton Homes, etc., skilful advanced guard work, 105; weakened, 105; Bastion Hill, 122; V. K., 200, 203, 218; Hussar Hill, 230; Cingolo, 236; unite in fire-action with artillery from Hlangwane, 278; pursuit after P. H. delayed, 283; cautious action, 286; reach Ladysmith, 286.

Mounted Infantry re-organised into four Brigades, 4; under General French to Dewetsdorp, 292, and under General Hamilton to Thaba Nchu, 293; distribution for advance to Pretoria, 297.

Musketry training, value of, 205.

Natal Army: Composition and distribution, 346–349, 350–353; casualties, 354–356; withdraws from Colenso and pauses, 63; strength, 68; supply arrangements, 68; distribution, 71; wanting in mobility, 86, 107; crosses Tugela, 96; after S. K. withdraws across Tugela, 178; reinforcements reach, 187; V. K., 198–218; redistribution, 220; repose and re-equipment, 221; final operation Relief of Ladysmith, 221 – 285; reaches Ladysmith and reposes, 286; strength, 296; advance northwards and halts, 299; guards railway S.E. Transvaal, 314; works in concert with Lord Roberts' Army, 316–319.

Natal railway working capacity, 68.

Naval guns, P. G., at extreme ranges, 15; Natal Army in corps troops, 348, 352; difficulties on march, 86; orders regarding, 95; on Mount Alice, 96, 97, 103, 125; S. K., ordered to summit, 159, 171, 172; V. K., 196, 199, 200, 204, 206, 209; Hussar Hill, 230, 234, 237; some taken N. of Colenso, 253, 254, 262; some on Hlangwane, 273: weights and mobility, 340.

Night attack, General Hart suggests, 104; possible value of after S. K., 172; suggested during V. K., 212.

Night marches, exhaustion caused by, 18, 144, 260.

Night operations and enterprises, comments on, 257, 260; withdrawal of compromised troops by, 123, 127, 238, 253.

Offensive, General Buller's adherence to, 188–195, 222–225; Boers fail in spirit of, 72, 187, 219, 226, 256, 257, 260, 269, 272, 325.

INDEX. 365

Officers armed with rifles S. K., 143; consequences of casualties among, S. K., 155; gallant exertions of, S. K., 156; lack training in fire-action, 329, mental grasp of needs in action, 331, "mutual understanding" in combined operations, 340.
Operations: Influence of Lord Roberts' on Relief of Ladysmith, 191, 192, 223–225, 248, 277, 285; purpose of General Buller's in N. Natal to support Lord Roberts in advance to Pretoria, 299; Clausewitz on pauses in, 45; General Buller on conduct of on Upper Tugela, 107, 133, 134; in Natal, termed "Fights for Positions," 272.
Organisation, talent for of Lords Roberts and Kitchener, 70; want of on Boer lines of communication, 130.
Orders, P. G., 6; march to Springfield, 78–83; General Buller's confidential to General Warren U. Tugela, 94; General Warren's to General Clery, 110; S. K., 136–140; V. K. 198–202; M. C.-Cingolo, 238; comments on, 243; advance to Ladysmith, 261–263; omission to communicate to all concerned, 153, 172, 270.
Over-reliance on Kaffir information, 191; on marksmanship without military training, 205.

Paardeberg victory, announcement of to troops, P. H., 278.
Pause in operations, after capture of Bloemfontein, 44, 290; after Battle of Colenso, employed in training troops, 63, 68, by Boers in entrenching, 76; after Relief of Ladysmith, 288; and after clearing N. Natal, 300; Clausewitz on, 45.
Peace manœuvres and training, illusions fostered in, 32, 50, 260, 344.
Personal reconnaissance by Generals—Lord Roberts, 4; General Kelly-Kenny, 9, 28, 48; General Buller, 87, 91, 217, 229, 248, 273; General Warren, 92, 109, 217; General Coke, 133, 136; Col. Thorneycroft, 136.

Personal relations, Generals Kelly-Kenny and French, 47; Generals Buller and Warren, 100, 107, 133; Louis Botha and Lucas Meyer, 227, 231, 247, 282.
Political considerations regarding Ladysmith, 60, 63, 189.
Pontoon bridges, construction of, 99, 196, 214, 251, 276, 277.
Pontoon troop, commendation of, 179, 251.
Poplar Grove, position and strength of adversaries, 4; Boer disposition, 5; Lord Roberts' orders, 6–8; action of, and comments, 9–22.
Position of head-quarters P. G., 8; S. K., 152, 169; V. K., 201; advance on Ladysmith, 262; Gen. Warren's and Gen. Hart's night 23rd Feb., 271.
Prisoners of war, British, release of, 305, 319; Prinsloo's commandoes captured, 310.
Public opinion, demand for further attempt Relief of Ladysmith, 224.

Qualities, characteristics, etc.: Action, promptness of British, 42, 157, 241, 243, 271, slowness of British, 92: adroitness and skill in selecting, entrenching and preparing positions—Boer, 7, 38, 88, 114, 126, 228, 246, 325; British, 196, 215, want of, 146, 330: caution, British, 11, 19, 284, 286: confidence in leaders, British, 187, loss of 67, 338: control, over-reliance on, British, 155, impatience of, Boer, 205, 310, 326, 336: coup d'œil, Boer, 163, 270; British, 241: courage, moral, British, 48, 61, 63, 174, 183, 189, 191, 304: determination, British, 216, 304: devotion to duty, British, 338: discipline, want of, Boer, 16, 41, 91, 187, 205: dulness, Boer, 228, 237, British, 165, 330: endurance, Boer, 177, British, 233, 304: energy, Boer, 177, British, 48, 242, 304, 338: enterprise, Boer, 291, 294, 303, 306, 308, 313, want of, British, 100, 102, 232, 237, 242, 248, 283, 286: eyesight, Boer, 240, ill-trained, British, 120, 240, 331: faint-heartedness, Boer, 17, 39, 40, 89, 119, 143, 160, 165, 276,

318: fixity of purpose, *British*, 223, 304: flaccidity, *Boer*, 227: grit, *British*, 20, 34, 219, 338: hesitation to incur losses, *Boer*, 269, *British*, 20, 48, 76, 111, 124, 194, 198, 244, 286, 298, 337, 338: home-sickness, *Boer*, 41, 64, 188, 226: horse-mastership, *British*, 44; inactivity, *Boer*, 97, 227, 247, 276: individual initiative, *Boer*, 147, 155, 207, 235, 256, 268, 271, 325, *British*, 122, 236, 271, want of, 155, 330: irresolution, *British*, 20, 178, 211, 231, 233, 237, 249, 250, 313, 338: keenness for fight, *British*, 73, 236, 284; lethargy, *Boer*, 64, 202, 226, 281: manliness, *Boer*, 160: marksmanship, *Boer*, 35, 155, 205, 240, 325: mobility, *Boer*, 119, 142: optimism, *British*, 149, 190, 191, 194: passivity of defence, *Boer*, 24, 65, 69, 327: pedantry, *British*, 102, 202, 204, 207, 335, 336, 343: pertinacity, *British*, 188, 193, 253: pessimism, *Boer*, 39, *British*, 59, 75, 213, 221, 336: procrastination, *British*, 92, 104, 231, 233, 249; rashness, *British*, 252, 266, 332, 335: self-conceit, *Boer*, 203, 272: self-confidence, *Boer*, 64, *British*, 186, 194, 202, decline of, 20, 338: self-effacement, *Boer*, 227, 282; *British*, 47, 95, 98, 100, 134, 182: self-reliance, *British*, 225, 304: unsteadiness, *British*, 258, 259, 271: vigilance, *British*, 27, want of, *Boer*, 228, 281, *British*, 126, 271: will-power, *Boer*, 177, weakening of, *British*, 20, 337.

Railway, governs general direction of British movements, 69, 192, 249, 253, 297, 304.
Rain, effect on S. African roads, 4, 84.
Ranges, Boer guns, 206.
Rapidity of movement entails sacrifice, 43; of Lord Roberts' Army, 305; of de Wet, 312.
Reconnaissance: Cavalry supported by Infantry, 23; effective, 27; absence of *Boer*, 65; inadequate *British*, 90, 92, 100, 113, 145, 249, 252; delay in discovering Munger's Drift, 194; Hlangwane crossing, 249, 273; *Boer* after S. K., 188.

Re-equipment Natal Army, 221; Lord Roberts' Army, 294.
Regimental system transport, 68.
Reinforcements, Natal Army, 187; Lord Roberts' Army, 294, 318.
Remounts abundantly supplied, 294.
Resistance, moral, Boers fail in, 119, 131, 143, 270.
Repose, Natal Army, 68, 186, 221, 226, 287; Lord Roberts' Army, 290; Boers snatch in action, 164.
Responsibility, delegation of, 94, 95, 110, 117, 134, 169.
Richardson, Colonel, prompt action regarding supply, 43.
Rivers, passage of, 87, 91, 97, 99, 179, 206-208, 218, 251, 264, 276.
Roads, affected by rain, 4, 84; same used by troops and transport, 86; repair of in action, 159; deemed necessary for transport during final operations Relief of Ladysmith, 249; de Wet's disregard for, 312.
Roberts, F.-M. Lord, preference for manœuvres and turning movements, 20, 29, 48, 75, 288, 298, 303, 306, 318; comments on, 337-340; talent for organisation, 71; on situation after Battle of Colenso, 75; report on S. K., 181; on defensive action in Natal, 192; sanctions advance *via* V. K., 194, and encourages bold action, 216; cannot reinforce Natal Army, and enjoins a waiting attitude, 222-225; at Bloemfontein, 290; advance to Pretoria, 297; tactics at Sand River, 298; looks for indirect support from Natal Army, 299, 300; intensity of resolution, 304; energy of command, 305; enters Pretoria, 305; delay on account of de Wet's operations, 308; secures second line of supply, 314; moves eastward, 317; at Belfast, 318; remark on British Infantry, 330.
Rolling stock, capture of by British, 39, 42, 320.
Routine, Boer in entrenched position, 65.
Ruse: Boer ambush discovered D. F., 27; Boers credit British with after Battle of Colenso, 65; Boer surprise-fire Brakfontein Heights betrayed, 205, same at

INDEX. 367

Onderbrook successful, 252; De Wet's, 291, 311.

Sacrifices, British hesitation to incur, P. G., 20; V. K., 198; Green Hill, 242 : paralyses delivery of decisive blow, 286, 298, and renders successes illusory, 338; entailed in rapid movement, 43; readiness to incur not expressed, 111; not severe, 338; Lord Roberts assumes responsibility for General Buller's, 216; Louis Botha hesitates to incur, 269.
Sanitary, Boer arrangements inferior, 65.
Shock-action, D. F., 36; difficulties attending proper choice of moment for, 50, well met, 51; British over-reliance on, 51, 85, 327, and frequent results, 331; further comments, 324, 332.
Signalling from and to Ladysmith, 61-63, 73-75, 93, 129, 135, 188-192, 231, 233; S. K., 148, 150, 152, 157, 159, 161, 163, 165, 166, 169 : overwrought operator, 151; need for supplementing, 169 : orders for arrangements P. G., 8; march to U. Tugela, 83; V. K., 201; observation of fire-effect, 116, 148, 201, 262.
Situation, review of, after occupation of Bloemfontein, 42, 290, Lord Roberts after Battle of Colenso, 75; on U. Tugela, 91-93, 107; General Buller's after S. K., 195; Lord Roberts after V. K., 223; at beginning of May, 296; September, 320.
Sixth Division, Lieut.-General Kelly-Kenny commanding, P. G., 7-10; D. F., 23-38, 46-52; casualties, 54, 55; Bloemfontein, 297.
South African Light Horse, Col. Byng commanding, B. H., 122.
Spicheren, ref. S. K. Artillery support to Infantry, 154.
Spion Kop, weakly held, 77, 91, 100; topography, 88, 89, 140, 141; General Warren proposes capture, 128; Battle of, 132-185; need of general action on whole of Boer front during, 132; British distribution, 134; General Woodgate in command *vice* Coke, 135; preliminary reconnaissance, 136; orders, 136-139; comments on, 139; limitation of action to local assault, 140; Boer position and distribution, 140-142; preparation of rallying-point, 143; Col. Thorneycroft guides and heads assault, 143; capture of summit, 144; neglect of further reconnaissance and consequent faulty occupation, 145; inadequate entrenchment and over-crowded firing line, 146; L. Botha's prompt action, co-operation of Boer guns, 147; fog on summit, hand-to-hand fighting, 148; sanguine report, 150; Boers creeping advance, 150; no British Artillery direct support, 153, 166; ill-judged dispatch of reinforcements to overcrowded summit, 154, 158, 167, 170; overpowering Boer fire, 156, 166; British retirement begins, 156; Col. Thorneycroft's resolute intrepidity, 157; confusion of command, 158, 167, 173, 174; General Warren's counter-measures, 159, and position on Three Tree Hill, 169; Twin Peaks captured and abandoned, 163; indecisive fighting at close quarters, 164; General Coke reports situation critical 5.50 p.m., 167; Col. Thorneycroft do. 6.30 p.m., 168; inadequacy of signalling arrangements, 169; exhaustion of both adversaries, 171; withdrawal of British ordered, 173; Boers also quit summit, 175; L. Botha's energy in restoring situation for Boers, 177; withdrawal of British across Tugela, 179; Lord Roberts' report, 180-184; Col. Thorneycroft's, 185.

Springfield, flank march to, 77-86; return to and garrisoning of, 218.

Springfontein, Guards' Brigade to, 41.

St. Hubert Farm, Gravelotte, ref. S. K., illogical reinforcement of attack on, 154.

Staff, General Buller's, advise turning movement N. of Cingolo, 248, 273; head-quarters' anxiety regarding line of communication in advance on Pretoria, 304.

Staff officer, promptitude on emergency of a, 271.

Steyn, President, leaves Bloemfontein, 40; urges energetic action, 72; at Lindley, 301; escorted by De Wet to Bushveld, 312; returns to Free State, 320.

Strategy: Annihilation of Enemy's living force prime object of all, 20, 21, 194, 295, 317, 318, 338, 339; a lost opportunity, 294; Capitals and territory, occupation of hostile an inconclusive form of, 20, 21, 317, 318, 338, 339. Combination of operations, *British*, in Natal and Western Theatre, 75, 191–193, 195, 221–225, 248, 287, 299, 315; on Tugela and in Ladysmith, 61–63, 73, 77, 93, 111, 129, 135, 136, 189, 191, 224, 285; in Orange River Colony, 293–295, 304, 309; during de Wet's movements, 308–313: *Boers*, on Tugela and investing Ladysmith, 73, 90, 106, 212, 285; during de Wet's movements, 308–313. Communications, *British* operations influenced by regard for, 23, 25, 42–44, 68, 128, 249, 261, 304, 306, 314, 315; *Boer* operations against *British*, 291, 303, 304, 311, 314, 315, 321; *Boer* regard for their own, 105; *British* destroy *Boer*, 39. Division of forces, 24, 47, 95. Front, breaking of *Boers* as effective as turning movement, 107. Guerilla warfare, *Boer* leaders in, 21, 321; methods of crushing, 321. Human weakness, influence on strategy, 45, 339. Space for manœuvre cramped on U. Tugela, 91, and N. of Colenso, 253. Theatre of war, Natal generally unsuitable for wide turning movements, 76, 106.

Strength: *Boer*, De Wet's record for beginning of War, 302; P. G., 4; D. F., 26; Colenso position, 65; U. Tugela, 90; General Buller over-estimates, 94: S. K., 142; V. K., 203: before British final advance, 227, 228; position N. of Colenso, 248; Biggarsberg, 288; under de Wet near Wepener, 292; in theatre of operations, 296; rallied after Relief of Mafeking, 301; N.E., of Free State under de Wet, 309, 310; near Irene, July, 316; on Delagoa railway, 320. *British*, P. G., 4; Natal Army, 68; U. Tugela, 90; S. K., 136; V. K., 203, 204; (in units) for final advance to Ladysmith, 230, 232; P. H., 275; in theatre of operations, 297.

Supply, delay for, 3; fresh channels needed, 25, 41; Col. Richardson's prompt action, 43; arrangements of Natal Army, 68; influence on operations, 69, 110, 300, 304; abundant, 70, 186; orders affecting, 81; absence of emergency rations, 104; fresh scale of rations, 221; replenishment of, 294; Natal Army waits for, 300; difficulties of, 304; Natal Army brings forward and opens second channel of, 314; *Boer* arrangements defective, 130, 131, 277. Columns not organised, 69; improvised, 70; difficulties encountered, 84, 104; unwieldy, 100; too advanced position of, 218.

Tactics:

Advanced Guards, *British*, Gen. Kelly-Kenny in front of D. F., 25; deployment of Welch Regiment forming, D. F., 29: skilful action Acton Homes, 105; capture of Hussar Hill, 232; *Boer* methods of combat suitable for, 326.

Ammunition, scale of *British*, 80; supply, *British*, shortness of D. F., 33, 34; *Boer* not organised on U. Tugela, 130; for rifles short S. K., 130.

Artillery ammunition, *Boer* defective D. F., 31; V. K., 206: cannonades, *British*, P. G. unnecessary, 13; Colenso Heights ineffective, 65; U. Tugela ditto, 99; T. M., good practice, 116; S. K., resultless, 150; V. K., powerful but inconclusive, 204, 209, 213 (mutual) ineffective, 217; from S. Bank Tugela, 244; during W. H. ineffective, 254; P. H. violent but poor in results, 277; General Warren's views on T. M., 116, 126, 128; comments, 328, 329, 334. Command, *British*, V. K., 199–201, 203, 204, 208; M. C.-Cingolo, 232, 234; N. of Tugela, 253, 254, 261, 273; S. of Tugela, 274, 276, 277; comments, 325,

INDEX. 369

Tactics—(cont.)
340 : concealment and protection, Boer, T. M., 114, 118, 122; S. K., 148; V. K., 206; N. of Tugela, 248; P. H., 277; British, Zwart Kop for V.K., 196; Hlangwane, 227; comments, 325, 329, 341. Concentration of guns, Boer, D. F., 30; British (see Command, above); comments, 325. Concentration of fire, Boer, S. K., 147; V. K., 206; British, D. F., 35; comments, 325. Dispersion of guns, Boer, T. M., 114; S. K., 147; V. K., 203; N. of Tugela, 247; comments, 325, 329. Dispersion of fire, vide Cannonades; comments, 325. Duel, D. F., illusory results, 31, 32; T. M., Boer decline, 118; V. K. resultless, 214. Enfilade fire, Boer, D. F., 30, 50; B. H., 123; T. M., 130; S. K., 149; British T. M., 130; a lost opportunity, Cingolo, 237. Fire over own troops, Boer, S. K. very effective, 149, 165; British D. F., ditto, 50; S. K. hesitation about, 150; H. H., 266; mishap, 269; comments, 329. "Get at the Enemy's guns," S. K., 166, 168, 185; comments, 341. Heavy, Boer mobility of, 154, 212, 237; position, action, etc.; V. K., 212, 214; N. of Tugela, 248, 285; British scale of ammunition, 80; severe march, 86; position, action, etc.; Colenso position, 65; U. Tugela, 90, 92, 94, 96, 97, 103, 125, 128, 130, 135, 136, 150; V. K., 196, 199, 200, 201, 203; M.C.-Cingolo, 232, 234, 239, 240, 244; operations N. of Tugela, 250, 253, 262, 264, 266, 269, 273, 274, 276-279; comments, 324, 340. Indirect fire, British, S. K., 148. Lyddite, moral effect transient, T. M., 130; S. K., 210. Moral effect, Boer "Long Tom" insignificant, 214; British over-rated T. M., 116; lyddite (see above). Observation of effect, signalled Boer S. K., 148; British T.M., 116; difficulty in, 266, 269, 278. Practice, Boer D.F., 31; S. K., 149; V. K., 206, 208, 209, 214; M.C.-Cingolo, 241; P. H., 279; British D. F., 33, 35, 50; Colenso position, 65; T. M., 116, 130; V. K., 213, 214; M.C.-Cingolo, 242. Ranges, table of Boer,

Tactics—(cont.)
206; measured by Boers S. K., 120; Boer guns outranged N. of Tugela, 251; British guns outranged P. G., 11; D. F., 27; passage of Tugela, 87, 91; S. K., 150; V.K., 206; M.C.-Cingolo, 237, 239. Reconnaissance approaches S. K. inadequate, 154; V. K. do., 198. Silencing Enemy's guns, uncertainty about, 277; comments, 341. Support to Infantry, close D. F., 31; needed at S. K., 159, 172; M. C., 237; H. H., 266; comments, 239.

Attack:
Command, confusion of in S. K., 135, 150, 153, 158, 167, 170, 173-175, 184; operations N. of Tugela, 270; over-centralised, P. H., 274, 280; unity of effective, D. F., 49, 51; generally wanting, 328. Communications, improved during action S. K., 147, 159. Connection, loss of, D. F., 37; do. Cingolo, 235; maintenance of U. Tugela, 105 (see Infantry and Defence). Co-operation and support in, of neighbouring commands not arranged, T. M., 111; but Lord Dundonald affords for own initiative, B. H., 122; Artillery with Infantry effective, D. F., 49, 50, 334; needed S. K., 159; M. C.-Cingolo, 240; H. H., 266; comments, 329, 340; Infantry with Artillery needed V. K., 213; dismounted Cavalry with Artillery fire-action, P. H., 278; comments, 330. Demonstrative, on Tugela during Wagon Hill fight, perfunctory, 74; Potgieter's Drift, transparent and prematurely closed, 92, 96, 102, 103, 108, 125; S. K., need of, 155; General Lyttelton's broken off, 161; V.K. by Wynne's Brigade towards Brakfontein Heights cautious and too distinct from main action, 204, 207; comments on, 337. Emergencies in, well met by Welch Regiment, D. F., 34, 35, 51; measures taken, at S. K., British, 150, 152-155, 159, 161-163, 171, 172; Boer, 177; by K. R. Rifles, W. H., 256; by Col. Harris, W. H., 258; by a Brigade-major, Hart's Hollow, 271. Energy in, M. C.-Cingolo

2 B

Tactics—(*cont.*)
deficient, 231, 233, 237; well directed, 241; W. H., K. R. Rifles, 256. Enfilade-fire, value of, D. F., 49; T. M., 130; S. K., 146, 152. Entrenchments in, T. M., 115; B. H., 123; S. K., on summit ineffective, 146; V. K., difficulties encountered, 211; General Hildyard's troops, 215; Lord Roberts' comments, 330. Enveloping, U. Tugela operations, 92; T. M., orders for, 110, 111; falsely directed, 115, 117; M. C.-Cingolo, 230, 234, 236, 241, 242; Sand River evaded by Boers, 298; Six Mile Spruit do., 305; Diamond Hill, Boers form fresh front, 305; comments on, 337. Fire-action, D. F., well-timed change to shock-action, 36, 50; T. M., over-reliance on Artillery, 116; V. K. do., 213; H. H., untimely interruption of, 267; comments, 326, 328, 331, 335, 341, 343. Fire-effect, D. F., gradual development, 35; paramount importance of, 49–52; self-deception regarding, 50; M. C.-Cingolo, 240; comments, 328, 329, 333, 337, 340. Fire-fight, T. M., over-reliance on Artillery, 116; V. K. do., 213; M. C.-Cingolo, Artillery delay in participation in, 239. Fire-preparation, D. F., thorough, 51, 335; B. H., results of absence of, 127; H. H. do., 266. Fire-tactics *v.* shock-action Onderbrook Heights, traditional British methods, 252; comments, 51, 324, 327, 331–335. Flank, D. F., movement for planned, 24; but not executed, 32; M. C.-Cingolo wanting in surprise, 243; P. H. do., 283; comments, 337. Flanks, protection of in operations S. of Tugela, 230. Front of S. K. too narrow, 132, 140, 155, 170; V. K. do., 207. Frontal, P.G., irresolute, 19; D. F., skilful, 33–35, 48; T. M., false direction of, 117; M. C.-Cingolo, tardily developed but effective, 235, 241, 243; Sand River, wanting in energy, 298; British commanders' aversion to, 20, 29, 91, 124, 319; comments on, 336, 337. Ground, influence of on, T. M.; 121; S. K., 145; V. K., 197;

Tactics—(*cont.*)
skilfully used in, D. F., 49; T. M., 117. Initiative in Lord Dundonald's at B. H., 122; Cingolo, 236; must be allowed to subordinate leaders, 139, 202. Isolated, B. H., 127; S. K., 132, 139. Line of direction of, V. K., maintained by Rifle Brigade, 209; H. H., departed from under flanking fire, 267; P. H. do., 279. Mobility in, deficient, 198. Night, suggested for capture S. K., 104; and on Boer front after, 172; and at V. K., 212; dangers of, *cf.*, W. H., 260. Orders for, S. K., 136–139; comments, 139; V. K., 198–201; comments, 202; W. H., 261; failure to communicate, S. K., 153; H. H. do., 270. Outflanked, T. M., 120; V. K., 210; M. C.-Cingolo, 241; Onderbrook Heights, 251; W. H., 255–259; H. H., 264, 267; P. H., 279, 280; comments, 331, 334, 340. Outflanking, Johannesburg, 303; Bronkhorst Spruit, 317. Phases of, T. M., over-emphasised, 116; V. K. cut and dried, 207, 208, 211; comments on, 328–331. Plans for, T. M., transparency of, 113; M. C.-Cingolo do., 231, 243; Onderbrook Heights do., 250; P. H. do., 276; not clearly expressed, 111; not communicated, 112. Position of General Commanding in, P. G., 8; D. F., 25, 28, 35; S. K., 137, 150, 152, 153, 173; comments on, 169–171; V. K., 201; before H. H., 270, 271. Rallying-point in, S. K., 143. Reconnaissance, for S. K., 133, 143; of summit deficient, 145; Onderbrook Heights incomplete, 248, 249; comments, 329, 331. Reinforcements in, S. K., errors concerning, 153, 158, 170; P. H., delay in arrival of, 280; comments based on 1870 War, 154, 335. Reserves, D. F., skilful employment, 35, 49; T. M.; unnecessarily large, 115; comments, 331, 332. Sacrifices, hesitation to incur (*see* Sacrifices). Space for manœuvre in, cramped at Potgieter's Drift, 91; and near Fort Wylie, 253. Support, mutual in (*see* Co-operation in, above). Surprise in, M. C.-Cingolo, element of lacking, 243;

Tactics—(*cont.*)
P. H., success of, 281; comments, 337. Visibility of movements for, U. Tugela, 91; S. of Tugela, 232; M. C.–Cingolo, 243; N. of Colenso, 249; P. H., 276, 283. Vital point in, M. C.–Cingolo, well-timed action at, 241; P. H., delay in pressing, 280.

Cavalry:
  Charge, Diamond Hill, 305. Dismounted action, Hussar Hill, 232; P. H. with Artillery, 278. Machine gun, Hussar Hill, 232. Outposts, D. F., vigilance of, 27. Pursuit, delayed and cautious after P. H., 284, 286: Reconnaissance supported by Infantry, 23; before D. F., merit of, 27; Natal Army, 90, 92, 100, 113. Turning movement by, failure of D. F., 30, 47, success at Cingolo, 236; lost opportunity for P. H., 283; Johannesburg, 303.
  Command D. F., unity of, 49; U. Tugela divided, 95, 111, 135, 181; T. M., 117; S. K., confusion in, 153, 158, 167, 173, 184; S. of Tugela, L. Botha and Lucas Meyer do., 227; comments, 328.

Defence:
  Advanced position, N. of Tugela, 247; W. H., 255; H. H. dangerous attraction of for Boers, 265; Co-operation, D. F., 35; of Artillery S. K., 147, 166. Concealment, D. F., 27; Tugela Hts., 89, 103; T. M., 114; Hlangwane, 228; N. of Colenso, 248; P. H. of guns, 277. Counter-attack, V. K. under cover of veldt fire, 214; W. H. in darkness, 256; H. H. at dawn, 269; Hart's Hollow by night, 271; P. H. opportunity for lost, 282; comments, 327. Cover, malign attraction of Tugela Hts., 89; S. K., 165, 176. Entrenchments, D. F., 27, 30; Colenso position, 76; S. K., 77, 142; Tugela Hts., 77, 90, 103; Brakfontein Hts., 91; T. M. specially effective, 114; S. of Tugela, 228; N. of Tugela, 246, 247; W. H., 255; H. H., 265. Field of fire, Tugela Hts., 88, 89; Onderbrook Hts., 251; P. H., 279. Fire-effect, D. F., 35; overwhelming at S. K., 156, 168; comments, 327. Fire-

Tactics—(*cont.*)
fight, Brakfontein Hts. prematurely opened, 205; comments on individual action, 325. Fire surprise, Brakfontein Hts., fails, 205; Onderbrook Heights, 252; comments, 331. Flank, unprotected Cingolo, 228; P. H., 281. Front, change of inaction Diamond Hill, 306. Invisibility, Colenso position, 67. Line of prolonged in action, P. H., 279. Mobility in D. F., 27, 46; Tugela Hts., reliance on, 103, 119, 142, 203; P. H., 279. Position and distribution in, Tugela Hts., well chosen, 88, 89; comments, 326. Ranges measured, T. M., 120. Re-inforcements, L. Botha's energetic action; S. K., 177. Reserves, D. F., 35; snatch useful repose, S. K., 164. Skill, individual in, comments on, 325, 326, 330. Surprise of unguarded flank, P. H., 281. Vital point, delay in re-inforcing S. of Tugela, 231, 233; promptly re-inforced, W H., 254; comments, 327. Withdrawal during cannonades, T. M., 129; comments, 328, 329.
  German Regulation on fire-effect, 52, 333.

Infantry:
  Advance, movements in, concealed, T. M., 117; Twin Peaks, 162; V. K., 210; H. H., 264; crawling and rushing P. H., 281. Ammunition supply, *Boer* deficiency in S. K., 160; *British* D. F., 34, 35; W. H., 256. Bayonet-assault D. F. well-timed, 36, 51; T. M. countermanded, 123; H.H., Irish Brigade gallant but premature, 267; P. H. evaded by Boers, 282; General Buller's reliance on, 85; General Warren's views on, 116; comments on, 324, 327, 332, 333. Close quarters, ebb and flow at S. K., 164. Deployment, T. M., premature of whole force, 115; on narrow front, 121: V. K. at 3,000 yards, 234; comments, 331, 334, 335. Direction, V. K. doggedly maintained, 209; H. H. deflected under flanking fire, 267; P. H. do., 279, 281. Distribution in fight, *Boer* unscientific, 326; *British* Sixth Division, D. F., 29, 48; T. M., 115, 118, 121 127; S. K., 144 Twin

INDEX.

Tactics—(cont.)
Peaks, 162; V. K., 204, 209; M.C.-Cingolo, 234, 239, 240; W. H. 254; H. H., 264; P. H., 274, 278, 280; comments, 331. Fire-control and discipline, *Boer and British* contrast, S. K., 155; V. K., 205; comments, 325, 343. Fire-effect, D. F., gradual development, 35, 49; comments, 333, 340, 343. Fire position M.C.-Cingolo, 235, 240; H. H., 265. Fire preparation insufficient, V. K., 210; Onderbrook Heights, 252; H. H., 266-268; comments, 329, 335, 341. Firing line over-crowded T. M., 119, 121; S. K., 146, 151, 166; unsupported Onderbrook Heights, 253; P. H., 279; comments, 331, 334. Flank, support of threatened V. K., 211. Formation P. G., 10; D. F., 29, 49; Colenso, 74; T. M., 118, 120; Twin Peaks, 162; V. K., 204-209, 214; M.C.-Cingolo, 237; W. H., 259; comments, 102, 334-336, 343, 344. Ground use and influence of, D. F., 30-34, 49; T. M., 117, 119-121, 127; S. K., 145, 151; Twin Peaks, 162; V. K., 197, 206, 209; M.C.-Cingolo, 235, 240; Onderbrook Heights, 252; W. H., 255; H. H., 264; P. H., 278-281, 283; comments, 325-327, 330, 342. Independent fire, *Boer* skill in, 155; comments, 325, 336. Long range fire, inadequacy of, S. K., 150; M.C.-Cingolo, 239. Re-inforcements, D. F., 50, 51. Relief of troops in action T. M., 124; V. K., 215; H. H., 267. Rushes in advance, V. K., 240; H. H., 266; P. H., 281. Volleys, D. F., 36; T. M., 120; S. K., 148. Issues, subsidiary, British overregard for, D. F., 48; U. Tugela, 104; T. M., 114, 117; comments, 331, 332.
Leaders' superior responsibility regarding re-inforcements, S. K., 154; subordinate, need of independent initiative among, T. M., 121; V.K., 202: result of casualties among, S. K., 155; comments, 327, 329, 337, 342-344.
Linear Tactics, 100.
Marksmanship T. M., 120; S.K., 155; V. K., 205; comments, 325, 330.

Tactics—(cont.)
Mental qualities, need of development, T. M., 121; comments, 343.
Mounted Infantry: Attack of Bastion Hill, 122; S. K., Position of horses, 161; Reconnaissance inadequate by N. of Tugela, 250; Pursuit impossible after P. G., 12; failure in D. F., 36; after S. K., 178, and V. K., 218; absence of after M.C.-Cingolo, 242; N. of Tugela delayed and cautious, 284.
Outposts, T.M., 126; S. K., 142; Hlangwane, 244; H. H., 268, 271.
Passage of rivers, Gen. Warren on, 91; Potgieter's Drift, 97; Trichardt's Drift, 99; unharassed, 178; Munger's Drift, duty of covering party, 206; for V. K., 207; unharassed, 218; Langverwacht Spruit, 264; Hlangwane Falls, 277.
Patrols, 65, 77, 188, 230.
Rearguard, P. G., 11; *British* V. K., 219: *Boer* holds ground S. of Tugela, 244; Bulwana Hill, 286.
Reconnaissance, *Boer*, 65, 77, 188, 230; *British*, 90, 92, 100, 145, 154, 284-250; comments, 329.

Teams Artillery, ten-horse, 13.
Tents discarded, 44.*
Thaba Myama, action of, 113-131; Council of War preceding, 109; instructions to General Clery, 110; comments, 111: insufficient report of intentions to General Buller,111; Boer position, 113, 114: all Woodgate's Brigade deployed, 115; Artillery phase, 116; unfavourable direction of attack, 117; General Hart to gain southern slopes, 117, 118; Boers unsteady, 118, 119; attack at a standstill, 120; overcrowded firing line, 121; Mounted Brigade captures edge of Bastion Hill, 122, 123; driving home of frontal attack countermanded, 123, 124; General Lyttelton's demonstration, 125; Boers withdraw, 126; attack on western slope, 127; reinforcements arrive, 128; alteration of General Warren's plans, 128; casualties, 125, 354.
Thorneycroft, Col., S. K., reconnoitres for, guides and heads

INDEX. 373

assault, 136-143; appointed to command on summit, 153; intrepid action, 157; asks for Artillery support, 166; reports critical situation 6.30 p.m., 168; not informed about counter measures, 172; decides on evacuation of summit, 173, which completed, 175; report, 185.

Topography, U. Tugela, 87; exceptionally favourable to Boers, 107; influence of T. M., 119; summit S. K., 140, 145, ill-appreciated; V. K., 197; Hlangwane, 229; Hussar Hill, 229; Monte Christo, 229; Cingolo, 235; N. of Colenso, 246; W. H., 255; H. H., 265.

Traction engines inefficient, 70.

Training during pause in operations, 68; of eyesight needed by British, 120, 331.

Transport: *Boer*, fondness for his wagon, 228, 277; in de Wet's movements, 310, 312; *British*, excessive escort for, 29, 47; regimental system, 68; on same road as troops, 86; unwieldiness and length of columns, 103-105, 109, 178, 179, 218; premature anxiety concerning road for, 129; in zone of fire, V. K., 218; influence of N. of Tugela, 249.

Trichardt's Drift, General Warren selects, 92; passage at, 95; withdrawal at, 178.

Troops, Colonial, 42, 291, 295; confidence in General Buller, 186; overcrowding of N. of Colenso, 253.

Tugela R.: Upper, topography, 87, 107; fatal delay in operations on, 92; passage at Potgieter's Drift, 97; Trichardt's Drift, 99; Munger's Drift, 194; withdrawals across unharassed, 178, 179, 218; Lower, topography, on S., 229; on N., 246; passage of N. of Colenso, 251; N. of Hlangwane, 273, 276.

Twin Peaks: Important offshoot of S. K., 146; skilful capture by K. R. Rifles, 162; abandonment, 163; Boer guns on for V. K., 203, 206.

Typhoid fever: *Boer*, 65; *British*, 290, 291.

Use of ground, D. F., 49; in allotment of troops in attack, 121, 145; at Krüger's Spruit for flank attack, 280, 281; comments, *Boer* gift for, 325; *British* failure in during attack, 330.

Vaalkranz, action of, 186-220; plans for, 196; topography, 197; orders for, 198-201; comments, 202; distribution of adversaries, 203; *British* Heavy Artillery, 203; demonstrative attack, 204; *Boer* fire surprise foiled, 205; *British* field guns outranged, 206; bridge construction smart though molested, 206, 207; resemblance of operation to peace manœuvres, 207, 208, 211; effective cannonade 209; Boers retire, 210; operations broken off, 211; entrenchments, 211, 215; *Boers* reinforced, 212; *British* standstill, 213; *Boer* counter-stroke, 214; British outposts, 215; General Buller's report, 215; Lord Roberts urges bold action, 216; action finally broken off and unmolested withdrawal to Chieveley, 218.

Veldt fire, Boer counter-stroke under cover of, V. K., 214.

Viljoen Ben, commands on V. K., 203; stunned by lyddite, 210.

Visibility British movements U. Tugela, 91; S. of Tugela, 232; N. of Tugela, 251, 276.

Volleys, D. F., 36; T. M., 120; S. K., 148.

Voluntary enlistment, baneful influence of, 21, 338.

Wagon Hill, action of, 72-75.

Warren, General Sir Charles, Commanding Fifth Division, 347, 351; on passage of rivers, 91; reconnoitres, 92, 109; crosses Tugela at Trichardt's Drift, 99; moves into Venter's Spruit Valley, 109; renounces Acton Homes route, 110; orders attack on T. M. under General Clery, 110; report to General Buller,112; on Artillery action, 126, 128; proposal for capture S. K., 128; decides on, 132; receives over-sanguine report,

149, alarming report, 159; appoints Colonel Thorneycroft to command on summit, 153; takes certain counter measures, 153, 159, 171; position during fight, 169, 170, calls General Coke to it, 173; reports to General Buller, 177; V. K., 199, 201, 204; reconnoitres, 217; at Council of War, 217; S. of Tugela, 232, 239, 243, 244; N. of Tugela, 251–257, 270, 271, 275, 278–281.

Water, supply in action, 8, 60, 62, 138, 233; need of, S. K., 156, 166; W. H., 257.

White, General Sir G., rejects suggested capitulation of Ladysmith, 61; offers co-operation, 62, 129, 135; after Wagon Hill, 75; anxiety about situation, 93, 189; suggests breaking out, 189; over-reliance on Kaffirs' information, 192; buoyancy of spirits, 195; proceeds to Cape Town, 287.

White flag, General Buller's instructions regarding, 85.

Wings of attack, S. K. operations, 134; P. H., 275.

Wood-fighting, General Buller on capacity of Natal Army for, 76, 217.

Woodgate, General, mortally wounded after capturing summit S. K., 150.

Wynne's Hill, attack on, 253–261.

Zwart Kop, Heavy Artillery hauled up, 196; effective cannonade from, 204.

www.ingramcontent.com/pod-product-compliance
Lightning Source LLC
Chambersburg PA
CBHW050924240426
43668CB00021B/2429